The Research Paper
A Guide to Library and Internet Research

THIRD EDITION

Dawn Rodrigues

*University of Texas at Brownsville
and Texas Southmost College*

Raymond J. Rodrigues

Skidmore College

Prentice
Hall

Upper Saddle River, New Jersey 07458

Library of Congress Cataloging-in-Publication Data

Rodrigues, Dawn.
  The research paper : a guide to library and Internet research / Dawn Rodrigues,
Raymond J. Rodrigues.—3rd ed.
    p. cm.
  Rev. ed. of: The research paper and the World Wide Web. 2nd ed. c2000.
  Includes bibliographical references and index.
  ISBN 0-13-184682-5
    1. Research—Data processing.   2. World Wide Web.   3. Internet in education.   I.
Rodrigues, Raymond J., date   II. Rodrigues, Dawn. Research paper and the World Wide
Web.   III. Title.

LB2369 .R585 2002
808'.027—dc21

                                                                    2002276246

Editor-in-Chief: Leah Jewell
Senior Acquistions Editor: Corey Good
Senior Marketing Manager: Brandy Dawson
Editorial assistant: John Ragozzine
Production Liaison: Fran Russello
Editoral/production supervision: Karen Berry/Pine Tree Composition
Buyer: Ben Smith
Art Director: Jayne Conte
Cover designer: Bruce Kenselaar

This book was set in 10/12 Palatino by Pine Tree Composition, Inc., and was
printed and bound by R.R. Donnelley. The cover was printed by Phoenix
Color Corp.

© 2003, 2000, 1997 by Pearson Education, Inc.
Upper Saddle River, New Jersey 07458

Printed in the United States of America
10 9 8 7 6 5 4 3 2 1

ISBN: 0-13-184682-5

Pearson Education Ltd., *London*
Pearson Education Australia Pty, Limited, *Sydney*
Pearson Education Singapore, Pte. Ltd.
Pearson Education North Asia Ltd., *Hong Kong*
Pearson Education Canada, Ltd., *Toronto*
Pearson Educación de Mexico, S.A. de C.V.
Pearson Education—Japan, *Tokyo*
Pearson Education Malaysia, Pte. Ltd.
Pearson Education, *Upper Saddle River, New Jersey*

Contents

PREFACE   **ix**
ACKNOWLEDGMENTS   **xi**

1 **THE RESEARCH PAPER IN THE INFORMATION AGE**   **1**

The Research Process and You, the Researcher   1
Research in the Information Age   2
What Is Research and What Do Professors Expect?   3
Varieties of Research Reports   4
   The Library Research Paper   *5*
   Experimental Research   *6*
   Field Studies or Observational Research   *8*
   The Case Study   *9*
   The Multimedia Research Paper Variation   *13*
Suggested Activities   16

2 **GETTING STARTED: DISCOVERING YOUR TOPIC AND STARTING TO SEARCH**   **17**

Explore Possible Topics First   18
Recognize the Expectations of the Discipline   19
Explore Your Topic in Several Ways   20
Learn to Use Your Library   21
   The Stacks   *21*
   The Reference Desk   *21*
   The Reference Section   *21*
   Microforms Sections   *22*
   Interlibrary Loan   *22*
   Archives   *22*

Create a Research Journal or Log   22

Browsing in the Library   25

    Browsing Library Databases   26

Browsing the World Wide Web   28

Your Initial Reading   29

Suggested Activities   30

3 FROM RESEARCH QUESTIONS TO RESEARCH PLANS   31

From Topic to Issue   32

Developing Research Questions   33

Narrowing the Research Question   35

From Initial Research Questions to Research Methods   36

Developing a Preliminary Thesis Statement   38

Implementing Your Research Plan   40

Field Research: Interviews, Surveys, and Observations   41

    The Effective Interview   42
    The Effective Survey   43
    Effective Observation   45

Suggested Activity   47

4 FINDING SOURCES   48

Exploring Your Library's Resources   49

    Finding Books   49
    General Reference Materials: Print Indexes, Bibliographies,
        and Online Databases   49

Searching Online Databases   53

Search Strategies: Keyword Searching   54

Search Strategies: Subject Searching   55

Exploring the Web   56

    Web Browsers   56
    Bookmarks   59
    Search Engines   61
    Boolean Terms or Boolean Operators   64
    Common Search Engines   65
    Metacrawlers   68
    Specialized Searchable Databases   69
    Subject Directories   71

Search Strategies   73

Field Research and Interviewing Expert Sources   74
>   *Email   75*
>   *Mailing Lists   76*
>   *Exploring Online Communities for Sources   79*
>   *Indentifying Potential Sources through Newspaper Reports
>   or Magazine Articles   79*
Suggested Activity   81

5 EVALUATING SOURCES   82

Evaluating Information: The Early Stages of a Research Project   83
>   *Content Criteria   83*
>   *Currency   84*
>   *Source of Publication   84*
>   *Coverage   85*
>   *Relevance   85*
Preliminary Evaluation of Web Sources   86
Is a Journal or Magazine Appropriate for Your Topic?   87
>   *Is an Online Journal Appropriate?   88*
The Importance of Exploring Varied Sources   88
Evaluation at the Drafting Phase   89
Determining What Kinds of Sources to Explore   90
>   *An Experience Validating Sources   90*
From the Précis to the Annotated Bibliography to the Evaluative
    or Critical Bibliography   93
>   *The Précis   93*
>   *The Annotated Bibliography   94*
>   *The Critical or Evaluative Bibliography   94*
Evaluating Interviews, Email Communications, Mailing List Postings,
    and Newsgroup Postings   96
Conclusion   97
Suggested Activities   98

6 ORGANIZING SOURCES AND NOTES:
PREPARING TO WRITE   99

Organizing Your Bookmarks   100
>   *Creating Bookmark Files   100*
>   *Creating Folders   101*
>   *Annotating Bookmarks   103*

Setting Up Your Electronic Workspace   105
   Electronic Note Cards   106
   Electronic Bibliography Cards   109
   Using and Organizing Email for Your Research   110
Using Your Computer to Organize Your Writing   112
   Draft Files   113
Summarizing the Organizational Process   115
Conclusion   116
Suggested Activity   117

7 TURNING YOUR RESEARCH INTO A WRITTEN REPORT   118

Writing Over Time   119
Writing in Increments   119
Revisiting and Revising Your Thesis Statement   121
Moving from Notes to First Draft   122
   Writing from an Outline   124
   Writing from Your Notes   124
   *Writing a Conclusion Appropriate for Your Academic
      Field   125*
   Writing Your Introduction   130
Preparing Tables and Figures   133
   Tables   133
   Figures   135
   Tables and Figures: Other Considerations   136
Revising and Editing   136
Maintaining Academic Honesty   137
   Copyright Law   138
   Plagiarism   138
Summarizing, Paraphrasing, and Quoting   139
   Summarizing   139
   Paraphrasing   141
   Quoting   143
   Quoting Primary Sources   145
Your Rhetorical Stance   146
Revising Your Paper   147
Suggested Activities   149

8 Documenting Sources   151

Guidelines for Citing Electronic Documents   152

Modern Language Association (MLA) Style   154

Internal Citation   154
Works Cited   154

American Psychological Association (APA) Style   159

Internal Citation   159
Reference Citation   159

Columbia Guide to Online Style (COS) Electronic Citation Style   163

General Style for Online Sources   163
Citations of Databases and CD-ROMs   164

General Electronic Style Guidelines for MLA, APA,
  and COS Styles   165

The Council of Science Educators (CBE/CSE) Manual Style   166

Internal Citation   166
Works Cited or Reference Citation   167

Chicago Manual of Style (CMS)   169

Internal Citation   169
Bibliography   171

Exploring Citation Problems   174

Copyright Considerations   175

Conclusion   176

Suggested Activities   176

Appendix A   Writing for the Web   177

Writing: In Print and on the Web   177

Different Kinds of Web Writing Projects   178

Posting to Online Forums or Submitting to Online Journals   178
Using a Word-processing Program to Transform a Traditional Essay
  or Research Paper into a Web Text with Links   178
Hypertext Essay   180
Class E-Zine or a Class Anthology   182
Collaborative Course Projects   183

Creating Web Pages   184

Design Basics   185

Designing a Website   185
Designing a Page   185

Review Questions: Website Design   186

The Basics of HTML   188

Adding Pictures or Graphics   190

Writing on the Web: Sites to Explore   191

APPENDIX B   CREATING A POWERPOINT PRESENTATION   193

APPENDIX C   SAMPLE RESEARCH PAPER—AMERICAN
PSYCHOLOGICAL ASSOCIATION STYLE   197

APPENDIX D   PARTIAL SAMPLE RESEARCH PAPER—MODERN
LANGUAGE ASSOCIATION STYLE   230

APPENDIX E   SAMPLE RESEARCH PAPER—COUNCIL
OF SCIENCE EDUCATOR'S STYLE   237

WORKS CITED   251

INDEX   253

Preface

If you have been assigned a research paper or project, we have organized *The Research Paper: A Guide to Library and Internet Research* to help guide you through the many research choices available to you and to give you suggestions to help you write your research in a way that you can be proud of.

We recommend a process that begins with understanding the assignment clearly, so that you start off in the right direction. We'll suggest ways to decide upon a topic that both meets the requirements of the assignment and, at the same time, interests you so that you feel motivated to make it the best report you can. Then, we'll help you determine how you want to pursue your research, whether using the library print sources or online sources, the World Wide Web, information from the field that you gather yourself, or, what is more likely, a combination of these.

You'll discover many sources of information, ranging from information that strengthens your ideas to information that is not at all reliable and possibly inaccurate. We'll give you guidelines on how you can decide what is worth using and what is not. We'll suggest ways you can organize your research, from the moment you first start thinking about it until you turn in your final draft.

Toward the end of this book, we offer suggestions on how to integrate what you have discovered into your writing so that it sounds like you and not a collection of other people's ideas. We show you how you can be intellectually honest, citing ideas that others have written, while making sure that your own ideas stand out. In addition to being intellectually honest, like other good researchers, you need to document your sources so that others who may want to read them can find them. Our intent has been to put it all together for you, guiding you through the complete process from drafting to revising to editing.

You'll find three different types of activities in this book. "Try It Now" activities have been designed to suggest immediate applications of what you are learning as you read and how to conduct research in the world of rapid technological changes. "Web Activities" lead you to the companion website where you will encounter both additional sources of help and exercises to test your understanding. Finally, at the end of each chapter you will find "Suggested Activities." We have designed these so that, by completing them, you move step-by-step to your final draft of your research paper or report.

The research skills you learn today will help you throughout your academic program and well into your careers, whatever they may be. We wish you many new discoveries along the way.

Dawn Rodrigues
University of Texas at Brownsville and Texas Southmost College

Raymond J. Rodrigues
Skidmore College

Acknowledgments

This book has undergone substantial revision from the two earlier versions of *The Research Paper and the World Wide Web*. For that, we have a number of people to thank.

First, we'd like to thank Corey Good, our editor at Prentice Hall, who has been a supporter and a source of good ideas from the very start. His knowledge of what instructors need has helped us reconceptualize many of the parts of this book.

Karen Berry, our production editor at Pine Tree Composition, has been enormously patient with our changes, has caught errors both accidental and just plain wrong, and has helped us to make this a more readable work. Tracy Metivier has checked the materials we quote and screen shots to determine whether to acquire permissions and has secured those permissions in what appears to us as an amazingly efficient process. Both Karen and Tracy have asked questions about our intentions and what we have said so that we could present the clearest possible explanations. For that, we thank them.

Three faculty members have read the early manuscript and offered suggestions that have helped us organize our ideas and directions: Jeffrey T. Andelora of Mesa Community College, Joy Chase of Evergreen Valley College, and Cindy Hardy of the University of Alaska–Fairbanks. Without the recommendations of these faculty, who know their students and what would work best for them, we might not have tried to revise the book as we have done.

At the University of Texas at Brownsville and Texas Southmost College where we work, an institution that is both a community college and a university, two colleagues have contributed in important ways. Alison Abell of the Biology Department, who works to help students write better, kindly let us read her students' research papers to determine which might make the best example of a paper written in CBE (now CSE) style by students in a science course. And of course we thank those students for allowing us to use their work. Librarian Kathleen Vanderslice has shared her insights gained every day from helping students learn how to search online databases. Her understanding of what students new to online research need to learn has contributed much to our own thinking and understanding.

And frankly, we probably ought to thank each other for still being willing to talk to each other after our debates, disagreements, clarifications, and gentle or not-so-gentle suggestions on what we should include, how we should say it, and even whether this organization or that organization would be more meaningful to students. We wish all the students who read the end product equally passionate and productive collaborations.

CHAPTER 1

The Research Paper in the Information Age

After completing this chapter, you should be able to:

- Explain the kind of research you are assigned.
- Use the companion website for this book to find links to resources.
- Log in to a library that has online resources and explore those resources.
- Describe the kinds of research that are typical for your field of study.
- Summarize the steps required of you to submit your research paper or report.

THE RESEARCH PROCESS AND YOU, THE RESEARCHER

You have probably never thought of yourself as a researcher before, but you will have many opportunities to carry out research in your courses and on the job. Therefore, we have organized this book to help you begin to think like a researcher, asking questions and gathering information in a systematic way. We begin by helping you to discover the topic that you would like to write about by using library, Internet, and real-world sources. We guide you through the development of the research project, establishing a timetable so that you meet your deadlines and the requirements of your assignment. We show you how to find sources, in the library, the Internet, and from the world around you. Because all sources are not equally valuable, we help you to evaluate those sources and take notes so that you save yourself time when you begin to write your research. We show you how scholars give credit to their sources of information and avoid unintentional plagiarism. We review the major documentation styles that researchers use. And then we put it all together, reviewing the entire process of writing the paper or project from your initial draft through revision to proofreading before you submit your

1

WEB ACTIVITY

Go online to the companion website for this book (http://www.prenhall.com/rodrigues) and complete the exercise on writing and research in different disciplines.

research. To answer key questions you may have, we have provided a guide to the chapters inside the front cover of this book.

RESEARCH IN THE INFORMATION AGE

Research as we know it has changed dramatically in recent years. With the advent of the Internet, suddenly we have all sorts of research material around us, combinations of online databases, websites, print journals, and, as always, books. Research writing in the Information Age involves challenges and opportunities that earlier research did not have to manage. In addition to searching through an overabundance of resources, researchers must seek information and conduct research in many new forms and in new places, such as online communities. Researchers must learn to both tap and unleash the power of the new technologies, such as sophisticated online databases and new and evolving search engines.

Depending upon your particular academic field, you may be asked to conduct a variety of research activities. For some, the research will be based entirely on print and online sources. For others, original research may be expected, such as experiments or observational studies such as building case studies. Even then, an essential part of your research will involve integrating print and online sources into the original research as academic scholars must do. Researchers don't live in a vacuum. They build upon what has been learned before by others and help those who read their research build upon what they have done.

Where do you begin? You probably will perform many steps at the same time. You will skim the Web for ideas, check the library for information to support the ideas, go to a database to identify sources, take notes, keep accurate information on your sources so that you or others can find them again, and even draft parts of your writing as you conduct your research. Staying organized is key to your ultimate success, and being able to make judgments about the value of the information you are finding is critical.

Today, not only do you have access to the many resources of the Web, including those developed by scholars at colleges and universities across the nation and around the world, but also you have libraries available to you from around the world. For example, under construction at the time this book is being written, the Bibliotheca Alexandrina, or the modern Library of Alexandria, has a mission to be a major public research facility for people from all over the world (http://www.unesco.org/webworld/alexandria_new/aswan.html). You can also search the databases at your library and either make use of them (access them) immediately online or order their materials through interlibrary loan.

■ **WEB ACTIVITY**

online to the companion website for this book, http://www.prenhall. com/rodrigues. There, in the activities for Chapter 1, you will find a set of links to various libraries that you may access online. Go to a few of those libraries to determine whether you can search their online catalog or databases.

The Web offers other possibilities that can expand your research:

■ You can locate experts on your topic and interview them via email (see Chapter 4).
■ You can search through newsgroups and see what other people think about your topic (see Chapter 4).
■ You can discuss ideas and collaborate with colleagues through listservs, forums, and even chat groups (see Chapter 4).

If you use the Web and online databases extensively for your research, your research process is likely to change. In the dynamic environment of the Web, research can become a dialogic process, that is, you can interact with databases and change your understanding of a topic through that interaction; you can communicate with other students or scholars and have your ideas shaped through those communications. A reference that you find through the Public Access Catalog or a search engine may cause you to shift the direction of your search. A note from another student exploring a similar topic or an announcement in today's news reported online may cause you to reexamine your topic or to think of new angles for your investigation. In other words, libraries online and the online world of the Web have caused information to be more dynamic, more available than ever before, and, likewise, much more necessary for you to exercise your judgment in deciding whether to use that information or not. In writing a paper about the development of weapons during the American Revolutionary War, for example, you are as likely to find a paper on the Web written by a junior high school student as you are to find one written by a recognized scholar on the subject.

WHAT IS RESEARCH AND WHAT DO PROFESSORS EXPECT?

Throughout *The Research Paper,* we stress a key theme to successful research: you write best what you know best and care about. Your professors may give you very specific topics for your research or may leave the topics very open.

Most likely, whatever assignments they give, those assignments will be broader than what they expect your research to be. Therefore, whether the assignment seems to be specific, such as "The Latest Research on One Form of Cancer and Its Causes" or "Analyze One of John Donne's Poems to Determine Its Philosophical Roots," you still will need to narrow your topic so that it is both manageable and interesting to you. Also, you need to be sure that your evidence is focused. Both Chapter 2, "Getting Started," and Chapter 3, "From Research Questions to Research Plans," guide you through the process of selecting and narrowing your research topic.

Different academic fields conduct different types of research and expect researchers to report the research using different formats. Be sure that you understand what your professor expects. Although the type of research may vary and the format for reporting it may differ from field to field, all researchers should be aware of previous research that has occurred regarding the topic of the research. Therefore, the skills that you develop for searching the library and the Internet will serve you well regardless of the type of research that you do.

VARIETIES OF RESEARCH REPORTS

Today, research is reported in a variety of formats: printed papers without illustrations, highly illustrated papers, reports submitted online to websites, PowerPoint presentations, and hypertext reports with links to sources and other explanatory or illustrative material. In addition, different disciplines structure their research reports differently.

The traditional research paper, sometimes called a "library research paper," is a generic form of research report that meets the requirements of many introductory classes and, in the humanities, in advanced classes. But today it is often supplemented by other forms of research in addition to library searches. For example, many composition classes now expect students to conduct "authentic" research, research that relates to their own lives or to the lives of others outside the classroom, research that matters to them personally or to topics and issues in their own communities. And most instructors expect students to make use of online databases and Web resources to flesh out their library research. In addition, students may interview people in their communities, experts in the topic being researched, and even people whom they never meet in person, but interview online.

After discussing the traditional research paper, experimental research, and varieties of case studies, we will discuss how different visual elements can supplement these papers and how the multimedia research paper can be created. Even scholarly journals have begun to make use of more visual and graphic components as writers become more aware of the value of visual elements.

The Library Research Paper

The organization of library research papers is often dictated by the standards of particular disciplines or academic majors. Pay particular attention to the style that your professor expects you to use in preparing your report. The most common styles are either MLA (Modern Language Association) or APA (American Psychological Association), but some disciplines will expect you to follow the CMS (Chicago Manual of Style) or the CBE (style manual of the Council of Biology Educators—recently changed to Council of Science Educators). Your school or department may even have developed its own version of one of those styles that it expects student writers to use. Beyond that, professional journals sometimes develop and require their own documentation style.

MLA style is the preferred style in several academic fields, most notably the humanities, such as literature. The standard organization for a paper written in MLA style is as follows:

1. Title page: Include this if an outline or abstract is part of the paper.
2. Outline: This serves a purpose similar to a table of contents.
3. Abstract: Summarize the purpose of the study, the main points discussed, and the conclusion. MLA style does not ask for an abstract, but your instructor may.
4. The body of the paper:
   a. Introduction: Introduce the topic, making sure that you have narrowed it to a manageable one. Provide information on the background of the topic, citing a few key sources to establish the history of research related to this topic or referring to original sources that flesh out the context for your work. Summarize what you write about in your paper, define key terms if necessary, and include your thesis statement somewhere in the introduction.
   b. The body: This is the heart of your paper. Here you discuss the background of your topic in detail and organize it according to a plan that is most logical for your paper. For example, you might organize the paper as a cause-and-effect paper, a historic chronology, a set of comparisons and contrasts, or a process. The organizational pattern should evolve from the nature of the topic and what you learn.
   c. The conclusion: Bring the reader back to the thesis for the entire paper. Summarize your findings and interpret them for the reader, stressing the main points that you want your reader to remember. If there are any implications for further research, state them.
5. Content Notes (Optional): Content notes are different from citations in that content notes are designed to provide information for the reader that may have been tangential to what the body of the paper discusses, but that is nevertheless helpful to understand. They are numbered sequentially throughout the paper with raised or superscript numbers.
6. Appendices: In the MLA style, the appendix is where illustrations, charts, tables, and graphs should go. In addition, compilations of data, such as survey results or analyses of numerical details, will go in the

appendix and be referred to in the body of the report. Pages continue to be numbered sequentially throughout the paper, and each appendix is labeled "Appendix A," "Appendix B," and so on.

7. Works Cited: This is your list of references or bibliography. See Chapter 8 for guidance on formatting the Works Cited or Reference sections. Although the paper format above follows the MLA style, professors in some fields might prefer that you use *The Chicago Manual of Style*, 14th ed. (Chicago: University of Chicago Press, 1993) or Kate L. Turabian, *A Manual for Writers of Term Papers, Theses, and Dissertations*, 5th ed. (Chicago: University of Chicago Press, 1987). We provide examples from MLA, APA, *The Chicago Manual of Style*, and the Council of Biology Educators (CBE or CSE) in Chapter 8. Be sure to learn what your professor prefers.

Appendix C contains an example of a traditional research paper written in APA style and Appendix D contains an example of what it would look like if it were written in MLA style. An example of a paper written in the Council of Biology Educator's Style (CBE or CSE) appears in Appendix E.

Experimental Research

The sciences and social sciences, including education, rely upon tightly controlled experiments, with clearly defined variables or influencing factors, and specific methodologies that other researchers could copy, or replicate. This enables researchers to determine whether the studies' conclusions held if conducted again or if certain variables were changed.

For the person reporting the results of an experiment, the language used should be clear and as free of value judgments as possible, if not totally free. The criterion that the research and its ensuing report be as objective as possible is absolutely accepted by researchers in fields that rely on experiment research. Even the format in which the research is reported has been accepted across their fields so that there is no question about what format the research report will follow. The typical experimental research report follows the following pattern:

1. Abstract: Many scientific fields expect an abstract of the study at the beginning. An abstract is a brief summary of the problem, the hypotheses tested, and the findings. Discuss what you learned from your research in relation to your findings. It enables readers to determine whether they want to read your study in detail.

2. Statement of Problem: Tell the reader exactly what you intend to learn and why. Is the problem an important one, and if so, why? Does it address a timely or otherwise significant issue? State the problem clearly. Perhaps use an anecdote or illustration to intensify the reader's interest in the problem.

3. Review of the Literature: What are the key findings in research before your research? You don't have to include as much research as possible to establish that you know the context in which your research occurs, but you should identify key studies that preceded yours. Did the find-

ings contradict one another? How does that contradiction relate to the problem that you have identified? Define the key concepts that the reader needs to know. In short, establish the scholarly context for your study through this review, perhaps even noting specific studies to which your research is related.

4. Development of Hypotheses: Hypotheses are *predictions* of what your research will prove. Place your hypotheses at the end of the Review of the Literature section. Your hypotheses should be clear, value-free statements that you intend to test. *Note:* A hypothesis is not specifically what you intend to *prove,* but, rather, a statement that you intend to test. If the results of your research demonstrate that your hypothesis was wrong, that is a valid finding. Discovering that something is *not* true is as important as discovering that something *is* true.

5. Methods: Describe the procedures that you used to test your hypotheses, including a description of the sample that you selected, the variables that you tested, and the method or methods for testing them. You should describe your procedures clearly enough so that another research could replicate or reproduce what you have done using similar samples, variables, and testing procedures. Use tables, charts, graphs, or illustrations if their use clarifies your written description of your methodology.

6. Results or Findings: Was your hypothesis true or not? Remember that a negative finding is a finding nevertheless. Discuss the findings so that your reader understands them in relation to the variables you worked with. Use tables, graphs, charts, and other illustrations to clarify or summarize what you have learned.

7. Discussion: Based upon what you have learned, what can you recommend regarding future research? Should your hypotheses continue to be tested, perhaps with different sampling techniques or populations? Should they be modified, including, perhaps, new variables or reconceived variables? Here you can begin to discuss factors that you did not include in your research, but that you may have observed or that your review of the literature might have included, and speculate about what might happen if they were to be included. But do be clear about what part of your discussion is based on fact or findings and what part might be going beyond those findings.

8. Conclusion: The conclusion is a summary of all that you have said before. What was the problem that you investigated, what hypotheses were you testing, how did you go about your investigation, what did you find, and what were the implications of your research?

9. References: In the scientific paper, follow either the APA style or *Scientific Style and Format: The CBE Manual for Authors, Editors, and Publishers,* 6th edition (Style Manual Committee, Council of Biology Editors; Cambridge, NY: Cambridge University Press, 1994). See Chapter 8 for examples of documentation style and Appendix E for a sample student research report.

(Note: In experimental research reports or the field study reports summarized below, it is normal to include subheadings, bulleted or numbered lists, and other aids to help the reader follow the organization of the paper. In fact, it is preferable. With the impact of the visual media upon the pubic, including both television and the Internet, writers include illustrations more than ever before, just as they include tables, charts, and graphs.)

Your professor may ask for a simpler, more concise form of experimental research report. Here is the typical format for such reports:

1. Abstract
2. Introduction
3. Methods and materials
4. Analysis or results
5. Discussion
6. Conclusion
7. References

Using this format, the Introduction includes the Statement of the Problem, Review of the Literature, and Development of Hypotheses. In some instances, the Discussion and Conclusion sections are combined into one section. This is most common when there are not many findings. When there are many findings, the reader will find them easier to comprehend if the sections are kept separate. See Appendix E for an example of a research paper in a science class.

WEB ACTIVITY

Go online to the companion website for this book, http://www.prenhall.com/rodrigues. There, in the activities for Chapter 1, you will find a set of links to science research reports. Note the formats that these reports use, the contents of the abstracts, and where references to the research of others appears.

Field Studies or Observational Research

When you conduct observational research in the field, you observe people or something else in their natural habitat. The primary value of observational research is its direct observation of behavior in a given context and situation. Survey research and self-reports may provide quick information for researchers and may actually be quantifiable, but they are at best indirect measures of behavior and subject to the biases, predispositions, and subjective opinions of those who are reporting on themselves. Observational research provides a way to determine how people really behave. For example, suppose first-year teachers are surveyed regarding whether their education as teachers helped them in their first year. Will those who respond to the survey honestly indicate their weaknesses? And what are we to make of those who do not respond? Are they angry at the education they received, or are they unwilling to take the time to respond? Observers watching, interviewing, and cataloguing the behaviors of those teachers while they teach might be able to determine what aspects of their education truly have been useful to them.

Observational research, however, does have its weaknesses: One of the factors that a researcher must handle is the researcher's possible influence over or even interference with the activities and behaviors being observed. Likewise, the presence of certain research tools, such as video cameras or tape recorders, can also influence the way people respond in their presence. So, not only must the researcher be objective in the recording of observations, but also the researcher must be objective in noting how the research process may have influenced the results.

Below are three types of field studies or observational research. The research report format for the case study can also serve as the format for the observational studies:

- The case study
- Participant observation
- Nonparticipant observation

The Case Study

Case studies make significant contributions to a number of professional fields, ranging from dentistry to education to management to marketing, fields where highly controlled experimentation may be impossible, given all the possible variables that attend human interactions with other humans and their environments. Some would argue that the highly controlled experiments of scientific research may be important to understand specific factors about what is being studied, but in "real life" we have little control over those variables. Thus, case studies serve a purpose.

A major use of case studies is for teaching others. A class or a group of business persons, administrators, or workers can discuss all the variables that are found in the case and debate what they might do in similar circumstances. From such in-depth discussions, learning occurs, often learning about how to manage processes rather than find the exact solution to a problem. Each human problem is different from other human problems, so knowing how to address types of problems is more beneficial than thinking that one solution fits all. While one case may not be enough to demonstrate anything conclusively, many cases of similar topics, with related conclusions, may ultimately lead to firmer conclusions.

Researchers must make careful observations of the "case" that they are studying, taking notes so that they can remember as many of the factors influencing the situation as possible. Because case studies can facilitate study of many variables at once, you should allow time for studying your topic in depth. That means that, after an initial review of the library and Internet sources, you may want to revisit the sources after your study to confirm your understanding of how those cases relate to yours. Different fields may vary the typical components of case studies, but the following outline encapsulates the most common components:

1. Abstract: A summary of the case, the purpose for the topic being investigated, the characteristics of the case, the methods used to study it, and the findings, as well as the conclusions.

2. Introduction: A brief summary of why the study was undertaken, specifically the key issue or problem and the value of studying such cases. Specify the type of audience that can benefit from studying this case. Establish the context for the study so that the reader can understand the situation in which the study occurred.

3. The Report: This is the heart of the case study. Describe what you had intended to learn and the importance of learning it.
   a. Context: Describe the context as thoroughly as possible, including the human players involved, the physical setting if it matters, and the conditions under which normal interactions occur. If biographical information is pertinent to the case, provide it, at least in brief.
   b. Methodology: Discuss the methods for the study: observation from outside the situation, observation from within (such as participant observation), whether specific technologies were employed (such as videotaping), and how the data were compiled and analyzed. What problems did the researcher encounter? What made the researcher's work more effective? How can other researchers conduct research like this?
   c. Findings: What specific information came from the study? If there are data, provide them, including tables, charts, graphs, and illustrations, if appropriate.

4. Discussion: Here is where you would include a review of the literature and where your library and Internet research will apply. Does the case fit into a set of similar or related cases described by others? How does your study differ from the previous studies, or were you attempting to replicate a similar study? Draw inferences or make hypotheses as a result of your experience with this case. Discuss the importance or the lessons learned from it. If your results fit a pattern revealed by earlier studies, note that. If they add new understandings or insights to the previous studies, note that as well.

5. Conclusion: Briefly summarize what you have learned from the study of this case and how it may apply to other, similar or related, situations. If there were limitations that readers ought to understand so that they are aware of them, include them here. Perhaps make recommendations for similar studies of like cases to help broaden the understanding of those who must work with situations such as those described in the case.

6. References. [Note: Some professors or publications may also ask for an annotated bibliography of studies that relate to this one but that may not have been pertinent for you to include in the body of your report.]

Below are some examples of case studies designed to indicate the breadth that their topics cover, but also designed to possibly stimulate your own ideas for a case study:

- The interactions of family members during the week. Study your own family. When do they talk to one another or work or play with one another? What is the nature of their interactions? What characterizes the ways that they communicate? Do they all perceive their interactions in the same way? What does the research tell us about communications in the family today? Does your case fit a pattern, or is the family you study different in some substantial way?
- The sales practices of used-car salesmen. Observe several salesmen in the same used-car lot. How do they approach potential buyers? How do the buyers respond to them? When are they successful? When are they unsuccessful? What makes a greater difference in whether someone buys a used car: the salesman or the buyer? What can this study contribute to developing better salesmen or better buyers?
- Occupational studies: A day in the life of a teacher, a doctor, a nurse, an auto mechanic, a plumber, a gardener, the CEO of a local business.
- Health practices: A young mother taking care of her first baby, elderly in a nursing home, an executive in a high-pressure business, the eating habits of your classmates.
- Advertising: Categories and times of TV ads throughout the week, floor plans and displays of stores and how buyers respond within them, traffic patterns in malls.
- Problem solving: Observe someone having to solve a problem typical for that person's job. How does that person go about it? Does the person read anything, talk to anyone, or seek help? Does the problem get solved? What can your reader learn from what you observed?

Participant Observation

In participant observation, researchers actually participate with or join the activities of those whom they study. By being part of the group being studied, the researcher is able to observe behaviors that the group might never reveal to outsiders, such as nonverbal behaviors and behaviors that the group might not want outsiders to know about. Such research may be open, with the group knowing that the researcher is studying them, or it may be covert, with the researcher concealing his or her identity for fear that the group might not even allow the researcher in if they knew what was happening. Some anthropologists who are members of specific ethnic or cultural groups have reported on their own families, with the family members aware that the researcher was going to report what they did. Other researchers, working with more secretive groups, have hidden their research. They have studied, among others, gangs, political dissidents, cults, government agencies, company governing boards, private clubs, and the internal workings of bureaucracies. In one case, a young reporter studied how border immigration agents responded to him when he dressed like a businessperson, like a student, and like a poor worker. In another case, Ted Conover, the author of *Coyotes: A Journey Through the Secret World of America's Illegal Aliens*, pretended to be an illegal immigrant seeking help in crossing the border from Mexico to the United States. His study placed him in contexts where he was subject to great personal risk.

A potential risk that the participant observer takes is becoming so much a part of the group that he or she is studying that objectivity is lost. Or having to take part in extensive activities over time may prevent the researcher from recording observations while they are still fresh in memory.

When you conduct a search of library or Internet sources, you will want to look at more than studies that are strictly participant observation. Remember, you are interested in knowing as much as you can about your subject, so you may want to read autobiographies, statistical studies, essays based on the writers' opinions, newspaper or magazine articles, and more. Be sure to evaluate the nature of your sources. You can use biased reports as part of your background research, but, if you cite them, do so as counterpoint to your study, which is to be as objective as possible.

Below are some possible participant observation studies designed to stimulate your ideas for what you might study:

- The study habits of your classmates. When do they study? How? Where? Under what conditions? Does their economic status or family context bear upon the answers to those questions? What do they say and think about what they are studying, if anything? What can teachers or other students learn from your research?
- The life of an athletic team. What is it like behind the scenes—in the locker room, on the buses, on the bench while the game is going on? What do they do when they are practicing as opposed to playing the game? Are there groups within the team? What specific personalities emerge and what is their effect on the team? What is the relationship of the coach to the team? How do they interact? Did you observe anything that surprised you? What can other athletes, coaches, families, or fans learn from your research?
- A day in the life of a college student.
- Working at a particular job.
- Conversations between members of the opposite sex.

Nonparticipant Observation

In nonparticipant observation, the researcher does not join the group or activity being studied, and the research may be open for all to know about or covert. Because the researcher is not involved in the study group's activities, the researcher may use a variety of approaches in combination: surveys, questionnaires, and interviews, as well as observations. As with participant observation, there is still the risk that the activity of the research itself may have an influence upon those being studied and thus distort the results. One of the most famous of such studies, the 1927 Hawthorne study of workers in the Western Electric Plant in Cicero, Illinois, has been criticized because the presence of the research team clearly influenced the results. The study sought to determine the effect of increased light levels upon worker productivity. When lighting increased, productivity increased. But a subsequent study found that when lighting decreased, productivity also increased. Worker morale was being affected positively, and thus their productivity increased, because they knew that the company was paying attention to them. Taken together, these studies are now referred to as "the Hawthorne Effect."

Here are some possible nonparticipant observation study topics that might give you ideas on research you can do:

- The grammatical usage of people with different educations: Study how students, faculty, staff, and administrators talk in different circumstances. Does their use of language change when they are talking to different groups of people or in different contexts, such as the student center, the classroom, or an athletic event? What does that tell us about grammatical usage?
- Worker behavior in a service-oriented business: How do they greet customers, deal with difficult customers, solve problems, interact with supervisors and workers who report to them? What can businesses that want to increase their business learn from your study?
- The responses of people in positions of authority to people who dress in a variety of ways.
- The daily lives of workers in a particular industry.
- The production of a major event, such as a play or a conference.

WEB ACTIVITY

Go online to the companion website for this book, http://www.prenhall. com/rodrigues. There, in the activities for Chapter 1, you will find a set of links to field studies and various forms of observational studies. The activities ask you to note specific features of the sample research projects, such as the degree of objectivity of the writers and the ways that the writers weave their resources into their reports.

The Multimedia Research Paper Variation

The traditional research paper is undergoing many different permutations as writers develop the visual literacy skills that today's readers expect. In essence, the format may be the same as the MLA format presented above, but now imagine what it might look like if the appendices were incorporated into the paper itself rather than attached at the end. Illustrations, graphs, charts, and tables are placed as close as possible to the words they are illustrating. In fact, given computer capabilities, the words may wrap around the illustrations, graphs, charts, and tables, if doing so does not detract from the visual impact of both the words and illustration, graph, chart, or table.

For examples of how various types of media are being incorporated into publications, class reports, and papers, explore sites such as these:

http://www.readingonline.org/research/explorer/
http://www.geocities.com/jazybones/midi/
http://www.ncrel.org/sdrs/areas/issues/methods/technlgy/te300.htm
http://www.neiu.edu/~ncaftori/students.htm
http://www.sciam.com/
http://www.rootsworld.com/rw/feature/vietnam.html
http://www.geom.umn.edu/docs/research/
http://www.sims.berkeley.edu/~pam/papers.html

Not all research reports are prepared solely for print now that we have the Internet as a publishing vehicle. See the companion website for an example of a publication using hyperlinks. Through the use of Web editing software programs, we can publish our report to the Internet and create links, or hyperlinks, to the very material we might have footnoted alone when we only had the capability of preparing our reports on paper. We can insert video illustrating key points; connect with specific sounds such as clips from interviews, music, and the author reading from the original work; or, when copyright law (see p. 175, Chapter 8) allows, send the reader to the original documents cited in the report. Letters, diaries, original manuscripts, evolving drafts of original writings—who knows what you might include in your hypertext research report that will bring it alive for the reader? We have, essentially, exploded the traditional research paper, opened it up to a multidimensional world, and

WEB ACTIVITY

Go online to the companion website for this book, http://www.prenhall. com/rodrigues. There, in the activities for Chapter One, you will find a set of links to reports and articles on the web that illustrate the varieties of ways writers have opened up traditional writing by using tools available on the web. Note the methods that these writers use. Which web features are new to you? Which can you incorporate into your research reports?

enabled our readers to move closer to the emotions that we may have felt when working with the sources and data that we have discovered.

Student research "papers" on the Web are exploring the many possibilities open to them. Consider the possibilities:

- An oral history project has taped one of the elders in the community speaking of her childhood and how her life changed as various new technologies appeared, moving from the electronic railroad to the automobile to the airplane, from the simple crystal radio set to today's television. As her voice plays on the computer, pictures appear on the computer screen illustrating her story, hyperlinks begin to appear linking the listener to comments by the student researcher and expert resources that the student research has located.
- A research project traces the gradual decimation of Western American Indian tribes. Beginning with a narrative on the screen, the student researcher links to images from early Western photographers to images taken today on the reservation. Other links capture historical documents such as treaties between the United States and the tribes, Bureau of Indian Affairs documents, and research reports on the economic, health, and educational conditions on the reservations.
- A research report demonstrates how colonial U.S. forces defeated the Hessians in Trenton during the Revolutionary War, this research report begins with a map of colonial New Jersey and Pennsylvania with hyperlinks embedded in the map. The reader can click on any particular site on the map and learn key actions, causes, and consequences, as well as interpretations by noted historians. Illustrations range from the tombstone of John Honeyman, the spy who gave Washington key information about the Hessians, to a winter photo of the Delaware River at the point of Washington's crossing.
- A research report on DNA and how researchers track the genetic propensity for certain diseases begins with a video clip of DNA and gradually introduces genetic models to illustrate the use of DNA research to seek cures for diseases. Hyperlinks in the paper take the reader to research reports and journal articles that the writer drew upon for the research.

Even when their reports are in print but not online, researchers are beginning to experiment with variations upon their formats. In the middle of a serious prose description, the writer might insert a poem that illustrates the point more effectively than dry prose does. An email message from a person who is a valuable source may be included, even a series of messages between the researcher and the source person. Photographs, videotapes, and audiotapes might serve as multimedia appendices for the report. The possibilities are expanding with every expansion of the resources available to us and the infinite ways that researchers view their subjects.

TRY IT NOW

Ask your professor or a research or reference librarian where you can find examples of research in your field. Read two or three published research reports that can serve as models for your writing and note:

- The format for these research publications, *that is,*
  - the major parts of the publication, and
  - the types of information in each section
- The degree of objectivity or subjectivity in the authors' conclusions
- The ways that the authors document or cite their sources
- The breadth or narrowness of the topics that they write about

SUGGESTED ACTIVITIES

1. Of all the sample research reports that you have read on the companion website, which type is the most appealing to you? What are its characteristics? How could you model your research upon that report in your course?

2. Summarize the research assignment that you have been given:
   a. What kind of topic should you research?
   b. Is there a particular format you should follow?
   c. What documentation style should you use?
   d. Are there any intermediate steps you must perform before submitting your final draft and when are they due? For example, does your instructor require a proposal to be approved or an annotated bibliography?
   e. Where can you find examples of similar research in the discipline?
   f. When is your final draft due?

Getting Started: Discovering Your Topic and Starting to Search

2

After completing this chapter, you should be able to:

■ Identify the kinds of research that researchers conduct in your chosen field.

■ List the possible topics that you would like to study.

■ List people who can help you consider possible ways to explore your topic.

■ Create a research log or journal.

■ Browse through the online resources of a library.

■ Browse through an online "subject directory."

■ Create electronic bibliography cards.

■ Identify possible research topics for your class assignment.

You have been assigned to conduct research and produce a research paper, either a traditional formatted report or an online variation. Given the assignment, what would you like to learn? Whether your professor has assigned you a broad topic or a narrow one, is there some aspect of the subject that interests you? When you are engaged with your topic, when it really means something to you, that's when you will be not only stimulated to do the research that is required, but you'll also be more stimulating as a writer because you'll have more to say about it. Think about it: How can any of us write well on something that we do not care about and know very little about? Not only will we have little to say, but our writing will be awkward, our sentence structure reflecting our lack of information and our lack of interest.

In this chapter, we're going to focus on finding that topic that will be both meaningful to you and will also cause your readers to recognize how well you have investigated the topic and presented the results of your research. We begin by exploring topics that give you room to demonstrate your ability to conduct research objectively, balancing out different perspectives. Then we consider how to browse both the Internet and the library to start finding good research topics. You'll establish your own research log so that you can keep track of both where you sought information and the results you had. You'll start keeping bibliographic note cards so that you can eventually document the sources you use. And finally, you'll begin to learn more about research in a particular discipline, such as the key journals and the citation styles that they typically use.

EXPLORE POSSIBLE TOPICS FIRST

Whether you know something about your topic or not, take time to explore it before you absolutely settle upon the exact topic. One of the mistakes that beginning researchers often make is to jump right into a topic before they have learned more about it. What have others said about this topic? Is there enough information available to give you some choices about what to include? Do other researchers differ in their points of view about the topic? Is it a topic

TRY IT NOW

Suppose you were assigned to conduct a research study about cancer. Might there be a personal connection between that very broad topic and your own life? For example, have you ever known anyone who has had cancer or perhaps died from it? Would you like to learn more about that type of cancer? Might there be family members or doctors whom you could interview as part of the research? What aspect of this topic seems most interesting to you? The causes? The possible cures? The impact upon family members? The economic impact? The accuracy of the media reporting? Each of those ways of looking at cancer will lead you to very different discoveries and interpretations.

Now write down the possible questions that you can ask about a topic you are considering for your research, such as:

- What do you already know about this topic?
- What are its causes? Its history?
- What impact does it have upon other topics?
- What are some different opinions that people have about this topic?

After you have answered those questions as best you can, save them to refer back to as you develop your research topic.

about which people disagree strongly, or do people agree on it so much that it is not worth writing about?

Your research project should be meaningful to you personally, whether it is assigned by a teacher or self-generated. If you select a topic that *you want* to investigate critically, then you are certain to benefit from the research process. If you customize and personalize assigned topics, you will enjoy research more.

RECOGNIZE THE EXPECTATIONS OF THE DISCIPLINE

As you work to focus your topic, keep in mind that it should also fit within the expectations of the discipline you are studying and the expectations of your professor. Each discipline tends to expect certain types of research and to use the specialized language of that discipline. So, for example, a literature course will probably expect you to analyze a work or works of literature and develop interpretations of the author's or authors' intents or techniques. A science course may expect you to summarize and synthesize the research related to the topic while also conducting an experiment of your own. A social science course or a behavioral science course may also expect you to summarize and synthesize the research related to the topic, but may ask for interpretations of the topic and applications to our understanding of it today. In addition, each discipline has within it specific journals and databases that are designed by scholars within that particular field. You will be expected to become familiar with some of them and to use those in your research.

Here are some questions to ask as you begin to explore possible topics:

WEB ACTIVITY

Whether your professor has already assigned a topic for your research or whether the choice is completely open at this time, take a few minutes to think about your answers to the questions below. Then go to the companion website for this book, Chapter 2, Exercise 1, and answer the questions.

1. What is the general topic for the research assignment?
2. What do I already know about this topic?
3. Is there any aspect of this topic that I am truly interested in?
4. Who are some individuals who might know something about this topic and whom might I consult before beginning to explore this topic?

■ What types of topics are appropriate for this discipline?
■ Am I expected to conduct a specific type of research, such as a literary analysis, a field study, or an experiment?
■ Which particular journals are most appropriate for research in this field?
■ Which particular databases should I explore?
■ Are there particular websites that will be best to use as I begin my research?

EXPLORE YOUR TOPIC IN SEVERAL WAYS

As you work to determine how you want to focus your research, you can explore in a variety of ways: browse your library's online catalog, read encyclopedia entries to give yourself a broad overview of the topic, go to the Web and use a search engine or subject directory, find a listserv on the topic and read what others have to say, talk to friends, or seek experts near you to talk to, perhaps your own professor or another professor that yours might recommend.

Where you actually begin depends upon your topic, whether you must discover the most recent information about it, and how much information you already have available to you. For example, if you are exploring a literature topic or a historic event, chances are that there are already many books in the library about that topic. Search the library catalog online or ask a research or reference librarian for some guidance. When you locate a few key books, scan the tables of contents to learn how those authors organized your topic. Perhaps one of the topics in the table of contents will suggest a topic for your research. Scan the index to determine what categories and topics the authors included in their books. The index can suggest keywords for your future research online. Look at the bibliographies or lists of references at the ends of the books to see whether there are other books on the topic that you should check. Perhaps the names of a few authors seem to appear quite often. Those are authors whom others consider to be experts and therefore authors you should check out as well.

If, on the other hand, your topic is one that is very current and likely to be changing over time, you probably will want to begin your research by exploring the resources on the Web. For example, the North American Free Trade Agreement (NAFTA) is relatively new, so new issues or data are always appearing online and in journals, magazines, and newspapers. If you are exploring a topic grounded in science, such as stem cell research or global warming, then you'll want to check out the latest journal articles online and other Web resources to discover new research findings and new interpretations of those findings. If you are seeking background on the scientific knowledge underlying stem cells and disease or biological ethics and religious beliefs, then the books in the library may provide the best information.

When you begin research, you start upon a process of discovery, not just of what others think, but also of what *you* think. Even if you are asked to submit a research proposal to your professor before you can officially begin, you can begin to explore the topic and start your research before you write that proposal.

LEARN TO USE YOUR LIBRARY

As soon as possible in your research, learn how to find books, periodicals, and other resources in your library. Learn the location of physical areas of the library as well as the names of people in the library who can give you help when you need it.

The Stacks

Books and journals are stored in stacks, with collections arranged either according to the Library of Congress cataloging system or the Dewey Decimal System. Most libraries have open stacks where you may browse all you want. Learn where books, journals, magazines, newsletters are stored. When you locate a possible source, copy the source information in your research log.

The Reference Desk

This is the place for you to find specialists called reference librarians, experts whose job it is to help you find the information that you will need. They will be able to direct you to the reference collection of the library and to suggest specific references for your research.

The Reference Section

Reference sources include general references such as dictionaries, encyclopedias, almanacs, and atlases. Specialized references include encyclopedias on specific topics and bibliographies of resources on topics in different fields. The following list gives you an idea of the kinds of specialized references you can locate:

Encyclopedia of Multiculturalism
Introduction to United States Information Sources
Information Sources in the Life Sciences
International Encyclopedia of Psychiatry, Psychology, Psychoanalysis and Neurology
Encyclopedia of Sociology
Biographical Dictionary of American Sports
A Selective Bibliography of Bibliographies of Hispanic American Literature
A World Bibliography of African Bibliographies
Shakespearean Bibliography and Textual Criticism: A Bibliography

The reference section also includes books called "periodical indexes." Indexes such as *The Readers Guide to Periodicals* contain listings of the titles and topics of many magazine articles and newspaper articles. To locate the full text of the periodicals, you need to search the online library catalog, where you will find if your library subscribes to the periodical (and, in many cases, where the periodical is kept in the library). Your library may also subscribe to some print indexes for specialized fields such as Humanities, Literature, Criminal Justice, or Education. In most cases, however, libraries have stopped subscribing to print indexes; instead, they have chosen to purchase subscriptions to online databases—digital equivalents of the print indexes, available through the World Wide Web or on CD-ROM. (See pp. 53–56 for an explanation of how to search for information in online databases.)

Microforms Sections

The periodicals section of the library keeps some reference materials on microforms, such as "microfiche." These may contain materials not received in other formats. For example, the Education Resources Information Clearinghouse (ERIC) documents contain a wide variety of education-related conference presentations and other papers. Sometimes old newspapers are found in microform format. Special reader machines allow you to copy pages found on the microforms.

Interlibrary Loan

When you have located a source that your library does not have, you can ask the Interlibrary Loan Office to order the book or a copy of the article from another library. It may take from a few days to a couple of weeks for the materials to arrive, so be sure to locate the sources you need early in your research.

Archives

Libraries often have special collections of material that they place in rooms called "archives." Archives are collections of important documents, such as rare books, maps, or the correspondence of a famous alumnus or politician. You will not be allowed to check out these materials, but you may be able to arrange for them to be copied. An archive in your library may provide a valuable source of material for a research project, so do learn whether your library has an archive and what is preserved there.

CREATE A RESEARCH JOURNAL OR LOG

Now is a good time to create your research journal or research log. A research journal serves as a log or research diary for you as you work your way through your research project. In it, you record information on key resources that you locate, bibliographic data, notes to yourself on what you want to pursue as your research proceeds, and other information that will save you time and effort. You can keep a research log in a notebook, but working with a computer, you can keep an electronic research log, saving it to disk as a backup and also as a portable research log that you can move from computer to computer.

In Chapter 8, "Documenting Sources," we describe a template that you can use to keep your documentation data so that you create your bibliography as you find sources, and in Chapter 6, we describe note-taking strategies in some detail. However, you can begin taking some notes in your research log. To create these templates, you will need to create a table with your word-processing program. If you are using Microsoft Word, click on "Table," then "Insert" on the drop-down menu, and then "Table." A menu will appear that asks how many columns and how many rows you want to create. You can create as many rows as you want, for you can always add rows and columns later if you need them. The menu will also ask you to size the columns. We recommend that you select "Autofit to Contents" so that you don't have to readjust the size later if you need a wider column. Table 2.1 is an example of what one type of electronic research log table might look like.

This research log entry is designed for the early stages of your research. Note that the researcher has listed titles of articles that appear to be worthwhile and the Electronic Collection access number so that it is easier to return to these articles if necessary. Note that the researcher also included the keywords that led to these sources. That's a good practice for you to follow as you locate more sources in online databases and search engines. (See Chapter 4, "Finding Sources.")

TABLE 2.1 Sample Entries in an Electronic Research Log

Date	Record of Activity	Results	Notes, To Do
9/15/2002	Conducted search of online library catalog	Located several books, but none is current on NAFTA	Learn how to search online databases.
9/17/2002	Learned how to search online databases. Searched Wilson Web and InfoTrac. Saved articles to disk.	InfoTrac results: "The Future of Hemispheric Free Trade" Electronic Collection A21206815 "A Different, New World Order." EC: A66894065	Do I want to do research on alternatives to NAFTA? Return to continue research. Note keywords that found these sources: protectionism, free trade, commercial policy.

Note that this researcher actually saved the articles to disk so that it would not be necessary to return to the online sources. The bibliographic data can also be saved to disk along with the article. We describe how other parts of the research journal can be used in future chapters, but below are some components that you can include in your research journal:

- a daily log of your activities, with notes to yourself about ideas that you develop as you use your sources and notes about future steps you want to take;
- bibliography cards;
- note cards with quotes, summaries, and paraphrases;
- bookmarks, or electronic placeholders for online sources;
- copies of email messages related to the research; and
- drafts of your paper.

WEB ACTIVITY

We have provided research log templates on the website associated with this book. Go to: http://www.prenhall.com/rodrigues to find them.

As you find sources, you can create bibliography cards electronically and save them to a separate file in your electronic research log and on your backup disk. Table 2.2 illustrates an electronic bibliography card template for books. We have provided this as an example, but you can find more of them in Chapter 8, "Documenting Sources."

By using your Copy and Paste commands of your word processor, you can duplicate as many of these as you want, whenever you want them. You

TABLE 2.2   Sample Electronic Bibliography Card for a Book

Author's name: Last, First Initial	
Book Title	
City of Publication	
Publisher	
Date of Publication	
MLA Format	Last name, First Initial. *Title*. City of Publication: Publisher, Date of Publication.

can create a separate format for each type of bibliographic entry, following the style required for your course. So that you don't have to be constantly looking up the correct bibliography format for your sources, the last row contains the format. The example above uses the MLA format, but you can easily design these for other style guides. If you want to create electronic bibliography cards now, then go to Chapter 8 or to the website for this book for guidelines.

WEB ACTIVITY

Go to the companion website for this book. There you will learn how to use your word processor to create electronic bibliography cards.

BROWSING IN THE LIBRARY

Not too many years ago, the only place that we could browse was the library. Now, not only can we continue to browse the library, but also we can find more avenues for browsing in the library. Fewer and fewer libraries have card catalogues anymore. Now they have Public Access Catalogues, online versions of the old card catalogs that allow you to search at a library terminal or even from your personal computer if you can log in to your online catalog from home. Ask your librarian whether you can access the online catalog from home and, if so, how you can establish your identity and password to log in.

When you begin your library research, you can look through the list of books available at your library to get a sense of how many works your library may have on various topics. Figure 2.1 illustrates how libraries now provide a variety of resources online.

When you locate a particular reference and find it on the shelves by using the call number of the book, don't stop there. Many researchers have found it helpful to look at other books with similar call numbers to the left and right of that book. Sometimes a book whose title did not appear to be relevant turns out to be a good source after all. If you don't know how to use the online catalog of the library, ask a reference librarian for help. That's their job, and they are always happy to help.

You can still use traditional bibliographies such as *Subject Guide to Books in Print, Books in Print,* or *Bibliographic Index: A Cumulative Bibliography of Bibliographies.* Specialized bibliographies may be more helpful to you if you already have a general field that you want to browse, for example, *Magill's Bibliography of Literary Criticism; American Ethnic Literatures: Native American, African American, Chicano/Latino, and Asian American Writers and their Backgrounds: an Annotated Bibliography; Humanities Index;* or the *MLA International*

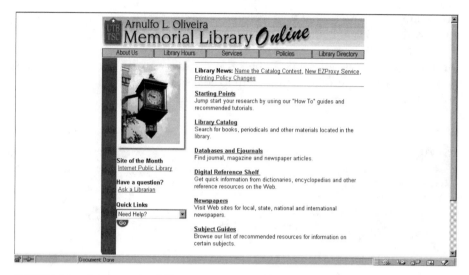

FIGURE 2.1 An example of library resources online. Permission granted by Oliveira Library, University of Texas at Brownsville and Texas Southmost College.

Bibliography are among many sources to start if you are writing a research paper for a literature class. (For a list of other literature sources, go to http://www.iusb.edu/~libg/guides/lit-crit.pdf or ask your librarian.) To learn what the U.S. Government Printing Office is producing, you can look through the *Monthly Catalog of United States Government Publications.* Whether your topic falls within the sciences, social and behavioral sciences, or arts and humanities, you will find bibliographies and catalogs online and in print that can give you leads on your research.

Browsing Library Databases

A *library database* is an electronic collection of articles that can be searched by using keywords. Figure 2.2 illustrates one library's page leading into its databases. Each database has its own system for searching, so you should either read the online guidelines if they are provided or seek assistance from the research or reference librarian at your school.

When you go to a particular database, you should first learn how to search with that particular database. Figure 2.3, for example, illustrates the online help at one library that is available to search WilsonWeb.

Note, for example, the Thesaurus link. Some databases contain a *thesaurus,* which consists of the standardized terms available for searching the database. You can search for synonyms, related terms, more general terms, or more narrow terms. This enables your search to be more effective within the structure of a particular database. Not only can you search within a given database,

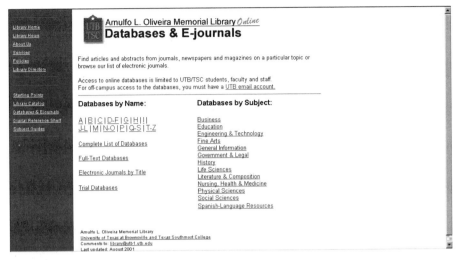

FIGURE 2.2   How one library organizes the entry into its databases. Permission granted by Oliveira Library, University of Texas at Brownsville and Texas Southmost College.

but you can also sort your results, save them, mail them, and print them. Once you have found one, two, or three databases that fit the nature of your topic, you can concentrate on learning how to search just those databases so that you save yourself time in your research.

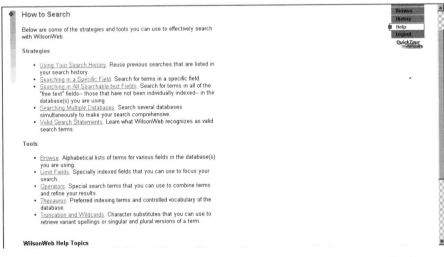

FIGURE 2.3   Instructions for searching the database WilsonWeb. Reprinted with permission.

TRY IT NOW

Go to your library, either online or in person, and begin browsing the online catalog and the databases to learn more about your possible topic. Maintain your research log as you browse.

BROWSING THE WORLD WIDE WEB

Online, search sites consist of subject directories and search engines. Use subject directories such as those available at Yahoo! (http://www.yahoo.com) or Galaxy (http://galaxy.einet.net/). Yahoo! is shown in Figure 2.4.

Subject directories or collections feature sites that scholars and others have collected and organized into categories. Notice the subject directory categories in Figure 2.4. These resulted from the keywords "Nafta U.S. Economy" being entered. On this page we see how Yahoo! returns with four sets of subject categories arranged in hierarchical order, from the most general to the more specific. By being organized hierarchically into categories, they allow you to browse in increasing depth to determine what possible subjects already have a great many resources available online and whether any of those can help you determine what you want to research. They are especially helpful when you

FIGURE 2.4   Yahoo subject directories.

really don't have any idea about what you want to research except in the very broadest sense.

Commercial *search engines,* such as Google (http://www.google.com) allow you to search by using keywords, and show the results or "hits" in a series of screens that list possible sites in some order of priority determined by the search engine program. For example, the priority may be set according to the most popular sites people have gone to. Search engine results may list so many hits that you find it impossible to use them for discovering your topic. ("Google" means the number one followed by one hundred zeroes, which symbolizes the amount of information that search engine can provide.)

In Chapter 4, we show you a number of strategies that will help you conduct your research using search engines once you have a general sense of your topic. For now, though, don't ignore these search engines because of the possible weaknesses in many search results, for their search results may lead to some serendipitous sources that turn out to be the very topic you truly want to explore.

YOUR INITIAL READING

Skim through the books and journal articles themselves, looking at the tables of contents, or glancing through the index to learn how that author has covered subtopics. Allow topic possibilities to percolate in the back of your mind. As you pour through a range of sources, you will gradually gain a sense of what interests you, and you will develop a sense of what has been said about your potential topics by others. Don't start taking detailed notes right away, for your initial task is to develop an overview of your subject so that, once you narrow your topic to a manageable one, you will be more knowledgeable about your research topic and able to choose one that will be best for you. Here are some questions to guide you as you browse and begin reading library and Web sources:

- What possibilities have I discovered for my research?
- What limitations in sources have I discovered about this or that topic?
- What standard library sources should I consult?
- What online library resources should I consult?
- How can a reference librarian help me?
- Do the possible topics lend themselves more to Web research than research with print materials or library databases?
- Are there collections of resources already available on the Web that others have gathered?
- What aspects of my possible topics are really intriguing?
- What do I already know about my possible topic?
- What do I need to find out?

SUGGESTED ACTIVITIES

1. Interview professors in your discipline. Find out what the key journals are and see if you have them in your library or in an online database.

2. Analyze a key journal in your field. What style for citations and bibliographies or lists of references do they follow? Do they begin with an abstract?

3. Find out what kinds of research faculty in your field do. Read several research articles.

4. Answer as many of the questions as you can in the bulleted list of questions above.

From Research Questions to Research Plans

3

After completing this chapter, you should be able to:

- Develop an extensive list of possible research questions about your topic.

- Draft an initial plan for how you will conduct your research.

- Develop a possible thesis statement for your research.

- Establish your timetable or set of deadlines to hold yourself to as you conduct your research.

- Start conducting field research.

Choosing a good research topic is important if it is to both be meaningful to you and meaningful to the professor who has assigned a research paper as part of the course. After you have had a chance to begin exploring the Web and library resources and have begun to find possible sources for research papers, concentrate your research efforts on developing a topic that is manageable and worth researching.

In this chapter, you'll learn how to develop inquiry questions that will help you focus upon what *you* really want to know. After you develop these research questions, you should be able to draft a preliminary thesis statement. Then you will be ready to develop a research plan and present it as a research proposal.

FROM TOPIC TO ISSUE

As you begin to browse, think about the possibilities that any topic might open up. Your professor is going to expect a balanced view in your report, not simply a report that reflects and supports your personal opinion. Recognizing divergent viewpoints or evidence is a characteristic of academic scholarship, even when the scholars ultimately come down on one side or another of an issue. Topics such as the following open up many opportunities to present evidence on the different sides of an issue before drawing your own conclusions:

- Did the North really fight the American Civil War to abolish slavery, or were their economic interests more important?
- Is the future of the United States inextricably tied to the future of Mexico, and if so, what should the United States do in the face of continuing illegal immigration by Mexicans seeking work?
- Is it ethical for business leaders to plan takeovers of other companies without letting their stockholders know?
- Is capital punishment morally wrong? Has capital punishment deterred violent crimes?
- Does spraying crops pose a risk to public health? For example, does spraying crops in south Texas cause a high rate of anancephaly in the newborn along the border, or are there other environmental factors or health practices at fault?
- Was Ethan Allan a patriot or an entrepreneurial accumulator of wealth who acted out of self-interest? For example, did he lead the Green Mountain Boys to Fort Ticonderoga out of a spirit of patriotism, or was there some self-interest involved?
- Is Robert Frost strictly a New England poet, locked in place by geography, or are his imagery and metaphors more universal in nature?
- Is the color of a flower the only factor that attracts insects to it or do variables such as weather, age of the flower, and availability of pollen play more important roles?
- Are there limits to patriotism? For example, in times of national crises, should we be willing to forego any of our constitutional rights in order to protect our country?

Your research about any one of these topics or others more pertinent to your assignment will uncover many facts and opinions, but it will be up to you to understand, interpret, and draw conclusions about them. You'll need to distinguish well-founded opinions and interpretations from those that are emotional or developed out of some form of self-interest or not based upon evidence. One of your personal challenges will be to examine the evidence as objectively as you can and then organize it so that your reader understands the different perspectives about the issue. Should you then draw your own conclusion about a controversial topic, your reader will recognize that you have taken into consideration the divergent viewpoints and not simply jumped to a biased conclusion.

DEVELOPING RESEARCH QUESTIONS

The pure quantity of information available to us today can be overwhelming. Thinking about the information available on any topic is like trying to understand the Gulf of Mexico. It is huge, contains a vast amount of water, and, as seas and oceans go, it is fairly shallow. Imagine that you wanted to conduct some research into the origins of its water. Where would you start? You could start with the Atlantic, but that's even larger. Therefore, you start with the Mississippi, the largest river that feeds the Gulf, and discover that there are many tributaries to the Mississippi, large and small. You decide to study large tributaries and find that the Missouri River is the largest. As you explore the Missouri, you discover all sorts of aspects you might research: Lewis and Clark's early observations; Mark Twain's depiction in *Huckleberry Finn*; the Pony Express at St. Joseph, Missouri; the Platte River. Perhaps you would decide to investigate the Platte. Where does it come from? What kinds of animal life surround it? How extensive is the agricultural industry along the Platte? Does the runoff carry pollutants, or have farmers developed new ways to control insects and weeds? Gradually, you start to focus in on your topic, but notice the branches and tributaries that you have followed.

Well, you say, if I had wanted to study sources of pollution along the Platte, I would have begun there. Right! That's why it's important for you to ask yourself what you are really interested in as you begin your research. If you want to study sources of pollution, you might even begin with your local community. Perhaps you have some personal experience or knowledge that gives you a starting point for your study of pollution. Good research begins with good research questions. Let's consider types of research questions and what they might lead to if we stay with the topic of river pollution and ask questions designed to fit certain categories. Below is a category–question technique to help you generate questions:

Category	Question
Analysis	What types of pollutants are in the Platte River or the Rio Grande or (the river near where you live)?
	How do scientists determine types of pollutants in rivers?
Evaluation	How accurate are studies of pollution in rivers?
	Is our local government able to judge and manage water pollution in our community?
Media	How accurate are media reports of pollution in rivers?
	Which media reports should the average citizen pay attention to if we are to be well-educated about river pollution?
Policy	How do federal government policies control river pollution?
	Should farmers be more restricted in their uses of pesticides?

Category	*Question*
Health	What is one of the most serious health risks from river pollution?
	What educational programs are designed to teach people about the health risks from river pollution?
Food	Are fish in polluted waters safe to eat?
	If farmers can't use pesticides, will our food supply be diminished?
Demographics	Have population shifts had an impact on river pollution?
	Have pollution controls had an impact on local populations?
Economics	Can we afford to have restrictive pollution controls along rivers?
	Which companies profit from controlling pollution along rivers?
Ethics	Which has greater value: controlling pollution or producing food?
	Do I have a responsibility to care about my uses of pesticides?

You can do this exercise with any topic that you would want to start exploring using the categories above or others, such as religious views, cultural issues, personal issues, education, family values, or history.

WEB ACTIVITY

Go to the companion website for this book (http://www.prenhall.com/ rodrigues) to do an online version of the category–question technique to generate research questions. Start with a broad topic that you want to explore and examine it from such perspectives as analysis, evaluation, media, policy, and history. Select those categories that are most meaningful to your subject. For example, if you are working on a literature subject, categories such as comparisons to other works, comparisons to other authors, symbolism, imagery, themes, style, and relevance to our lives today might help you best.

NARROWING THE RESEARCH QUESTION

Once you ask your initial research questions, you can begin to build your research agenda. Below we use the general topics "NAFTA" and "Technology in Colleges and Universities" to demonstrate how you can move from your initial research questions to your actual research. After you have settled on a topic or issue, you need to narrow it down to something manageable within the required length you are expected to write. Both "Technology in Colleges and Universities" and "NAFTA" encompass an enormous number of possible areas to focus on, certainly more than we could list here.

DEVELOPING RESEARCH QUESTIONS

1. State your topic as a question.

   Topic: Technology in Colleges and Universities
   Broad Question: Is incorporating technology into college instruction educationally sound?

   Topic: The North American Free Trade Agreement (NAFTA)
   Broad Question: What are the strengths and weaknesses of NAFTA?

2. Pose several subquestions.

   Topic: Technology in Colleges and Universities
   Subquestions:
   Is learning through distance education as effective as learning in a live classroom?
   Do today's faculty support the use of research using the Internet?
   How has the introduction of technology in the classroom made learning easier or harder?
   What methods of integrating technology into the curriculum have been demonstrated to be effective nationally?

   Topic: The North American Free Trade Agreement (NAFTA)
   Subquestions:
   Has NAFTA taken jobs away from our citizens?
   Are the economies of Mexico, Canada, and the United States stronger as a result of NAFTA?
   Are *maquiladoras* environmentally safe?
   Should we ease our immigration laws as a result of NAFTA?

FROM INITIAL RESEARCH QUESTIONS TO RESEARCH METHODS

Below is a scenario of how a researcher like you might begin to take your research questions and turn them into a plan of action to do the research. We start with "NAFTA" and "Technology in Colleges and Universities" as examples.

1. **How has the North American Free Trade Agreement affected industry and business in the United States?** First, what is NAFTA? Has NAFTA hurt or helped U.S. industries? (See Chapter 5, "Evaluating Sources," for an example of how we might evaluate sources discussing that question.) What organizations measure the effects of NAFTA? Are their reports objective or biased? How should I narrow this subject? What is the impact of NAFTA on Mexican labor rights? How safe is the food imported under NAFTA regulations? If we allow Mexican trucks and drivers on United States roads, are we putting our safety at risk? How do Canada and Mexico feel about NAFTA? What do Central and South American countries think about NAFTA?

Possible Research Plan

- Search the Internet to learn all you can about NAFTA before proceeding with your research plan (see Chapter 5 "Evaluating Sources").
  - Locate descriptions of NAFTA.
  - Read trade agreements in NAFTA.
  - Search government documents, including Canada and Mexico.
  - Identify sites with clear political biases pro and con.
- Ask your reference librarian for suggestions on where to search in the library, including the library online.
  - Academic reports
  - Journal articles
  - Government documents
- Interview business or labor leaders in your community or region.
- Focus on a few areas that are beginning to interest you, for example:
  - The impact of *maquiladoras* on the Mexican economy
  - Economic development councils
  - Labor union perspectives
    - United States
    - Mexico
    - Canada
  - Food imports and health
  - International truck safety
- Join a listserv that discusses NAFTA-related topics.

2. **To what extent is technology changing instruction on campuses across the nation?** What do you mean by "technology"? Research technology? Instructional technology? If instructional technology, what is driving its growing use: a desire to improve instruction or a dream of saving money? Are stu-

dents satisfied with their access to computers on your campus? Do many of your faculty teach with technology? If at least some do, how do they teach with technology? Do some students have more experience than others in using technology for learning? How does your institution provide for different levels of student experience? Are distance education and its tools starting to show up on campus, and under what conditions? How effective is it? How does your campus compare on all these questions with universities across the nation?

Possible Research Plan

- Search the Internet to learn all you can about computers and instruction before proceeding with your research plan (see Chapter 4, "Finding Sources," and Chapter 5, "Evaluating Sources").
  - Locate descriptions of teaching with computers, syllabi, and other examples.
  - Read online journals about educational technology and instructional computing.
  - Find information on instructional support and other resources available to faculty and students.
- Ask your Reference Librarian for suggestions on where to search in the library, including the library online.
  - Academic reports
  - Journal articles
    - General higher-education journals, such as *Educom Review* (http://www.educom.com)
    - Specialized teaching journals, such as *Kairos* (http://english.ttu.edu/kairos/)
  - Government documents
- Interview faculty, administrators, and students in your college or university about their perspectives on computer-intensive teaching and learning.
- Focus on a few areas that you find most intriguing, for example:
  - Teaching writing or mathematics with computers
  - The impact of learning with computers on art or business courses

TRY IT NOW

Create the table on the next page for your research log. Save it as a file in your research log folder and title it "Preliminary Research Plan." Given what you know about your topic, complete each of the items. Brainstorm responses. Don't worry about whether you can accomplish all of this plan. For now, you are creating a research plan that encompasses all the possible sources and steps that you might take. As you proceed with your research, you can always return to this table to revise it.

Preliminary Research Plan

At this point, what is my general topic?	
I will search the Internet to learn all I can about the following research questions:	
I will ask the reference librarian for suggestions on:	
I will interview:	
I will focus on a few areas:	
I can join this listserv:	

- Distance education tools in the classroom
- Taking distance education classes on your own campus
- Student economics and campus computing expectations
- Student support services for learning with various technologies
- Join a listserv on the more focused topic that you are interested in, such as:
  - ITForum (http://itech1.coe.uga.edu/itforum/home.html)
  - The American Association for Higher Education listserv: (http://www.fredonia.edu/tltr/index2h.htm#aahe_listserv)

DEVELOPING A PRELIMINARY THESIS STATEMENT

A *thesis statement* is the statement of the argument that you are going to make in your research paper. At this point, having begun to explore your topic, you should be able to draft a preliminary thesis statement. It is preliminary because you may discover, after having continued your research, having read and thought more about the topic, that you want to change your original thesis. Not only is that appropriate, but it is also indicative of your ability to weigh evidence and shift your conclusions if the evidence indicates that a change is warranted.

A thesis statement is usually a statement that someone else might disagree with. You will be presenting evidence in favor of your thesis statement, and someone else might present different evidence to counter your thesis statement. To be a good thesis statement, it should be somewhat controversial. Statements such as "Robert Frost was an important American poet," "There are many different attitudes toward the North American Free Trade Agreement," or "The World Wide Web can be a valuable research tool" are not worth defending, for no one would disagree with them.

A thesis statement should not be so broad that you cannot possibly cover it in a relatively brief report. These are examples of thesis statements that are too broad: "Robert Frost's poetry is hard-hearted," "NAFTA has done more harm than good," or "The World Wide Web contains much information that is biased." For your preliminary thesis, you should begin with a topic that you believe you can manage in the amount of space you will need. Therefore, you might focus on two or three of Frost's poems to prove that he could be hard-hearted or show how NAFTA has caused jobs to be lost in the United States or focus on a particular type of bias that shows up on the World Wide Web.

Design your thesis to be appropriate for your discipline. In the humanities, the arts, or the social sciences, you may be expected to argue a position that others would disagree with. Daniel A. Wagner, introducing his essay "Literacy Futures Revisited: Five Common Problems from Industrialized and Developing Countries," provides a thesis that summarizes his personal opinion, even though it is the result of careful research and consideration:

> It is my view that, while there is a tremendous cultural variation, a number of the basic "problems" of literacy cut across every society and, therefore, provide an opportunity for synthesis. (Wagner, 5)

In the natural sciences and often in the social sciences, you will be expected to demonstrate what the evidence shows, and so your thesis will either be an objective conclusion of what you have observed or a summary of what you will report. The introduction to "The Cloverleaf Site: A Late Archaic Settlement on the Walloomsac River in Southwestern Vermont," by Belinda Cox, Ellen R. Cowie, and James B. Peterson, provides an example of an objective thesis statement summarizing what will be reported:

> This report provides preliminary information about the setting of the Cloverleaf site, a brief history of investigations, and salient observations about the site's archaeological contexts and artifact assemblage. In addition, its implications for local and regional Native American history are briefly explored. (2000, 17)

Write your thesis as clearly as possible. Your reader should know what you are reporting or arguing in your research report and not have to figure it out. As you will see when you begin drafting your paper, the thesis will relate to the introduction, the body of the paper, and the conclusion, so it is critical that it be well-conceived by the time you have finished your research.

In short, a good thesis:

■ states a claim that you will defend with your evidence;
■ expresses a controversial point of view;
■ focuses on some aspect of your main topic that you can cover in the relatively short length of your paper; and
■ is appropriate as a thesis for research in your discipline.

For now, at the very beginning of your research project, try to draft a reasonable preliminary thesis, but don't worry if you need to change it as you learn more. Changing one's point of view or conclusion is a normal result of good scholarship and a natural part of the research process. You still need to find good sources of evidence, evaluate what you read, and begin to write your paper. Your preliminary thesis will help you begin the research that will be the heart of your work.

TRY IT NOW

Draft a preliminary thesis for your research paper. Share it with at least one other student in your class and check each other's thesis statements to determine whether they meet the four criteria above.

IMPLEMENTING YOUR RESEARCH PLAN

You've been assigned to prepare a research project or paper. You've started to narrow down your topic, and you've already found a topic and developed a preliminary thesis. Before you proceed, let's consider how much time you're going to need to complete it. Below, we suggest a series of steps for you to proceed through to completion of your topic. Take some time now to consider the steps you will need to complete and when you will need to complete them if you are to finish on time.

TRY IT NOW

Create the table below for your research log. Save it as a file in your research log folder titled "Research Deadlines." Fill in the dates you need to complete each of the steps in your research project:

Your Task	Projected Completion Date
Read broadly to determine your topic and narrow your thesis statement.	
Seek approval for your topic by submitting a research plan, if that is required.	

Your Task	Projected Completion Date
Conduct your research and develop a working bibliography.	
Organize your ideas, notes, and sources.	
Write your first draft.	
Revise what you have written.	
Edit the final draft before submitting it.	
Submit the final draft. Due date.	

WEB ACTIVITY

Go to the companion website for this book and complete the exercises on good research plans and good thesis statements.

FIELD RESEARCH: INTERVIEWS, SURVEYS, AND OBSERVATIONS

All writing, even personal writing, involves different kinds of research. In Chapter 1, we explained the formats for different types of research studies, such as case studies and reports of experiments. You may want to include your own research in the field to add personal or local depth to your research. When reporters cover a story, they need to learn about the topic, ask questions, take notes, and then synthesize their findings. When scientists conduct research, they ask questions and record their observations before they analyze what they have observed and synthesize their findings. Depending upon the type of research you are conducting, you may use a variety of techniques beyond searching the library and the Web. Three techniques can provide greater depth and insights into much of your research: interviews, surveys, and observations. Whichever technique you use, you must prepare carefully by having read as many related sources as you can, deciding upon the techniques you will use, and, after having gathered your information, interpreting and evaluating your results honestly before submitting it to an instructor or a publication.

The Effective Interview

Effective interviews have to be planned carefully. Good reporters have learned that, if they have time, they need to prepare methodically before they begin an interview. They do some background research on the topic so that they are better able to structure their questions and think of follow-up questions. They consider what they know about the person being interviewed, whether this is a person of power, an expert about the topic, or an ordinary citizen. The more the person being interviewed realizes that you have prepared for the interview, the more serious that person's answers will be. Make an appointment to interview the person at a mutually convenient time, and then be there on time.

Take your written questions with you to the interview, as well as a pen and paper. If you want to tape-record the interview, ask the person's permission first. Make sure that your questions are not simply ones that can be answered with a yes or no answer. For example, rather than ask someone, "Do you believe that drugs such as cocaine or marijuana should be legalized?," ask the person to respond to an idea, such as "Some people believe that drugs like cocaine or marijuana should be legalized. What is the position of your organization on that proposal?" Be prepared to ask follow-up questions, since sometimes the first answer to your question is very brief: "Could you talk a little more about the reasons for that?" "How did your organization come to that conclusion?" "Could you explain what you meant by . . . ?" If the person being interviewed refers to certain documents as having more information, find out whether copies can be secured, since you are liable to forget complex details that the interviewee may have summarized. And if the interviewee refuses to answer a question, be respectful. Indicate that you understand the concern and that you were simply trying to learn more. Before leaving, some interviewers ask whether they may call the person in case they need to clarify a few points. Most people appreciate the offer.

After the interview, as soon as you can, write a draft of the results of the interview before you forget key information or the logic of the person's answers. Note direct quotes and check your notes to determine whether you have summarized answers accurately. Then, just as you would with library or Internet sources, evaluate what you learned. Does what the person said corroborate what you have read about the topic or contradict it? Did the interviewee provide any evidence for what he or she said? If the person is an expert, why is he or she an expert on the topic that you discussed? Does the person have experience with the topic, or has he or she learned about it in some other way? Sometimes you may want to interview people who are not experts, simply to get their opinion. That may be enough, but at other times you may want to learn how the person formed his or her opinion.

A special kind of interview is the *focus group*. A focus group is a group of people selected for a group interview because they have something in common, such as all being students or women or shoppers in a particular mall. As an interviewer, you should take the same care with a focus group as you would with an individual, only this time be sure that you do get responses from all the members of the group and do not allow a few individuals to dominate.

Finally, when you write your report, be sure to cite the interview accurately, just as you would cite an article that you read.

WEB ACTIVITY

Please go to the companion website for this book and complete the exercises on conducting effective interviews.

The Effective Survey

Surveys allow you to gather information quickly from a group of people. However, surveys typically explore people's opinions or attitudes, and so they may not give you information about facts. You can survey people by sending them a questionnaire, by calling them on the telephone, or by giving the survey to them personally and waiting while they respond. Each type of survey has its own strengths and weaknesses. Mailing a survey may give you more responses, but you'll need to mail more copies than you need to receive, for many people never return them. Calling people may catch them by surprise and lead to guarded answers. Giving the survey to people personally helps insure that most respond, but limits the number of people you might reach. And personal interviews allow you to ask follow-up questions, but the number of people you can interview may limit the breadth or depth of your survey.

Before you construct your survey, read about the topic as thoroughly as you can. Then ask yourself why you want to conduct the survey: what is it you hope to learn? Knowing exactly what you want to learn can also help you determine which individuals you want to survey. Do you want to corroborate information you've read about? Do you wonder whether a different population will lead to different results from those in the literature? Do you want personal information about people or general attitudes or impressions? Do you need to provide particular information about the topic before asking questions about it? Your answers to those questions will help you structure your questions.

If you are at a university, there probably are specific guidelines on survey research and other types of research involving humans. You may need to submit your survey to a human subjects committee for approval before you can distribute it. Ask your professor for guidelines on campus policies.

You can structure survey questions in a number of different ways, for example:

- Information followed by a question:
  - "In 2001, following the attack on the World Trade Center by terrorists, Congress passed a law that allowed law enforcement officials to search the home or workplace of a suspected terrorist without informing the individual. Do you believe this law was justified?   Yes _____   No _____

■ Open-ended questions:
   ▪ What is the most serious safety issue on this campus?
      • _____
■ Multiple-response questions:
   ▪ How many people do you categorize as "close friends"?
      • A. 1 or 2 _____   B. 3 to 10 _____   C. more than 10 _____
   ▪ Illegal immigration poses a threat to the security of the nation.
      • Strongly agree _____   Agree _____   No opinion _____
        Disagree _____   Strongly disagree _____

The way in which your survey is organized on the page matters. Items should be clear and easy to answer. Put the answers in a location where you can read and tally them easily. Don't mix the position of the answer from question to question. Begin with information that you need to know about the respondent, such as the person's age, sex, or educational level. Start by asking questions that should be easy to answer and move then to the more difficult or more sensitive questions. Before you actually give the survey to your real respondents, give it to a few people to take as a test of the survey. Ask them if any of the questions were confusing or ambiguous. Were they offended by any of the questions? Then, based upon their answers, revise the survey so that it is as effective as possible. Try it once more with another small group of people before being satisfied with it.

If you are mailing your survey or handing it to a large group of people, prepare a letter or cover sheet explaining the purpose of the survey and giving any directions you may need to provide. Thank them for participating. If it is mailed to people, including a stamped, self-addressed envelope will result in more surveys being returned to you.

Determine how you will analyze the results before sending out the survey. If you are asking only a few simple questions, you can simply tally the results and report percentages. But if you are trying to determine something more complex, such as correlations between the demographic data of the respondents and their responses, then you'll either need to analyze the results statistically or give them to someone who can and who can then explain to you what those analyses mean.

You will then need to interpret your results as accurately as you can. Using the sample question above on illegal immigration, for example, it will make a difference if 50% of the people strongly disagree and 50% strongly agree, as opposed to a distribution of answers in which 10% strongly disagree, 35% disagree, 10% have no opinion, 35% agree, and 10% strongly agree, even though the responses are divided equally on both sides of the issue. If you have not asked follow-up questions to determine why people held the opinions they held, you might not have learned very much except that they disagree with one another. Can you safely say that the respondents are divided on the issue when you do not know why they answered as they did?

In short, while surveys provide quick data from a number of people, they risk leading to faulty conclusions when they are not constructed and analyzed well. The ability to analyze the data statistically does not ensure that the analysis is correct if the questions have not been well considered and well written.

For that reason, some researchers combine interviews and surveys. They may survey a large group of people first and then follow that up with specific, more in-depth interviews of a few individuals to try to understand why people responded as they did.

WEB ACTIVITY

Please go to the Web Activity on survey research to learn how to do an e-mail survey.

Effective Observation

Whether you are observing the behavior of students in a library or the number of insects attracted to different-colored flowers on a prickly pear cactus, your observations must be systematic and careful. You will need to take notes and interpret the results accurately. And you should have read sources that have dealt with similar observations or research questions so that you can design your observations appropriately and have them fit into a context of related research.

If you are observing people directly, you will have to determine whether you want them to know that you are observing them or not. (See "participant observation" and "nonparticipant observation" in Chapter 1.) If individuals know that you are watching them, they may change their behavior to protect themselves from some perceived intrusion or to behave in the very way they think you want them to behave. To avoid that, you may want to be less direct and less systematic, observing individuals in an informal way, without taking notes. Each has its advantages and disadvantages. If you do not take notes while you are observing, you may not accurately capture the data you seek. Yet, by not taking notes at the time, people may behave more naturally.

To prepare for an observation, first read the literature related to your topic. Being familiar with observational methods and questions in the literature, you can decide more clearly what it is you want to observe. Define what it is you are looking for. Identify the variables that you will be collecting information about. Decide how you want to collect that information. Observations of events as they occur will be more difficult than observing products of behavior. So you need to decide which method or combination of methods will yield you the best results.

For example, will you take notes, will you use a tape recorder or a video recorder, or will you use a checksheet that you follow? Checksheets allow you to record data quickly by checking the categories of the checksheet. Tape and video recorders allow you to replay the observations so that you can verify your data collection and try to verify whether you have missed anything. Taking notes while you are observing allows you to provide more in-depth observations, but may not allow you enough time to capture all you need to capture.

If you are observing products or artifacts of behavior, such as the writing samples of high school students, then you will have more time to analyze the artifacts, categorize them according to a scheme that you have developed, and reexamine them to verify your observations. Composition instructors, for example, have often used rubrics to guide their evaluations of student writing when their purpose is research or assessment of student writing of large numbers of students. For example, their rubric, or checklist of analytic factors, might include: (1) organization, (2) syntax, (3) usage, (4) mechanics, (5) use of supporting material, and (6) overall effect. They might weight each of these categories differently, knowing that some of those factors are more critical when judging effective student writing. The categories they choose to observe and the weight that they give their categories will determine the nature of their results and whether the results actually give them worthwhile information to use. If, for example, the composition instructors are interested in knowing whether students can construct an argument critically, the categories above might not be the best ones for them to use. Rather, they might more effectively use categories such as the student's ability to conceptualize a theme, the student's selection of appropriate sources, and the student's ability to integrate those sources into the student's own ideas.

Scientific experiments involve observations as well. In the case of classroom or field experiments and observations, all factors must be as tightly controlled as possible. Working in a laboratory, the researcher can design the appropriate conditions to provide the experimental controls needed. These may involve such matters as materials, temperature, ventilation, catalysts, equipment, space, and time. Such tightly controlled experiments may enable researchers to draw more definitive conclusions about causes and effects. So the ability to describe what is involved is as critical as the ability to analyze and interpret the results.

Working in the field, the researcher will be subject to many variables that the researcher cannot control. Therefore, deciding how to control for the possibility of extraneous variables becomes critical before the observation even occurs. For example, if a researcher is observing the number and types of insects that are attracted to various flower colors on prickly pear cactus, the researcher needs to decide such matters as which colors to observe; how many flowers will be observed on how many plants; whether the observations will take place under consistent time, weather, and temperature conditions or a variety of time, weather, and temperature conditions; how long each observation will take place; and how not to interfere with the natural behavior of the insects.

Having completed your observations, you will need to describe them accurately, clearly explain the variables and methods of observation, and interpret the findings for your reader. If there are any doubts about any aspects of your conclusions, you should honestly reveal those. If you draw conclusions that are based upon what you have observed, without recognizing possible alternative explanations, then you may not have provided appropriate information for your reader.

Observations in the field are subject to many different variables. Given your time, your budget, and the physical conditions in the field, you may not be able to control all the factors that you want to while conducting your observations. Most researchers who work in the field recognize that as a reality. An archaeologist, for example, may try as hard as possible to not disturb the artifacts and surrounding soil, structures, or related artifacts while digging, but that archaeologist may not have been able to control the ground squirrels that dug through the site hundreds of years ago or yesterday. What matters is that the researcher describe what he or she observes as thoroughly as possible and draw conclusions that account for the possible variables that may muddy the findings. Other researchers will respect that. And if you do the same, so will your reader.

WEB ACTIVITY

Go to the companion website for this book (http://www.prenhall.com/rodrigues) and complete the activities on field studies.

SUGGESTED ACTIVITY

Complete your research plan, including your preliminary thesis, and submit it as a proposal to your professor for approval. For topics in the humanities or social sciences, include the following categories:

- Preliminary thesis statement
- Purpose for conducting the research or preliminary research questions
- Possible sources of information that you can use

For a science research project, include the following:

- Preliminary research question or hypothesis
- Possible sources of previous research that you can use
- Proposed research methodology

4

Finding Sources

After completing this chapter, you should be able to:

■ Use the library to find sources.

■ Use search engines to explore your topic online.

■ Find library databases that have resources related to your topic.

■ Discover which key words are most productive for you to use.

■ Determine whether there are specialized databases on the Web on your topic.

■ Identify mailing lists on your topic.

■ Identify online communities on your topic.

In this chapter, you'll learn to search for sources in the library itself, using the online library catalog, online databases, search engines and subject directories, and by using mailing lists and newsgroups to identify possible people to interview via e-mail. **Note: You may wish to begin organizing and evaluating sources as you work. If so, refer to Chapters 5 and 6 before reading this chapter.**

Search strategies that you use to find books in the library will help you when you search the Web and online databases. As new technologies emerge, you will be able to search across many databases and library catalogs simultaneously. Already, in California, students can access a search tool called "Searchlight" that makes it possible to search across multiple databases and book catalogs in the same search.

Where you concentrate your research efforts depends somewhat on the search tools available to you, but also on your topic and discipline. If your topic is a contemporary issue, you may be able to find useful information on the Web. You would also use periodical indexes and full text databases to locate recent information in magazines and journals. If, however, you are researching an established topic or field, then you should locate books that have been published on your topic. Newspapers are fine starting points for information related to local statistics, such as the number of children growing up in single-parent homes in New York, or the crime rate in Chicago.

EXPLORING YOUR LIBRARY'S RESOURCES

Today's libraries include physical and online collections. As you refine your search and gather information, make sure you do not overlook any library holdings. Start with general references such as encyclopedias and dictionaries (see Chapter 2, Finding a Topic); then continue gathering information using the resources described in this chapter.

Finding Books

To locate books, you need to learn how to search the online catalog at your institution. Books are arranged using one of two main systems: the Dewey Decimal System or the Library of Congress system.

Most catalogs can be searched by author, title, key word, and subject term. To find a book on the shelf, you need to either print the page you retrieve from the online catalog or copy the exact location of either the Dewey or the Library of Congress number. Then find where books in that category are shelved in the library and retrieve the book. (Enjoy browsing in nearby books, too. Often you'll find additional useful information that you hadn't been looking for overtly.)

Other ways of finding books include searching libraries on the Web and exploring library websites (which often include valuable information and specialized bibliographies). Catalogs of books available at a large number of other libraries are available if your library subscribes to the OCLC WorldCat. You can also search many different libraries through the Library of Congress website or a website called LibWeb. Finally, you can order books through interlibrary loan.

General Reference Materials: Print Indexes, Bibliographies, and Online Databases

Indexes and databases often help researchers identify articles in periodicals—magazines, journals, and newspapers that are issued at regular intervals. (Note: The term "index" is usually used for print collections of references to articles; the term "database" tends to be used for online collections.) Bibliographies (lists of information in various sources) can also help you hone in on the best sources for your topic.

The following general reference materials will help get you started:

Bibliographic Index: A Cumulative Bibliography of Bibliographies
Biography Index
Biography and Genealogy Master Index
Books in Print
Book Review Digest
Cumulative Book Index
Dissertation Abstracts International
Library of Congress Catalog: Books, Subjects
Paperbound Books in Print
Publishers Weekly
Subject Guide to Books in Print

To learn how to interpret the entries in these reference works, look at the pages in front. There you will find explanations of abbreviations and the type of information provided for each entry. As an example of the type of information in a key reference, Figure 4.1 illustrates an entry in the *Biography and Genealogy Master Index* and the type of information contained in it. Organized by the names of people who have had articles or books published about them, this reference helps you identify those sources so that you can then search for them.

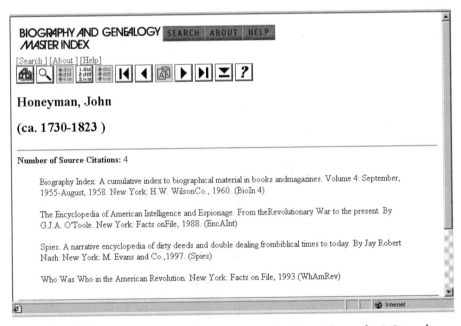

FIGURE 4.1 Biography and Genealogy Master Index. From *Biography & Genealogy Master Index* "Honeyman, John" © 2001 The Gale Group. Reprinted by permission of The Gale Group.

Figure 4.2 illustrates an entry in the *Book Review Digest* and the type of information contained in it. *Book Review Digest* will give you a sense of specific books published in the year covered by the *Digest* so that you can determine whether those books might contribute to your research.

The following indexes will help you identify journal and magazine articles:

Reader's Guide to Periodical Literature
Applied Science and Technology Index
Biological and Agricultural Index
Business Periodicals Index
Current Index to Journals in Education (CIJE)
Education Index
Humanities Index
International Index

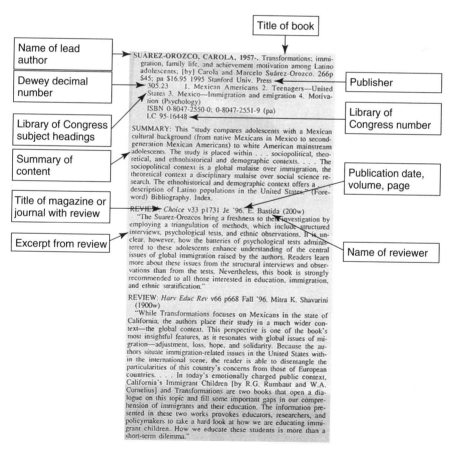

FIGURE 4.2   Sample entry, *Book Review Digest*. Book Review Digest, 1997, 93rd Annual Accumulation March 1997 to February 1998 inclusive. Copyright © 1998 by The H. W. Wilson Company. Reprinted with permission.

Resources in Education (RIE)
Social Sciences Index

Figure 4.3 illustrates an entry in the *Reader's Guide to Periodical Literature* and the information provided in the entries. The *Reader's Guide* includes many popular magazines, such as *Newsweek, Esquire, Jet, Fortune,* and *Condé Nast House & Garden,* which typically are not as scholarly as research articles in the academic disciplines. Nevertheless, those magazines might give you ideas about other sources you should look for that will be more scholarly. Many include surveys and quotes that might provide you with fascinating material that can add interest to your introduction. In particular, consider such magazines as *Archaeology, Psychology Today, Science, National Geographic, American Scholar,* and *Natural History.*

Newspapers are good sources for the most current information, as well as occasional in-depth articles on a variety of topics. Newspaper writers do not always cite their sources, but they do sometimes provide names of experts or topics of current research. Some newspapers are considered "world class," and therefore may be worth your reading to understand more about your topic, especially if you are conducting research on a topic of current interest. The following indexes will help you identify newspaper articles in several of the major newspapers of the world:

Bell and Howell's Index to the Christian Science Monitor
The New York Times Index
Official Index [to *The London Times*]
Wall Street Journal Index

If a work has been cited often in various articles, that source may be one of the key readings you should seek out.

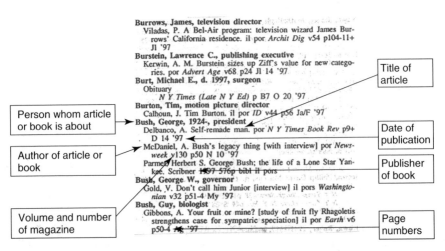

FIGURE 4.3 Sample entry, *Reader's Guide to Periodical Literature.*

Citation indexes will help you identify articles recognized by others as worth reading. If an author is cited often, that means that others writing in the same area considered that author's work noteworthy. Among the citation indexes are:

Citation Index
Source Index
Permuterm Subject Index

United States Government offices publish a wide variety of material, from official government reports to "how-to" publications. The following indexes are your key sources for publications of government and legal documents:

Monthly Catalog of United States Government Publications
Public Affairs Information Service Bulletin

Finally, virtually every academic discipline has an index to its publications. Ask your reference librarian to guide you to an index for the academic discipline of your research.

SEARCHING ONLINE DATABASES

Some of the indexes described in the previous section may only be available online. Many libraries are no longer subscribing to print indexes, for online databases allow users to locate material much more efficiently.

You use online databases to locate not only specific citations (titles, abstracts, and publication information), but also—in some databases—full-text articles on your topic. Many online databases allow you to control your search in various ways: (1) You may be able to indicate whether you want to include only "peer reviewed" publications (scholarly journals that have been approved by experts in the field before publication) or newspapers; (2) You

STEPS TO LOCATING JOURNALS AND MAGAZINES

1. Identify your topic.
2. List key terms.
3. Identify appropriate journals or indexes or databases. (If your library lists journals separately, you can click on the journal you want to search, and you will be directed to the appropriate database for that journal.)
4. Find citations (names, dates, titles of articles, page numbers of useful sources).
5. Use the online catalog to find out if the library carries that item.

may be able to search "backfiles," older collections that have been digitized but that are not included in the standard searches; (3) You may be able to search film, television, or image collections.

Infotrac
Popular database that also includes scholarly articles for research in all the academic disciplines including social science journals, humanities journals, science and technology journals, national news periodicals, general interest magazines, newswires, and *The New York Times.*

Lexis Nexis Academic Universe
A favorite of many business researchers, this database includes news, business, legal, medical, and general reference information.

PsychINFO
PsychINFO is an especially important source for medicine, psychiatry, education, social work, law, criminology, social science, and organizational behavior. It indexes information dating back to 1887.

Cinahl
An index to journals in nursing, occupational therapy, and other allied health fields.

ProQuest
Comprehensive collection that covers many disciplines, and includes full-text.

Academic Search
Academic Search (EBSCOhost) provides access to journal articles in most academic areas of study. It also includes *The Wall Street Journal, The New York Times,* and *The Christian Science Monitor.*

SEARCH STRATEGIES: KEYWORD SEARCHING

In most cases, you will start your online searching by using keywords, the key terms that authors use when they write about your topic. You might be able to guess which keywords will yield the most relevant sources based upon what you already know about your topic. As you read about your topic, note the key terms that various authors use, for those may locate similar sources for you when you search for more information. Other than that, the following technique will provide you with keywords that will be most promising.

If you have found at least one key source on your topic, search for that source using the online catalog. When you find that source, you should also see a list of subject terms that help identify that source. Then, go back to your search and use those terms, either all of them or a combination of some of them.

SEARCH STRATEGIES: SUBJECT SEARCHING

Another way to search is to begin by locating subject headings. The subjects into which librarians sort sources are based on official categories that librarians have agreed to nationally. The set of volumes called the *Library of Congress Subject Headings* (large red volumes that are in the reference section of the library) contains the official list of subject headings agreed on by librarians. If you look up a term using the *Library of Congress Subject Headings,* you will find a range of optional terms that you can use to search for your topic. For example, looking up "presidents" will lead you to alternative subject headings that might be useful to you. "Heads of state" is a broader term, identified by the abbreviation BT. Broader terms include presidents, kings, prime ministers,

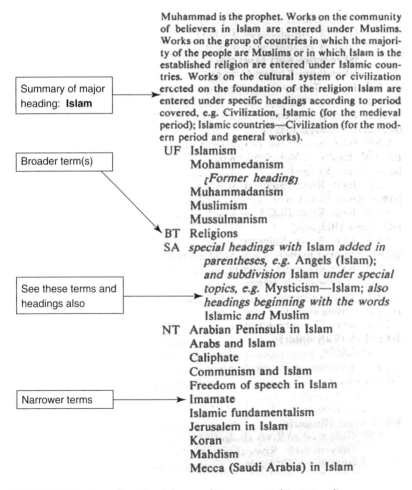

FIGURE 4.4 Sample entry, *Library of Congress Subject Headings.*

and other terms to designate the person who leads a nation. "Children of presidents," "grandchildren of presidents," and "women presidents" are narrower terms, identified by the abbreviation NT. "Ex-presidents" and "executive power" are related terms, identified by the abbreviation RT. Figure 4.4 illustrates subject headings found under the term "Islam." Immediately following this entry are a number of other categories related to Islam, such as charities, government, and history. These may suggest other terms for you to use in your catalog search. The abbreviation SA means "see also," which can suggest other topics that you could explore.

WEB ACTIVITY

Go to the companion website for this book (http://www.prenhall.com/ rodrigues) and complete the exercises on finding sources in the library.

EXPLORING THE WEB

The basic search strategies for personal searches of the Web are not much different from those you will use for searching online databases. However, because the Web is not organized into official categories, if you will be using the Web for research, you will need to understand more than the general searcher needs to know. You should learn how to distinguish between search engines on the basis of which search engine is best for locating which types of resources. You should also understand the differences between search engines and subject directories so that you can determine which will work better at different phases of your research process.

Four strategies for navigating the Web will help you get started:

- using a Web Browser;
- entering a specific URL into the location panel;
- using search tools and search strategies; and
- using bookmarks.

Web Browsers

A *browser* is software that allows you to access the Web and move from one site to another. There are two main browsers that most computers have: *Netscape Navigator* and *Microsoft Internet Explorer*. Figure 4.5 is a screen shot of *Netscape Navigator*.

The *navigation panel* near the top of the screen has several "buttons" that you can click on to execute specific commands:

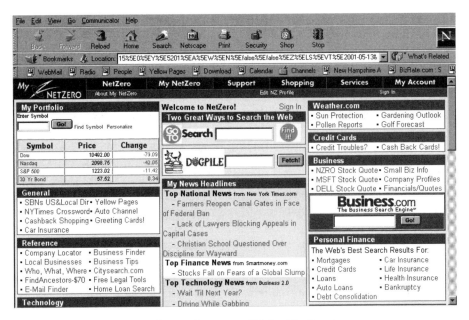

FIGURE 4.5 Netscape Navigator. Courtesy of United Online, Inc.

- *Back* will move you to each previous screen that you accessed, moving from the most recent screen to the one farthest back.
- *Forward* moves you from where you are in all the screens that you have accessed toward the most recent screen that you accessed.
- *Home* will return you to the startup page for Netscape Navigator.
- *Print* will start the commands for you to print the site page where you are currently located.
- *Stop* will stop whatever search your browser is attempting to carry out. This is a particularly useful command when, for whatever reason, the browser is having difficulty locating the site you are searching for.
- *Go* is better to use than *Back* or *Forward*. *Go* lists the most recent sites where you have been. By clicking on *Go* and then clicking on the site that you want to go to, you do not have to work your way through each site that you have just visited.

The *location bar* is the area where you can enter the site addresses that you wish to go to. When you are at the site, the location bar will show you the Web address or Universal Resource Locator (URL) of the site. A typical URL has the following parts:

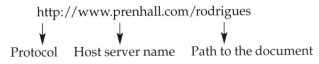

The *protocol* designates the method that the Web browser will use to exchange data with the file server where the document you are searching for is located. For most searches, the protocol will be *http,* or *hypertext transfer protocol.* But other protocols for the Internet are *ftp* or *file transfer protocol, telnet,* and *gopher.* Most of the time you will be using *http.* In fact, since it is most common among URLs, you do not even have to type it in when using the location panel of your Web browser. You could simply type, using the example above, www. prenhall.com/rodrigues.

To go to a new Web address or URL, move your cursor to the location bar and click on it. The background will be highlighted a different color. At that point, simply start typing in the new URL, and when you are finished, press the *Enter* key on your keyboard. Be sure to enter the correct address, character by character and case by case. If you make a mistake, you will either be sent to the wrong site or you will be sent an error message, indicating that the site may have moved to a new address or that you need to check your URL.

Figure 4.6 is a screen shot of *Internet Explorer,* the other most common Web browser. *Internet Explorer* has many of the same buttons as *Netscape Navigator,* with a couple of exceptions. The *Favorites* button is the same as the *Bookmarks* button on Netscape Navigator, but once you click on it, the procedures are slightly different.

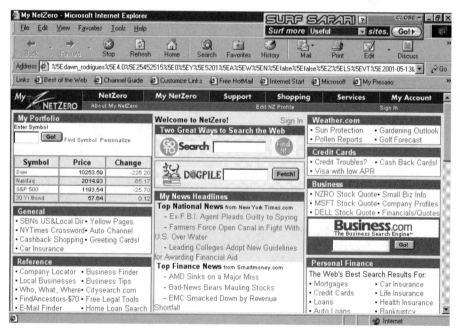

FIGURE 4.6   Internet Explorer.

TRY IT NOW

If you have never used a Web browser, go to a computer and load either Netscape Navigator or Internet Explorer. Experiment with the various commands. Use the *Help* button if you need to learn how to use a particular command.

Bookmarks

Once you have located sites on the Web that appear to be useful to you in your search, you can save those sites through a process called *bookmarking*. A bookmark on the Web is just like a bookmark in a book: it is a placeholder so that you can return to that spot in the future. Rather than type the entire Web address or URL every time you want to return to a site, all you do is open your bookmark file and click on the site you want to revisit. In Netscape Navigator, the term that appears at the top of the page is "bookmark." In Internet Explorer, the term is "favorites." When you bookmark a site, you electronically tag it with the electronic address of the site and a name for the site.

Not only can you save your favorite sites by bookmarking them, but also you can organize them into folders and subfolders. You might, for example, create a folder called "documentation" and bookmark sites that provide advice and models for documentation. (An excellent site to start looking for online documentation guides is the University of Wisconsin writing center: http://www.wisc.edu/writing/Handbook.) If you are beginning with a broad search for NAFTA articles and data, you might create a folder called "NAFTA," but within that create subfolders such as "economic data," "environmental impact," or "trade regulations."

When you have located a website with valuable information for your research and while the site is still online, go to your bookmark or favorites menu and choose **Add Bookmarks** (Netscape Navigator) or **Add to Favorites** (Internet Explorer). Click and your bookmark is saved. That is, the site you have identified will automatically be added to a bookmark list. Then, whenever you are online, you can go to your bookmark or favorites list, click on the bookmark that you want, and your browser will take you to that site. Note that the bookmark is actually saved on the hard disk of your computer, not online someplace, so you will only be able to access the bookmark online from the computer where you saved it.

As you add bookmarks, each bookmark will be added to the bottom of the list of bookmarks. When you are first starting to work with bookmarks, this is an adequate way to store your bookmarks. However, as you find more and more sites to bookmark, you will want to organize your bookmarks so that you can quickly find the particular sites that you want. This is especially important because, while you might begin storing bookmarks for your paper on marketing automobiles, stem cell research, or Robert Frost, if you are like most people, you will be discovering other sites that relate to your personal interests, hobbies, and projects that you will work on when you are not preparing your research report. Naturally, you will want to bookmark those as well. Soon, you will discover that your bookmarks are all mixed together and increasingly difficult to identify unless you develop a strategy for organizing them. In Chapter 6, "Organizing Sources and Notes," we explain how to organize your bookmarks.

TRY IT NOW

If you have not already done so, go to the companion website for this book (http://www.prenhall.com/rodrigues) and bookmark it so that you can return to it easily.

Saving Bookmarks to a Disk

Suppose you are working in your university's computer lab or library, pursuing your research and finding good sites as sources. If you save your bookmarks on the computer where you are working, then you can only use that computer to relocate your bookmarks. In the meantime, someone else may have gone to that computer and Web browser and changed the bookmarks, perhaps deleting your bookmarks. What you can do in this case is save your bookmarks to a disk.

If you are using Internet Explorer:

1. Make sure you have a disk in your A drive.
2. Go to your desktop. (*Note:* You will have to minimize your screen or screens if you want to return to it after you save your bookmarks.)
3. Double-click the **My Computer** icon. Then you will see a screen with icons representing your drives and printer and any other peripherals you may have.
4. Double-click the **C:** icon for the C drive. Now you will see a group of folders representing what you have on the C drive.
5. Double-click the **Windows** folder and click on **Show Files.** You will now see all your folders.
6. Right-click on the **Favorites** folder. A menu will open.
7. Choose **Send to:**
8. Choose 3½ **Floppy [A].**

If you are using Netscape Navigator:

1. Make sure you have a disk in your A drive.
2. Click **Bookmarks.**

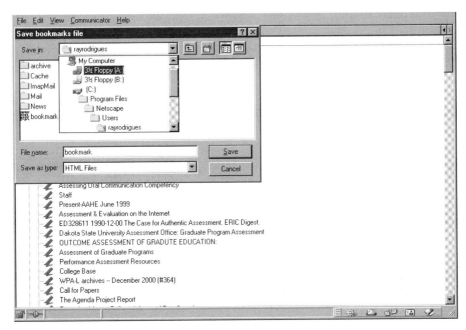

File Edit View Communicator Help

Save bookmarks file

Save in: rayrodrigues

- archive
- Cache
- ImapMail
- Mail
- News
- bookmark

My Computer
- 3½ Floppy (A:)
- 3½ Floppy (B:)
- (C:)
  - Program Files
  - Netscape
  - Users
    - rayrodrigues

File name: bookmark   **Save**

Save as type: HTML Files   Cancel

Assessing Oral Communication Competency
Staff
Present-AAHE June 1999
Assessment & Evaluation on the Internet
ED328611 1990-12-00 The Case for Authentic Assessment. ERIC Digest.
Dakota State University Assessment Office: Graduate Program Assessment
OUTCOME ASSESSMENT OF GRADUTE EDUCATION:
Assessment of Graduate Programs
Performance Assessment Resources
College Base
WPA-L archives -- December 2000 (#364)
Call for Papers
The Agenda Project Report

FIGURE 4.7 Saving bookmarks to a disk with Netscape Navigator. Netscape Communicator browser window © 1999 Netscape Communications Corporation. Used with permission. Netscape Communications has not authorized, sponsored, endorsed, or approved this publication and is not responsible for its content.

3. Click **Edit Bookmarks.**
4. Go to the **File** menu.
5. Click on **Save As.**
6. And then, in the **Save in:** menu, select your A: drive.

Figure 4.7 illustrates a *Netscape Navigator* screen as it would look in step 6 above. You will now have saved all your bookmarks to your floppy disk in the A drive. You can take the disk to another computer, open your browser, and then open the file with your bookmarks. From that point, you can use them as you normally would.

In Chapter 6, "Organizing Sources and Notes: Preparing to Write," we describe how you can organize your bookmarks into folders and subfolders. If you would like to learn that now, go to pages 100–103. Now we will look at where you can locate sites that you will want to bookmark.

Search Engines

Browsers can take you to specific sites when you know those sites. Search engines will search for sites that contain information you want. You can access search engines through your browser by typing in the URL of the search engine or clicking on the bookmark or favorites address of the search engine.

Unlike the library, the Web has no common set of subject headings. Web publishers are not required to file their pages using preset terminology. Fortunately, Internet search engines have been developed to help Internet users locate information. By adopting efficient search strategies, you can become proficient in locating sufficient appropriate material on your topic.

When you search using search engines, you will not suffer from a lack of information. In fact, if anything, you will encounter more information than you could possibly use, some of it useful, much of it useless. When you enter search terms, your search may lead to scholarly articles, commercial advertisements, papers written by other students and loaded on a website, and more resources than you know what to do with.

For example, suppose you were to search Google, one of the search engines with the highest number of sites available, for whatever you can find on poverty. See Figure 4.8. The "results" line at the top of the page indicates that your search led to about 2,640,000 hits. What are you going to do with all this information? Maybe all you were looking for was some U.S. census data. In that case, you got lucky. But the odds are that you are looking for something more narrow, something more specific about poverty. In that case, you still have to find ways to narrow your search, to focus in on a reasonable set of results or "hits."

What if you really don't know what you want to write about poverty? In that case, a broad search such as the one you conducted might help you look for more specific topics. The search engine has become one huge brainstorming tool, one that will give you a lot to think about before you decide upon the

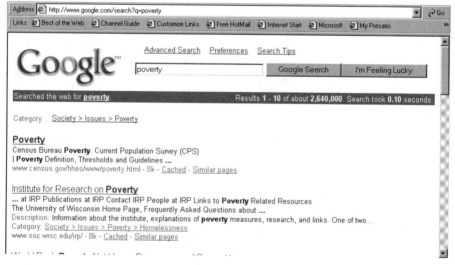

FIGURE 4.8 Google search results.

topic you want to write about. At this point, you can read through the topics, and perhaps a reasonably narrow topic will jump out at you. You can explore some of the sites that you've found to see whether they lead to a suitable research topic. You might be interested in child poverty and go to the National Center on Child Poverty home page. Or you might notice that the University of Wisconsin site has Frequently Asked Questions (FAQs). So you go there and find questions that interest you, such as "How is poverty measured in the United States?" and "What are good sources of information on basic trends in poverty, welfare, and related issues?" Clicking on the latter question will lead you to new possibilities: teenage pregnancy or health insurance issues.

Now, imagine that you decide to narrow your search by searching for sources on teenage pregnancy and poverty. You go back to Google and type in the two terms, *teenage pregnancy* and *poverty*. This time, instead of over 2 million hits, you only get 60. And some of those are leaflets and newsletters of various organizations—not particularly useful unless you are writing about organizations that work with pregnant teenagers. So, somewhere out there on the Web is the information that you can use.

TRY IT NOW

Log on to the Internet and your browser. Type the URL for Google (http://www.google.com) into the location bar of your browser and press "enter." When Google comes up, enter some keywords on your topic. Note the number of "hits" or results. Are any of the results on the first page potential sources? Which ones? Now go to the bottom of the page and click on "search within results." Add a new search term and press "enter." Do you have more or fewer results? Are any of the sources good potential sources? Do this a couple more times, adding new terms and deleting terms that seem too broad.

Record the results of each of your searches in the table below, which you can create yourself:

Keywords used:	Number of results:	Potential sources on first page:
Ex: poverty	2,640,000	Census Bureau, http://www.census.gov/hhes/www/poverty.html
		U. Wisc. Instit. for Research on Poverty, http://www.ssc.wisc.edu/irp/

Boolean Terms or Boolean Operators

When you search electronically using your library databases or search engines, you need to be familiar with "Boolean searching." Boolean terms or Boolean operators are a few words that allow you to designate which keywords you do and do not want to appear in your results. For example, if you type in the keywords *united* and *states,* the search engine will look for terms as shown by the following diagram:

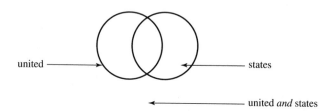

Thus, you will get sites that have *only* the word *united* in them and results that have *only* the word *states* in them. Your search results will also include sites that have *both* the words *united* and *states* in them, but not necessarily sites that are only about *the United States.* For example, your results could include sites on the "united Confederate states" of America or *states* that have *united* in certain interstate treaties. (A recent search with Google identified about 3,890,000 sites with the words *united* and *states* in them.)

Use other Boolean terms, such as *or* and *not* to narrow your search results further. Most search engines automatically enter the term *and* when you type in your keywords. Learn which terms the search engine you are using recognizes. Two common terms are:

a. OR, which means that either of the terms will be found. That is, if you enter *juvenile or justice,* some of the sites will have only *juvenile,* some only *justice* and some both.

b. NOT is a Boolean search term that allows you to narrow your subject more. If you enter *justice not juvenile,* you will locate sites that do not deal with juvenile justice, but do deal with all sorts of other justice issues. *Note:* Each search engine may accept slightly different Boolean commands. For example, some use the minus sign (–) instead of NOT.

Some search engines allow you to search for specific phrases by putting those phrases in quotation marks. As we illustrated above, if you enter *united states,* most search engines will search for both *united* and *states.* You will get many hits, ranging from unions that are united to foreign states to united states. When your search engine allows you to use quotation marks in your keywords, if you enter "united states," you will get sites that have information about the United States, as well as possible other united states such as the United Arab Emirates.

You can combine your Boolean search terms as well. For example, if you enter *"juvenile justice" NOT "United States" OR Canada,* you will get sites that deal with juvenile justice anywhere but the United States and Canada. (Even then, a recent search of Google using these keywords and Boolean operators led to about 84,700 hits. Even the more narrow search with Boolean operators turned out to still be a very broad search. When we instructed Google to look only for sites with the .edu domain, which designates education sites, we narrowed the results to about 9,860 sites.)

To learn which terms are recognized by the search engine you are working with, click on the "advanced search" button on your search engine's home page. You will then read a number of good hints on how to make your search with that search engine most effective.

Finally, you should understand "stem searches," sometimes referred to as truncation. If your search engine supports stem searches, that means that it will look for your search term and automatically include both prefixes and suffixes that are attached to the term. Such a search engine, if you typed in the keyword *digest,* would also look for the following terms: *digests, digested, digestion, indigestion, digestible, indigestible,* and, of course, *Reader's Digest.* If a search engine does not support stem searches, then you must type in the prefixes and suffixes that you want it to search for. (Search engines use different symbols to instruct the computer to return all versions of a word: $, ?, and * are the most common characters used.)

Common Search Engines

Below we list some of the most common search engines that you will be able to choose from, followed by basic descriptive information about each. Be aware that, because these are commercial sites, some may go out of business or be bought out by another company. So their addresses and structures may change over time.

Search engines are commercial enterprises. Each sells advertising space to the people who pay their bills—the companies that advertise overtly with banner ads and other techniques to get your attention. You can ignore those fairly easily. What you cannot ignore so easily and what is less evident is another practice of the search engine companies to make money: selling positions on the search results or "paying for placement." In some search engines, the rankings of search results depend less on how closely the site matches your search terms and more on how much the company has paid the search engine company to buy placement in the results. Sometimes the company is featured in a box at the top of the results page.

Alta Vista
http://www.altavista.com
Alta Vista accepts Boolean search terms, such as AND, AND NOT, OR, and NEAR. If you use upper- and lowercase in your search, Alta Vista will search for the words as typed. If you are searching for a phrase, put the phrase in quotation marks. You

may customize the way the results are formatted. A nice aspect of Alta Vista is its "Related Searches" section, which may suggest refinements to your search. Among its features, if you want a specific title, you can type *title:* followed by the actual title. If you are searching for a very specific topic, rather than a general search, Alta Vista is an effective tool. Alta Vista sells search result spots to advertisers. See, for example, Figure 4.9 below.

Dogpile
http://www.dogpile.com
Dogpile searches a variety of search engines at the same time. We recommend that you go to the area of Dogpile that lets you select the search engines you want Dogpile to search, for without that you will be receiving information that may be very commercial and may not suit your evaluative criteria.

Excite
http://www.excite.com
Excite's advanced search feature does not require special punctuation or Boolean terms. You may, however, use Boolean search terms and quotation marks to identify specific phrases. An advanced feature is the ability to designate *exact word order, specific domain,* and *language* to narrow your search.

Fast
http://www.alltheweb.com
Fast claims to be the largest search engine of all, but other search engines are always challenging that claim. You can customize Fast by selecting to filter offensive language and choosing to have your search terms marked in search findings. *Advanced features:* You can select the language in which you want search results and filter words so that the results must include the terms and must not include certain words. In addition, you can filter by domain.

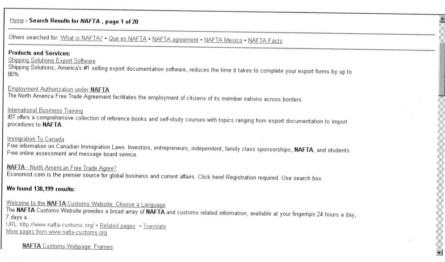

FIGURE 4.9 A search for the keyword *NAFTA* using the search engine AltaVista. Credit to come.

Google

http://www.google.com

Google, one of the two largest search engines, has features that make searching easy. The word **and** is automatically inserted between all your search terms, so you can refine your search simply by adding new terms to your original search. It ignores common words like **the** and **of** unless you specify that you want the word included by using the + sign before the word. It does not do stem searches, so you must specify, for example, **hits** if that is what you are searching for, not **hit***. The **categories** section at the top can be helpful when a search term might lead to topics you are not interested in. For example, searching for **white house** could lead to information about the President's home or Executive Branch of the U.S. government, or it could lead to games. The **categories** section can help you refine your search. **Advanced features:** You can search for phrases (e.g., University of Texas System) by placing the entire phrase in parentheses, can leave certain words out of the search by placing a minus sign before the word you do not want included in the search, and can limit the search to specific domains, such as **edu** or **org**.

HotBot

http://www.hotbot.lycos.com

HotBot automatically inserts *and* between words that you enter. If you do not want that, HotBot's drop-down menus allow you to narrow your search in other ways, such as **the exact phrase** and **the Boolean phrase**. You can narrow the search by date, by location or domain, by page depth, by allowing stemming, and by sites that contain particular media. You can search within the initial results with one step. Be aware that HotBot sells spots on their site to companies. As a result your search might lead directly to commercial sites. So it is critical that you evaluate the results of your HotBot searches carefully.

Infomine

http://infomine.ucr.edu

Infomine is first and foremost an academic search engine and is very useful if you have a broad academic topic that fits one of their databases. With sources selected by humans, the databases can be searched by subject, title, keyword, and author. You can choose to use stemming or not; and you can search for a description of the article or the full text. The quality of the descriptions allows the user to find the academic information that is most relevant to that person's search. For academic subjects, whether the life sciences, K–12 instructional resources, or social sciences and humanities, the results are sound sources. The major limitation is that the sources are relatively few compared to those found by search engines that work by computer selections rather than human selection.

Lycos

http://www.lycos.com

By selecting the advanced search capability, you can narrow the types of sites that Lycos will search. You can indicate if you want to search **all the web** or **all the words.** Lycos also suggests other words that you might search for when you receive your results. This search engine may allow you to find key sources for your research more rapidly than some of the other sites.

Northern Light
http://www.northernlight.com
Northern Light, one of the largest search engines, puts results into various categories. One of the best features of Northern Light is "Power Search." Using it, you can search by subject, source, document type, and/or date. By using the "tips" section, you can learn the techniques recommended by Northern Light to give you the best results using this search engine.

WebCrawler
http://www.webcrawler.com
WebCrawler allows you to use keywords, quotation marks around phrases, and Boolean search terms. Since it is owned by America Online (AOL), AOL users may find it comfortable to use. The relevance of sites located is determined by the ratio of the keywords to the total number of words in a document or site. If you choose, WebCrawler will list your search results without summaries. This is an advantage if you prefer more "hits" per screen.

TRY IT NOW

Load a search engine and practice searching for terms that might give you the results you want. Keep a record of the terms you use, noting which give you the best results. Now load another search engine and try using the same terms, noting the differences in results. Continue doing this with other search engines. Of the search engines you have tried, which do you prefer?

Metacrawlers

Metacrawlers search databases that search engines have already generated. Some people prefer them because they allow the searcher to find resources through more than one search engine at once. They do not, however, offer the advanced search techniques that many search engines offer. Below are some of the popular metacrawlers:

Dogpile
http://www.dogpile.com
You can search according to a specific list of search engines, directories, and specialized search engines. The results are grouped by search engines.

MetaCrawler
http://www.metacrawler.com
This is one of the oldest metacrawler sites, and it has given its name to the general category of metacrawler sites. The results will also list the search engines searched.

qbSearch

http://www.qbsearch.com

The metacrawler qbSearch (qb = quick browse) has, in addition to metasearch capabilities, a "Quick Link" capability that allows you to move from one link to another without having to return to the original listing.

Search.com

http://www.search.com

Search.com allows searches of the Web and specialized search engines. You can search through categories or with keywords.

TeRespondo

http://www.terespondo.com

This search site will search (buscar) in English or Spanish, but will return descriptions in Spanish. Like Ask Jeeves, TeRespondo allows the user to phrase questions for the search.

Vivísimo

http://vivisimo.com

Vivísimo not only returns results, but also organizes the results into categories that you might search further if they fit your research topic.

TRY IT NOW

Try several of the metacrawlers, using the same search terms that you used before with the regular search engines. Compare the results you get with the results that you get when you search by following the categories in those metacrawlers that are organized by category. Note which gave you the best results.

Specialized Searchable Databases

A number of specialized searchable databases are available that you can use if you are seeking specialized information. These have come to be called the "invisible Web," for they are not the best known sites for searching. For example,

■ Lawcrawler (http://www.lawcrawler.com) can be used to seek legal documents. It uses Alta Vista as its search engine and can be narrowed to search the U.S., California, other U.S. sites, and International. ABA LawInfo (http://www. abalawinfo.org) claims that it provides information that persons can use in their regular lives.

■ Psychcrawler (http://www.psychcrawler.com) is sponsored by the American Psychological Association and will enable you to search psychology journals and other sources relevant to the field of psychology. Users will find that it provides a number of specialized commands for narrowing one's search. For example, by using the *thesaurus* command, you can ask the search engine to search for synonyms of the search terms you have selected.

■ ArchNet (http://www.archnet.asu.edu/archnet) is a virtual archaeology library at Arizona State University that will lead you to sources about museums, lithic technology, site reports, and other archaeological sites.

■ Earth Resource System (http://ersys.com/usa) is an excellent source of data on major communities across the nation, providing data on education, health, weather, and a variety of other topics.

Be aware that some of these searchable databases are quite narrow in focus and many really are commercial in nature. When conducting research, you'll need to be selective.

If you are seeking specialized search engines, you might start with <http://www.searchability.com>. A search for "literature" databases turned out sites ranging from American Studies Web to the Perseus Project at Tufts University, sources on archaic and classical Greek history. You can also explore Direct Search (gwis2.circ.gwu.edu/~gprice/direct.htm), compiled by Gary Price, which will point you to searchable database categories ranging from Congress to statistics to Canadian shipwrecks. For scholarly sources, try Infomine (infomine.ucr.edu/search.phtml), which will help you search articles, reports, and data. The categories available at this searchable database range from agriculture to the visual and performing arts. For example, if you go from Infomine to the United States Geological Survey Site, you might find everything from the proposed federal budget for the USGS to reports on chemicals in humans.

TRY IT NOW

Try finding specialized databases in the area of your research by using both the Lycos Invisible Web Catalog and Infomine. Which database yields the best results for your research area?

As with all the search tools available to you, the more you use the Web to search for information in the area that you want to research, the more you will become familiar with the specialized search tools that can save you much time and effort.

WEB ACTIVITY

Go to the companion website for this book and try the activities for this chapter. They are designed to give you practices using regular search engines, metacrawlers, and specialized searchable databases.

Subject Directories

Subject directories are websites that invite readers to look for information by first exploring general categories such as Arts and Leisure, News and Views, or Health. Subject directories are compiled by people, not by a computer or Web-searching software (called "spiders"). Therefore, you will not find the enormous numbers of hits that you find by using search engines. However, what you do find may be more useful if they locate categories that include information you want. You can often locate specialized subject categories ranging from agriculture to space technology. Subject categories or subject directories are most useful at the beginning of the search process, when you need to explore broad categories to get a sense of what your topic encompasses. Once you have determined the extent of your topic, you can then go to a search engine for a more productive search.

Below are two major subject directories:

Yahoo!

Yahoo! Is the premier subject category search site on the Web. Yahoo! lists websites by various categories. The sites listed are those recommended by people, not those identified by a search engine. If you know the category of what you are searching for, you can begin with the categories offered by Yahoo! and narrow the search by selecting categories within those categories. You can use keywords, phrases in quotation marks, and + or − symbols to narrow your search. Yahoo! does not accept Boolean search terms, but does accept the field terms *t* for *title:* and *u* for *url:.*

The World Wide Web Virtual Library

The World Wide Web Virtual Library might best be thought of as a library of subjects. When you access the home page, you find a list of categories for various subjects. By clicking on any of those subjects, you can narrow your search within the total subjects that have been entered into the Virtual Library. The "library" is compiled by over 200 "maintainers," whose job it is to update the library on a regular basis. Searching this site is much like using an encyclopedia. You may not find exactly what you want, but if you need to learn more about your subject or narrow your subject before beginning to use search engines, this is a good place to start. See Figure 4.10 for an example of the Virtual Library home page with categories and Figure 4.11 for an example of what results of a search look like in the Virtual Library.

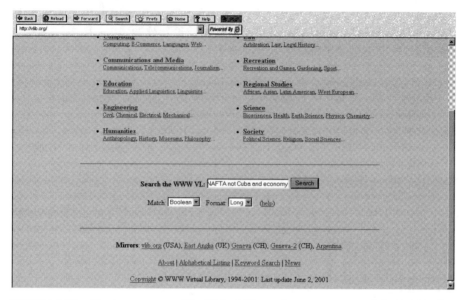

FIGURE 4.10   The home page of the Virtual Library. Image courtesy of the WWW Virtual Library, http://vlib.org.

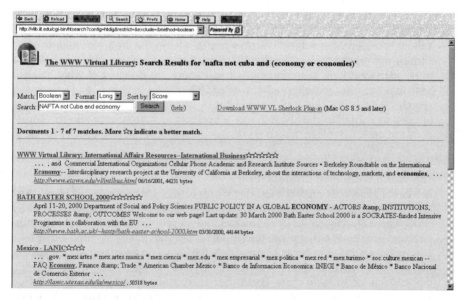

FIGURE 4.11   The results of a search on the Virtual Library. Image courtesy of the WWW Virtual Library, http://vlib.org.

SEARCH STRATEGIES

Even though you can get reasonable results without much trouble when you search, you will get better results if you develop efficient search strategies. Here is a list of tips for searching that are just as useful in the library or commercial database as they are on the Web:

1. Keep track of your keywords and subject terms when you use search engines and library databases. Record them in your research log so that you know which terms led to the best results and which did not.

2. If you use standard terminology used in the field of your research, you are more likely to have successful "hits" when you start than if you guess at the terms. For example, if you are conducting research on children or adolescents in prison, you probably will have better initial success locating scholarly academic material if you enter the keywords *juvenile justice* rather than *children prison* or *adolescents prison*. If you are interested in learning how to teach literature, you can enter the keywords *teach literature,* but if you enter terms such as *reader response,* you are more likely to find sources that reflect the results of scholarly inquiry rather than a miscellaneous collection of sources. As you read the literature of your field, keep a list of standard terms that scholars use in your field, especially those terms that appear in the literature often.

3. Learn to use Boolean search terms, or Boolean operators, such as *and, or,* and *not.* As you become familiar with various search engines, note which Boolean search terms you need to use with your search and which you do not.

4. Think in terms of synonyms, antonyms, and phrases to find more sources that fit your topic. Jot down a list of keywords that come to mind, and then list synonyms for each word. Use the thesaurus of your word processor to help, being careful to select words that have the right meaning for your purpose. So, instead of *juvenile,* you might use *youth, adolescent,* or *child.* Instead of single words, think in terms of phrases or clauses. Suppose your broad topic is *affirmative action:*
   - Synonym phrases: *equal opportunity, fair employment*
   - Antonyms and antonym phrases: *discrimination, unfair housing*
   - Clauses: Think "Is affirmative action fair?" and enter: *"affirmative action" and fair*
   - Think "Is affirmative action another form of discrimination?" and enter: *"affirmative action" and discrimination or "reverse discrimination"*

5. Before you use a commercial database (such as Ovid or InfoTrac) take time to familiarize yourself with the way that the search engine works. Each commercial database uses different terms and different rules for searching. Locate directions for using these databases either within the program itself or at your library or at another library's Web page. Ovid, for example, provides a checkbox that allows you to "map the term"; that is, the program itself will suggest appropriate "subject heading" terms. These subject heading terms will, in turn, allow you to check

Ovid's thesaurus of terms. The thesaurus, in turn, will allow you to narrow your search terms or find related terms.

6. If your library doesn't provide directions on how to use its databases, find a library that does and bookmark that page!

WEB ACTIVITY

Practice finding sites on the Web that you want to return to and recording both the URL and productive keywords or search terms. Go to the companion website for this book, where you will find all the research log charts that we discuss here.

Name of Site	URL	Description	Keywords

Note: If you know how to create tables with your word processor, you can also create your own charts.

TRY IT NOW

Go to the Web and start searching for a topic that interests you. When you find a website that you want to return to sometime, go to the **bookmark** or **favorites** area of your Web browser and click on **add bookmark** or **add to favorites.** Your bookmark is now saved on the hard disk of your computer. To view your bookmark, simply return to the bookmark area, and you will see your bookmark title displayed. Click on it, and you will be sent back to your website.

FIELD RESEARCH AND INTERVIEWING EXPERT SOURCES

Interviewing experts in the field can be one of the most productive strategies for your research. In this section, we describe three ways to conduct research using the electronic capabilities available to you:

1. Email (electronic mail)

2. Mailing lists or listservs and forums (electronic mail to a group of people with common interests)
3. Newsgroups

Email allows you to write messages to people throughout the world who are specialists on your subject; mailing lists help researchers and specialists (as well as students conducting research) to share ideas quickly; and newsgroups, programs that function like bulletin boards, enable groups of people, both expert and nonexpert, to post messages called *articles* to topical areas that can be searched for later retrieval. Forums—somewat similar to listservs—allow individuals to post messages in a systematic way and are often designed to focus upon very specific questions and topics. Many distance education courses use forums and bulletin boards as places where assignments can be posted and students can work together in groups to do those assignments.

Email

Use email to write to experts in the subject that you are researching, but realize that these individuals often have very limited time to respond to every message that they receive. Therefore, be polite, but scholarly. Show your reader that you care about the topic and that you have done some preliminary reading in preparation for your inquiry. Make your inquiry as specific and concise as you can. Individuals who receive many email messages seldom have time to read long messages. A good rule of thumb is to not send messages that are longer than one screen in length.

How can you find email addresses of experts?

1. One way is to join a mailing list or listserv on your topic. As you read the messages that individuals post, you can begin to determine which, if any, of the individuals might be knowledgeable enough to help you with your research.
2. Another way to find experts is to use the search capabilities of various search engines. If you have read an article by someone whom you would like to communicate with, you can search for that person's name. Often one of the sites that you locate will have an email address for the person.
3. One website designed to link you with experts is the "askanexpert" site: (http://www.askanexpert.com). There you can search by categories for experts in the field. Internet service providers (like America Online, Compuserv, or Prodigy) often have email address books that you can use to try to locate experts.
4. If the scholar is at a university or a corporation, go to the home page of that institution or organization. Most will have a search function to locate individuals within the organization. Similarly, the U.S. Congress and state government sites all provide ways to contact elected and appointed government officials.

5. If the expert has his or her own Web page, then you might be able to use Who's Who Online (http://www.whoswho-online.com)

6. For lists of specialized email directories, go to: http://www.555.1212.com/DIR/Index.jsp or http://www.emailaddresses.com/email_lookup_specialist.htm

7. Finally, many specific disciplines have their own address sites, such as:

- Worldwide Directory of Finance Faculty (http://fisher.osu.edu/fin/findir/)
- Economists with Web Pages (http://www.amherst.edu/njsirens/ewwp.html)
- By Region Artists and Musicians Directory (http://www.byregion.net/memberlinks.shtml)
- Home Page of Astronomers (http://www.aas.org)
- Directories of biologists (http://www.biosis.org/zrdocs/desktop/BIOL_DIR.htm)
- Directory of African Historians (http://www.sul.stanford.edu/depts/ssrg/africa/history/historians.html)
- Directory of Law Sites on the Web (http://www.dm.net.lb/tmalouli/links/legsites.htm#firm)
- Zoologists (http://www.indyzoo.com/zed/)
- The Directory of Theater Professionals on the Internet (http://www.stetson.edu/departments/csata/thr_guid.html)

When you begin communicating with experts, you will want to save both your email messages and their responses. In Chapter 5 we show you how to save your email messages in folders, both in your email program and in your word-processing program.

Attaching Documents to Email Messages

Your email program will allow you to attach long documents or websites to your email messages. Attaching them rather than copying them allows the recipient to download your file and then open it with a word processor or other program. To attach a document, go to the icon on your email program that symbolizes the attachment function, click on it, and follow the directions. Being able to attach documents or websites is especially helpful to you as a researcher. If you are working online at a library, for example, you can capture the document or website address that you want to keep and send it to your own email address. Figure 4.12 shows what one attachment pop-up box looks like just before the writer selected the particular file to send via email.

Mailing Lists

Mailing lists, or email lists, allow one-time discussions among a large group of people without having to send a separate email to each. A mailing list is a computerized list of electronic addresses for sending email to a group of people all

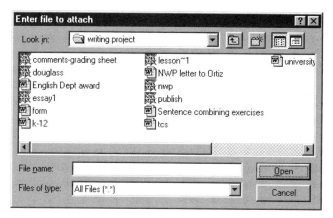

FIGURE 4.12 Email pop-up attachment box. Netscape Communicator browser window © 1999 Netscape Communications Corporation. Used with permission. Netscape Communications has not authorized, sponsored, endorsed, or approved this publication and is not responsible for its content.

at once. Two of the most popular mailing-list programs are LISTSERV, created by Eric Thomas, and LISTPROC, created by Anastasio Kotsikonas. Messages are sent to everyone on the list. The list may be monitored or not. If it is monitored, that means that someone reads all the messages before they are posted to see whether they are relevant and whether they conform to the standards of the list. If the list is unmonitored, the messages go to everyone on the list automatically. That means that some lists may have a lot of garbage in them, so you should be very selective in using those messages as sources. One site to search for online discussion groups related to your research is Topica (http://www.liszt.com/). You can even start a mailing list discussion there.

Subscribing to a Mailing List

To subscribe to a list, send a simple request to the appropriate list address, which follows the form <list-request@hostname>, for example:

listserv@ncte.org.

Do not write anything in the subject line, but do write the following in the message portion of the email:

Subscribe <listname> <yourfirstname yourlastname>

For example:

Subscribe ncte-talk Raymond Rodrigues

When you are correctly subscribed, you will receive a message from the list computer, such as:

You have been successfully added to the list NCTE-talk.

Here are some important commands that you will need to know:

Sub or **subscribe**	To subscribe to the list
Signoff or **unsubscribe**	To unsubscribe from the list
Info	To get information about the list
Review	To get a list of all subscribers
Help	To get help on how to use the list

There are other commands as well, and you can learn them by asking for help.

Finally, mailing lists have a particular etiquette, or "netiquette." Here are a few rules:

- Always sign your name so that readers know who sent the message.
- Be courteous, even if you disagree with an individual on the list. Impolite behavior is referred to as "flaming."
- If the list has many different discussions going on at once, refer to the one you are responding to. For example, "When Jane Doesmith commented on X . . ."
- Make the *subject* of your message as clear as possible so that people know what your message is about before they read it.
- If you are seeking information for your research, let people know why you are asking. The responses you get will be more useful to you.

How can you find mailing lists that are useful to your research? Some websites compile lists. One, for example, is **tile.net** (http://www.tile.net). Another is Topica (http://www.topica.com).

WEB ACTIVITY

On the companion website for this book, we have provided links to various mailing lists on a variety of subjects. Find a mailing list that relates to your research topic and join it. Read the messages on the list, perhaps going into the archives, and identify one individual who appears to have expertise in the topic of your research. Write to that individual and record what happens in your research log.

Exploring Online Communities for Sources

As the Internet has evolved, more and more people are finding it to be an excellent way to come together and share their ideas and information with others who have common interests. The manner in which these online communities communicate with each other changes as the technology itself changes. The ease of creating websites has led to a number of sites specifically created by and for people with common interests. You may want to explore some of them to find groups whose interests coincide with the topic of your research.

To find various online communities, you can search for "online community" using a search engine or go directly to a site. Three sites to start with are Online Community Report (http://www.onlinecommunityreport.com), Yahoo Groups (http://groups.Yahoo.com), and Suite 101.com (http://www.suite101.com). Each of these provides a variety of broad topics that you can explore as you narrow your search for more specific online communities. Some of these communities have been created as a result of a commercial venture or the publication of a specific book. For example, one site is devoted to creating active learning communities for students: http://www.CreatingLearningCommunities.org/etcetera/welcome.htm. Another specific site is ProfNet (http://www3.profnet.com/profnet_home/index.html), designed for journalists to share information and ideas.

An earlier version of these sites was the "newsgroup," essentially a bulletin board where individuals post messages. Google has acquired Usenet, one of the largest collections of newsgroups, and has now archived twenty years of Usenet discussions. Go to http://groups.Google.com. You will need to read the instructions and advice at this site to learn how to best use these newsgroups.

In short, the many online communities allow you to browse groups and messages to discover both information and possible experts to interview. You will need to be selective, for both amateurs and experts appear at these sites. But they may give you good leads for further research either in the library or on the Web.

Identifying Potential Sources through Newspaper Reports or Magazine Articles

A major reason for you not to use newspaper reports or magazine articles in your research is that they often have been compiled by reporters who have done their own research, but who are not constrained by the standards of academic reporting to cite their sources accurately. The reporter may actually have done considerable research in putting the article together, but for you to cite it as a source for your paper may be the same as citing another student's research paper.

When you find a news or magazine article that appears to have valid information in it, you can send a message to the reporter at the newspaper or news service and ask for recommendations on the sources that the reporter used. If you cannot contact the reporter or cannot find the sources, you can choose not to use the information or you can cite it, being careful to note that you have not been able to verify the information. Nevertheless, when a news report or popular magazine article refers to experts or other published reports, then you have a good lead where to go next. Use the Internet to find out more about the source and to locate additional information.

Consider the following article that appeared in *USA Today*, "Food Industry Is Making America Fat":

> The American Institute for Cancer Research (AICR) is asking Americans to buck a food industry trend that is contributing to the nation's obesity epidemic. "Value marketing" appeals to the consumer's desire for bargains by offering more product for less money. AICR Director of Nutrition Education Melanie Polk maintains that this marketing strategy is having a measurable and unfortunate long-term effect on national health.
>
> . . . Today, more Americans than ever—55%, according to the National Institutes of Health—are clinically overweight, while one in every four is obese (severely overweight). In fact, figures released by the Centers for Disease Control and Prevention show that the nation's obesity rose six percent between 1998 and 1999 alone.
>
> . . . When it comes to bigger portions, representatives of the food industry insist they are only responding to consumer demand, not creating it. "Last I checked, it's the consumer who's shoveling all that food into his mouth, not the food industry," notes John L. Stanton, professor of food marketing, St. Joseph's University, Philadelphia, Pa., an industry consultant, lecturer, and coauthor of *Twenty-One Trends in Food Marketing*.

This kind of newspaper report is ideal to help a researcher interested in its subject, for it gives both the names of researchers and where they work. Some also mention the journal, article, or book from which the story was taken. All the researcher has to do is find that journal article or book through a search in the library. Then, after having read it and others on the same subject, it might be

WEB ACTIVITY

Go to the companion website for this book and complete the Web Activity on finding experts and resources in newspapers.

TRY IT NOW

1. Compile a list of at least five mailing lists that deal with a topic you are interested in researching. Keep a log of all the choices you are given and the ones that you choose. Keep a written record of the purposes of the lists you subscribe to. After you have had a chance to read the messages posted to the list, discuss the list with your classmates. Which list or lists would you recommend for particular research topics?

2. Compile a list of at least five newsgroups that deal with the topic you are researching. Keep a written record of what the newsgroups are about. After you have had a chance to read messages on the newsgroups, discuss them with your classmates. Which newsgroups would you recommend to them for particular research topics?

3. Find at least one person on one of your mailing lists and one person who has posted to one of the online communities that you identified and send them an email message asking something about the research topic that you are interested in. Use your best netiquette. Tell them that you will be sharing their responses with other students in your class. Then share the results of your email research, discussing what worked to get good information and what did not.

appropriate to contact the researcher if there are questions remaining that cannot be answered through more library research or research on the Web.

SUGGESTED ACTIVITY

Review your notes and this chapter to verify the methods to find sources in the library and on the Internet. Then, in the time available to you, search for as much as you can about your topic. Record your successes and failures. What keywords and subject terms worked best, which search engines were most useful, which library databases were most productive, and which mailing lists or online communities did you locate related to the topic, if any? If you had to judge your top five sources now—regardless of where you found them—which would they be and why?

Evaluating Sources

After completing this chapter, you should be able to:

■ Evaluate sources on a website and in a library database, using the following evaluation considerations:
  - Content
  - Currency
  - Source of publication
  - Coverage
  - Relevance

■ Evaluate email communications, mailing list postings, and newsgroup postings to determine whether they are valid sources for your research or can lead to valid sources.

■ Create a précis, an annotated bibliography, and an evaluative or critical bibliography.

The more sources you read for your research paper, the more you will continue to learn about your topic. Your knowledge of the topic is, however, only as sound as the sources you use. You want to find authoritative sources, sources that are well written and well documented. You also want to find sources that provide you with a thorough background on an issue, supplying information that both you and your reader can believe. Your goal should be to locate authoritative, accurate, unbiased, current information on your topic—not always an easy task. To get a good idea of what is available in your field, you need to search widely—shuttling between the library and the Internet as needed, perhaps even checking with people who are knowledgeable about the topic, including your professor or individuals your professor might recommend that you consult with. As a result of the Internet's growth, there are many more sources immediately available to you than ever before. For that reason, many people, especially university and college faculty, have expressed their concerns about the validity of sources found on the Internet. But you should realize that all sources need to be evaluated, even books and journal articles you locate in your library. All sources represent *some* kind of bias. If you aren't aware of the bias, you are likely to misconstrue the ideas in the source. And as you become more knowledgeable about your topic, you will be better able to judge whether the sources meet your needs as a researcher.

EVALUATING INFORMATION: THE EARLY STAGES OF A RESEARCH PROJECT

This process takes time and commitment. Plan to spend several weeks locating and conducting a preliminary evaluation of your sources before you begin drafting. Gather both Internet sources and library sources so that you develop a sense of the range of information available on your topic. Before you begin, evaluate your information needs by answering the following questions:

What do I know about my topic?
What do I need to learn?
What kinds of sources are most likely to help me?
What exactly am I looking for?
What types of Internet resources are likely to help?
What kinds of library resources are likely to help?
Are there people I should seek out who can help me understand my topic better?

As a writer, you have different reasons for evaluating information resources. At the early stages of information gathering, you want to sort and sift quickly. You can gather sources and read them quickly to get a sense of the topic, but don't take detailed notes on your topic until you have read widely to get a sense of the breadth and depth of the subject. Once you have done that, you'll be better able to judge how good your sources are.

It is important to evaluate *all* your sources, both as you proceed and then again before you determine whether to use the source in your research paper. When you locate a possible source on your topic, you need to evaluate its value to your research. After you have a working knowledge of your topic and a sense of the range of issues, you are in a position to begin evaluating sources in depth. Ask yourself questions such as the following:

Content Criteria

1. Is the source valid? Factual? That is, do you have reason to think that it is accurate information? Does the author appear to have done a thorough job locating and researching the topic?

2. Is the topic treated thoroughly? Does the source cover the topic in an appropriate breadth or depth? By having read widely when you start, you will be better able to judge whether or not your source is sufficiently comprehensive.

3. Is the treatment biased? If the author acknowledges the bias, you will have an easier time deciding whether or not to use the source. The problem is that many authors do not admit their bias: information is often put on the Web for the sole purpose of promoting a particular point of view; thus, many sites have "hidden agendas." Always check to see if you can learn more about the organization that sponsors the website or the background of the writer. The author of a book or journal article probably has a specific purpose in writing, and that purpose may be biased toward a particular perspective. In and of itself, that is neither unusual nor wrong, however, to judge the value of the source, you need to be aware of the bias or perspective that the author has.

Currency

1. Is your information current? Avoid out-of-date books or journal articles, unless you use the sources to establish a point. (For example, you may want to demonstrate what books in the early part of the century said about your topic or summarize their perspectives on that topic.) Sources in the sciences must especially be as current as possible. Sources in history or literature need not be the most current, but even in those fields current knowledge may add substantially to our understanding of the subject.

2. The type of information may determine how critical its being current is. For example, a source based upon a survey may need to be as current as possible. Respondents' attitudes change over time. A source using business data to support a business technique may be more valuable if it is recent. An interpretation of a Shakespearian sonnet or of an historical event need not be current, but the theoretical perspective of the source might matter, so more current theories should not be ignored.

Source of Publication

1. Is the author an expert on your topic? Find out something about the author. What are the author's credentials? Check the author's Web page to see if he or she has published widely in the field. Check the bibliography or references the author includes. Do these sources appear to be current? Do other sources often cite this author or this particular work? If so, this citation indicates that others consider the author an authority. Checking an appropriate citation index through your library may indicate the number of times other authors have referred to the one you are considering as a source. Among the citation indices are the following:

   Science Citation Index
   Computer Science Directory
   Social Sciences Citation Index

Arts and Humanities Citation Index
Bio Sciences Citation Index
Chem Sciences Citation Index
Clinical Medicine Citation Index

3. Is the source reliable? If you used a scholarly source, such as a source from an academic press or from an educational institution, it is likely to be reliable, for it probably has been objectively evaluated before being published. If it is a popular source such as a magazine, you need to be sure that you are using the best source on your topic. If it is a source on an organization's website, then you need to know more about the organization and the purpose of the website.

Coverage

1. How complete or extensive is the coverage of the topic? You may be able to use a source that doesn't cover a topic thoroughly, but be sure to supplement it with other sources.
2. Does the source include specific detail? When you quote or summarize information, you want to be using material that is not written in general terms that anyone might know or think.

Relevance

1. Is the source relevant to your own research question? Even in the early phase of your research, you can weed out many sources that in isolation would be good sources. If they aren't related to your needs, they aren't good sources for you.
2. Even if the source is relevant, does it simply repeat information that you have found in another source? If so, choose the more current or more authoritative source for your paper. If multiple sources stating the same thing strengthens the point you are making, then do cite them.
3. Is the information significant or important within the context of your research? You probably will not be able to make this judgment when you are starting your research, but as you become more knowledge-able, you will be more able to make that judgment.
4. Note whether the website is a commercial site. Search engines generally are commercial ventures, designed to make money. The common way most have made money is by selling banner ads to advertisers. You, as the user, can choose to ignore those banner ads. As it turns out, most users do ignore them, so now many Web search engines are selling places to businesses that allow their business to show up as a "hit" when someone is searching the Web. Some search engines overtly indicate which hits are in fact commercials, but others do not. With experience, you will soon recognize these "covert advertisements." If the URL is that of a "dot com" (.com), that automatically identifies it as a commercial site. For example, in searching one search engine that gives high ranking to commercial sites, upon entering "NAFTA," we received,

among the hits, a site titled "Immigration to Canada." The URL for this site was http://www.webimmigration.com. We would have to evaluate this site to determine whether the information was of the type that we could use.

Any given source you find is not necessarily valuable for your topic: it may be overly biased, it may be out-of-date, and it may not have been published by a respectable press. Learning which sources are the most appropriate for your paper comes later in the research process, but is only possible if you have done a good job sorting and sifting early on.

PRELIMINARY EVALUATION OF WEB SOURCES

You can weed out many sources quickly by learning what to look for in a "good" source and what to avoid. Methods used to evaluate print sources, such as journal articles and books, can also be applied to sources you find on the World Wide Web. In addition, you should be aware of some ways to evaluate Internet sources.

- Check to see if there is a tilde (~) in the URL, which often means that the information is part of someone's personal website. Personal sites may be created by people very knowledgeable in their fields; by people who are knowledgeable in one area, but who have created a website that has little to do with their expertise; by people who simply want to proclaim their opinions; or even by other students who post their research papers, travelogues, or other very personal items. Do not automatically reject these sites. Judge their quality by considering the other criteria we have summarized for you.
- Check the URL to see if it ends in **edu** (education), **com** (commerce), **gov** (government), **mil** (military), **net** (telecommunications), or **org** (organization). Different types of information can be found on any of these sites, but being aware of the type of site you are looking at can help you make a judgment. For example, if you are investigating the status of medical research on arthritis, you will want to question information that you find at the website for a pharmaceutical company. Is the information strictly public relations and commercial promotions or scientific reporting?
- Examine the style of writing and the level to which it has been edited. If you find incoherent passages and occasional grammar or punctuation errors, you should be wary.
- Look at the date the site was created or last updated. If the site is out-of-date, you can eliminate the site as soon as you see it listed in the search engine's report.
- Note the relationship between author and publisher. For example, if the author is a university professor, and the source was published on a commercial web site, ask why. Scholarly articles are more likely to be published at an educational site or at the site of an academic publisher.

■ If the website is owned by an organization, society, or club, try to learn as much as possible about that group before accepting what they publish to the Web. Check their mission statement or membership of their governing board or other statements that indicate their particular orientation or bias.

One of the biggest problems some students have is trying to use sources that are simply not "meaty" enough to provide them with in-depth information on a topic. Sometimes, even an out-of-date book on a topic can provide a more thorough introduction than a cursory Web page. Don't use a source merely because it is the most convenient one. Determine whether your topic demands that you use a more authoritative or thorough source than is available on the Web. For more readings on evaluating sources, go to the Cornell University Library: (http://www.library.cornell.edu/okuref/research/webeval.html) or the Voice of the Shuttle site (http://vos.ucsb.edu/index.asp/). For some entertaining exercises in determining validity of online sources, try those at the UCLA library (http://www.library.ucla.edu/libraries/college/instruct/hoax/evlinfo1.htm).

WEB ACTIVITY

Go to the companion website for this book and complete the activity on evaluating websites.

IS A JOURNAL OR MAGAZINE APPROPRIATE FOR YOUR TOPIC?

The term "journal" and the term "magazine" are sometimes used interchangeably, but research librarians make a distinction that you should be aware of. Magazines generally are aimed at a general reader, the so-called "popular press." Journals are typically aimed at the more academic or scholarly reader. Another distinction worth noting is that magazines do not always have volume and issue numbers, and as a result citation style for magazines is different than citation style for journals (see Chapter 6).

Journals vary, too. Sometimes an entire volume—a year's worth of issues usually—is paginated simultaneously. Other times, each issue has its own pagination. Citation styles for these two variants of journals are different, too (see Chapter 6).

How can you tell whether a given publication is an academic or a popular magazine or journal? Some guidelines are included in Table 5.1.

An increasing number of journals that have migrated to the Web have developed online versions of the journals that differ somewhat from their print counterpart. Some of these are scholarly journals; others are popular journals. Your research paper topic and the demands your teacher or employer have given you will determine the extent to which you can use Web journals.

TABLE 5.1 Differences between Magazines and Scholarly Articles

Scholarly Article	Popular Article
Aimed at a college-educated reader—often one with an advanced degree	Aimed at the general reader
Uses citations to document sources	Often refers to information without giving any indication of the source
Uses academic language	Uses popular language
Often includes charts and graphs	May contain many pictures

Is an Online Journal Appropriate?

Online journals have been maturing rapidly, but most are still relatively new, and the form is still evolving. Take time to determine whether the online journal is a serious undertaking or a casual production. Some "zines" (online magazines) depend on volunteers and are not monitored for consistency.

Online journals continue to evolve and become more substantial, both in content and in quality. Many make creative use of the hypertext capabilities available today, providing links to their own sources and to information illustrating the points of their authors. Readers can actually surf the Web while reading scholarly articles. Project Muse (http://muse.jhu.edu/) provides access to over 100 scholarly journals in the arts, humanities, social sciences, and mathematics. EBSCO (http://www-us.ebsco.com/) allows searches of many journals online. For samples of how the Web has expanded our ability to communicate, these sites will give you a taste of the range of possibilities:

RSNA Electronic Journal (http://ej.rsna.org/)
Kairos (http://english.ttu.edu/kairos/)
Chronicon (http://www.ucc.ie/chronicon/)
Arts and Letters Daily (http://www.aldaily.com/)

THE IMPORTANCE OF EXPLORING VARIED SOURCES

Don't start taking notes just to take notes. You have to read a while before you can recognize the kinds of data that you might be able to use or before you can spot bias. You may locate a useful source early in your research process, one that gives you adequate background on your topic. But should you cite this source in your paper? You can't begin to evaluate a source until you understand the range of material available.

Keep the purpose of your research in mind as you work on your research paper. Are you investigating an issue? Examining different viewpoints? Arguing a point? Or providing an objective summary of research? Your selection of sources is related to your research questions and your purpose for researching. When you are drafting your paper, you will want to select from your collection of credible sources those that further your investigation or support your argument best. Only when you determine how you will *use* a source in your paper will you be able to determine whether it is the best source possible for that purpose. Are you going to use a student interview to establish a point about local school violence? If so, your source may be better than a scholarly article at that point in your draft. Are you going to use some highly biased reports that you find on the Web to demonstrate opinions that are not objective? Then do so, but do so consciously, letting your reader know why you have included them.

EVALUATION AT THE DRAFTING PHASE

Many students who have located information about their topics on the Web are amazed to discover the different level of sophistication and the depth of analysis of issues in the journals they locate in proprietary databases.

You can get reasonably good results on the Web without knowing a lot about searching, but when you use commercial databases you need to understand that they are targeted toward more professional users and require that you learn how to navigate them. That's why it is important to explore all the databases available to you so that you can locate those that have the most useful information for your field or for the topics in which you are most interested. Here are some questions to ask yourself if you are about to start drafting your research paper, whether you are searching the Internet, exploring a library, or using field studies:

- Is the information I have located relevant to my topic and to my argument? (Just because a source is valid does not mean it is appropriate for your topic.)
- Does my source fit the context of my paper?
- Is my source the best source I can find on the topic? (Unless you have collected more sources than you can use, you won't know the answer to this question.)
- Is my source the right type of source for my topic? (For example, you probably need primary sources if you are exploring a legal issue. You can find state and Federal court cases on the Web or in government documents at the library. For history papers, you can find many historical documents on specialized websites. And many government, business, and private organizations now publish their original documents to the Web for easy access.)
- Have I explored my topic thoroughly? (You typically need more thorough coverage of a topic than that provided by a Web source, and so you should supplement your Web sources with sources located through your library.)

■ Have I examined the point of view of my source? (You need to be sure that the point of view expressed in your source is compatible with the point you are making in your paper.)

Databases store large amounts of information, ranging from numerical data to journal articles. Although online databases, especially those found in your library, are more likely to contain useful sources of information for many of your topics, don't assume that all journals you locate through a database are good sources. Consider issues such as the following:

■ When was the database updated?
■ Do I have to search a print index for earlier titles?
■ Are there better sources in the library that are not available online?

DETERMINING WHAT KINDS OF SOURCES TO EXPLORE

Sometimes its not a matter of evaluation, it's a matter of knowing where to go to look for a topic. In "Books, Websites, or Journal? The Information Cycle" (http://www.farmingdale.edu/library/inflow.html) the librarians at Greenley Library look at topics in the context of when they happened. They suggest that you use time as a guideline to help you determine whether a source is appropriate for your topic. Ask the following question: When did events related to my topic occur? Your answer will often determine where you look for information.

If the events are recent, the Web may be appropriate. If the events took place several years ago, the library is probably a better starting point.

If the event *just* happened, the Web is likely to be a good source of information, along with newspapers, television, and radio. A week later, however, a better source—one where the author has had time to reflect on and digest the information—would be a popular magazine. Six months later, a good place to locate information might be in a peer-reviewed academic journal on the topic; over time, books on the topic may prove even better sources of information, for they allow in-depth coverage of a topic. Of course, books may be biased, too, for they do contain the author's slant on the topic and they may be sponsored by a professional organization or political group with its own bias. After more time goes by, the event may be included in reference books, which are generally neutral, but may be published by a professional association or political group.

The example below of a search and evaluation of sources before using them demonstrates how your search and evaluation might proceed.

An Experience Validating Sources

In Chapter 2, we used the North American Free Trade Agreement (NAFTA) as an illustration of how you can focus your research questions and plan your research. Now, to demonstrate why you need to evaluate your sources, we illustrate a search process to identify sources for information on how NAFTA has influenced U.S. business.

Using Google (http://www.google.com), we typed in the keywords *NAFTA* and *impact*. At the very top of our list of hits, we came across a report from the Heritage Foundation (http://www.heritage.org/library/categories/trade/fyi160.html). This report is a very positive one, giving examples of the benefits of NAFTA.

Then we decided, because we needed to know whether the Heritage Foundation might have a particular bias one way or another, to search for *Heritage Foundation*. We discovered that there were many organizations calling themselves the "Heritage Foundation," ranging from the National Heritage Foundation, dedicated to preserving and restoring national historical landmarks, to the New Orleans Jazz Heritage Foundation, to the Alberta, Canada, Heritage Foundation, to a host of others. The organization we wanted was simply The Heritage Foundation (http://www.heritage.org/whoweare/).

We learned the Heritage Foundation is a think tank dedicated to promoting a "conservative public policy" and "free enterprise." Those terms indicated to us that this site was probably oriented toward advancing the interests of business.

To try to understand what types of people might be leading the Heritage Foundation, we clicked on *Board of Trustees*. That gave us a list of people who were mostly CEOs of major businesses, including Steve Forbes, the publisher of *Forbes* magazine. The information on NAFTA at that site was not wrong, but the interpretations of NAFTA's impact were biased with a business sector perspective.

Next, we found a speech of Ambassador Oliver Garza to the Brownsville, Texas, Chamber of Commerce (http://usembassy.state.gov/posts/nu1/wwwhd45.html). Ambassador Garza was also positive about the benefits of NAFTA. Since Brownsville, Texas, is on the border of Mexico, a twin city of Matamoros, Tamaulipas, Mexico, where many U.S. businesses have "twin plants," or *maquiladoras*, we knew that the Chamber of Commerce in Brownsville would be vitally interested in the future of NAFTA. After all, their economy is closely tied to that of Mexico. But what did we know of Oliver Garza? So we typed his name into Google and found, among other hits, his biography (http://www.state.gov/p/wha/bio/index.cfm?docid=1911). We learned that he had many years' experience as a senior foreign service officer and was appointed by President Bill Clinton in 1999 to be Ambassador to Nicaragua. Nothing in any of the sites indicated overtly whether Ambassador Garza would be biased one way or another toward NAFTA, but, since President Clinton was a supporter of NAFTA, we might assume that his appointees might also be. While we were not certain of Ambassador Garza's bias, we knew that we had to recognize the possible basis for his opinions.

Next, we found an EPI position paper citing losses of businesses and jobs in the United States caused by NAFTA (http://www.epinet.org/briefingpapers/nafta01/impactstates.html). Now we had a negative source, so we needed to find out something about the EPI. When we entered the keyword *EPI*, we immediately hit (http://www.epinet.org/index.html). We discovered that the EPI, the Economic Policy Institute, is a "nonpartisan think tank." "Nonpartisan" should indicate that they are unbiased and balanced in their perspectives. Just to be sure, we clicked on *Board of Directors*, and discovered that they were mostly U.S. union leaders, as well as others such as Robert Reich, the former Secretary of Labor under President Clinton. Because we had followed the early arguments for and against NAFTA, we knew that American labor leaders were much opposed to NAFTA for fear that it would take away union jobs in the United States. If we wanted to confirm that, we could search for various union opinions about NAFTA, reviewing past newspaper articles as well as websites. So, the EPI also has a clear perspective—like the Heritage Foundation, not necessarily wrong, but exhibiting a bias.

In our evaluation of these sources, our initial sources were clearly biased on both sides of the issue. So, how can we find out the truth about the impact of NAFTA upon U.S. businesses? One thing we can do is determine whether the biased reports agree upon any of the facts. We can also continue looking down our list of hits to try to locate unbiased reports, rather than opinions, speeches, or think tank interpretations. University research or teaching centers are supposed to be unbiased, although one should approach their reports with a cautious mind as well. Looking for sites that end in *.edu* is therefore a good step. One of the sites we found was a center at the University of Colorado (http://ucsu.colorado.edu/~slusarz/nafta/nafta_li.htm). But that site proved to be dated, last updated in 1995, and many links were obsolete. So we entered the keywords *NAFTA university research,* and that identified many good sites, such as Mexico Online (http://www.mexonline.com/nafta.htm). That site provided us links to NAFTA resources that, in turn, led us to many other sites having varying degrees of bias. At last, some supplied straightforward data, such as U.S. Census reports, and one link led to a University of Texas NAFTA center. So finally we had identified sources containing data, as well as biased reports.

Given the topic, we should search for U.S. government reports on NAFTA by looking for hits that end in *.gov*. Seeking more immediate access to government sources, we can turn to our own library and check the *Guide to the National Archives of the United States* and *Select List of Publications of the National Archives and Record Service* to search for reports on NAFTA. We should also search the online databases, trying *Fedworld* and *Thomas.* Since NAFTA has a great impact upon states such as Texas and California, searching their government documents may also provide information that we can use.

If our thesis statement deals with the opposing perspectives of whether NAFTA benefits the U.S., then the initial hits locating biased sources give us key documents to frame our research. Such a thesis statement might be: The conflicting opinions about the value of NAFTA do not lead to a single conclusion. If, however, we wish to discover unbiased facts about NAFTA's impact upon the U.S., then we have to expand our search and constantly ascertain the nature of our sources so that our conclusions are not grounded in mere opinions.

TRY IT NOW

Evaluate at least one source related to your topic from a website, library data-base, journal article, or book that you have located so far as you are develop-ing your research strategies, and share your evaluation criteria and results with your classmates.

FROM THE PRÉCIS TO THE ANNOTATED BIBLIOGRAPHY TO THE EVALUATIVE OR CRITICAL BIBLIOGRAPHY

As an intermediary assignment, or even as a terminal assignment, some pro-fessors require that you submit an annotated bibliography. A bibliography is the list of sources that an author has used. It appears at the end of a chapter, a book, or an article. (In the style of the American Psychological Association style [or APA style] and in the Council of Science Editors style [CBE or CSE style], the bibliography is titled "References." In the Modern Language Asso-ciation style [or MLA style] and in the Chicago Manual of Style [or CMS style], the bibliography is titled "Works Cited" or "Sources Cited.") The annotated bibliography is a bibliography with summary comments and observations on the particular book, article, or website. That summary is sometimes referred to as a précis. Below, we describe the précis and the annotated bibliography. Then, we introduce a variation upon the annotated bibliography that is alto-gether new now that evaluating our sources has become so critical: the critical or evaluative bibliography.

The Précis

The précis consists of a brief summary of the work that is being cited. Typi-cally, this summary is not more than three or four sentences. Your writing in the précis needs to be a good synopsis of the work you are citing so that the reader knows exactly what its content is. You may use quotations in the précis.

Here is an example of a précis in MLA style:

Newman, Leah. *Robert Frost: The People, Places, and Stories Behind His New Eng-land Poetry.* Shelburne, VT: The New England Press, 2000.

Newman has collected 36 of Frost's poems, arranging them chronologi-cally according to when they were written or based upon her educated estimate if an exact date for his writing the poem is not firm. Writing for the ordinary reader and not for scholars, she comments on both the auto-biographical evidence in each poem and on literary analyses of it. Her appendices include a chronology of Frost's life, "How to Start a Frost Poetry Circle," and thematic groupings of the poems.

The précis may also have included evaluative comments on the work as well. So, the above précis might have begun:

> In a clear and comfortable style designed to interest the average reader, Newman has collected. . . .

The Annotated Bibliography

An annotated bibliography is a collection of bibliographic entries and their summaries (or a précis for each entry). It is arranged alphabetically by author's last name. Some professors ask for an annotated bibliography at the end of a research paper instead of a simple bibliography. The key questions for you to use in judging your annotated bibliography are:

■ Have I summarized the work in a few sentences?
■ Have I included all the main characteristics or components of the work?
■ (optional) Have I made any evaluative comments in the summary?

The Critical or Evaluative Bibliography

With the Internet now providing a vast number of sources, ranging from the inconsequential to the highly pertinent and scholarly, readers of your research will want to know why you have judged the sources that you have selected as worth including. In this chapter, we have discussed many of the criteria that you should use in judging your sources, whether you find them in the library or on the Internet. Use the skills that you are gaining in evaluating sources to write the Critical or Evaluative Bibliography.

The Critical or Evaluative Bibliography is simply the Annotated Bibliography with a twist. While you may evaluate your sources in the Annotated Bibliography, in the Critical or Evaluative Bibliography you make overt the standards that you have used in judging your source. With the **changes in bold,** here is how the above summary of Newman's book on Frost might now look:

Newman, Leah. *Robert Frost: The People, Places, and Stories Behind His New England Poetry.* Shelburne, VT: The New England Press, 2000.
> Lea Newman, **a former college literature professor who has been president of both the Hawthorne Society and the Melville Society,** has collected 36 of Frost's poems, arranging them chronologically according to when they were written, or based upon her educated estimate if an exact date for his writing the poem is not firm. **The introduction summarizes key Frost scholarship for those who wish to read further.** Writing for the ordinary reader and not for scholars, she comments on both the autobio-

graphical evidence in each poem and on literary analyses of it. Her appendices include a chronology of Frost's life, "How to Start a Frost Poetry Circle," and thematic groupings of the poems.

Note the evaluative comments that have been added: (1) a biographical statement about the author's experience in the field of literature and (2) a judgment that the author is aware of the research on Frost and his poetry.

Here is an entry to a Critical or Evaluative Bibliography (APA style) on a source for a paper on NAFTA:

Organization of American States. (1992, December 17). *North American Free Trade Agreement between the Government of Canada, the Government of the United Mexican States, and the Government of the United States of America.* Retrieved July 4, 2001 from the World Wide Web: http://www.sice.oas. org/trade/nafta/naftatce.asp.

This document is the original NAFTA agreement. As such, it contains the objectives, definitions, and matters related to tariff issues, rules of origin, customs procedures, energy, agriculture, sanitary measures, emergency actions, environment, government procurement, investment, cross-border trade services, telecommunications, financial services, competition policies, temporary entry of businesspersons, intellectual property, reviews and dispute procedures, and exceptions. As the original document, it provides the starting point for anyone investigating the issues surrounding and evolving from NAFTA.

Notice the key evaluative criterion at the beginning of this summary: this is the original NAFTA agreement. Therefore, it is a *primary source.* If the research is about some aspect of NAFTA, this criterion is enough.

The following entry, based upon a report of the Dallas region of the Federal Reserve System, demonstrates other criteria for including it in research about NAFTA:

Taylor, L. (2001, April). *Regional Update.* Retrieved July 4, 2001 from the World Wide Web:

This recent report from the Dallas region of the Federal Reserve System noted that economic conditions in Texas related to technology and Mexico "have weakened." Consumer confidence had fallen, exports from Texas were down, but employment remained strong. This report demonstrates that the economy of Mexico influences that of Texas, for the purchasing power of the peso had declined, and the *maquiladoras* are closely tied to the U.S. economy because they produce materials for automobiles and high technology, which have both declined in the United States. Because the Federal Reserve System must monitor actual economic conditions, this report provided a useful check on the relationship between *maquiladoras* and the U.S. economy.

Note the evaluative comments: the report is "recent," an important criterion because economic conditions are not stable and do change over time. The rationale is important to the writer's research, for it relates to the thesis that there is a strong relationship between the economies of Mexico and the United States as revealed by *maquiladora* production. A reader might rightfully ask whether this one report is the best source for the paper. Wouldn't a report that tracks trends over time, perhaps another Federal Reserve report, be more meaningful? Note the date that this source was read from the Web. At that time, there was no more recent regional Dallas Fed report. However, considering this one bibliographic summary alone, we might not be able to judge whether this is a better report that the writer might have found, so we would need to look at the entire Critical Bibliography to determine whether it is a balanced scholarly effort.

The criteria for effective critical bibliographies:

■ summarize the work in a few sentences;
■ include all the main components of the work; and
■ provide evaluative comments that clearly indicate the basis for the evaluation.

WEB ACTIVITY

Go to the companion website for this book and complete the exercises on annotated bibliographies and critical or evaluative bibliographies.

EVALUATING INTERVIEWS, EMAIL COMMUNICATIONS, MAILING LIST POSTINGS, AND NEWSGROUP POSTINGS

By now, you should have a pretty good sense of what sources in the library or on the Web are worth including in your research. If you are interviewing individual experts, whether in person or through electronic mail, you can apply similar criteria to their comments. Even if you are quoting mailing list or newsgroup postings, you can apply those criteria. Here are criteria for you to apply to those individual communications:

■ What is the expertise of this individual?
■ Do the comments of this individual reflect any particular bias toward the topic?
■ Do any comments made by this individual add something new to your research, something that you have not found elsewhere?

As you are drafting your paper, think about how you might use the comments of an individual, whether interviewed personally or electronically, whether the comments are in response to a question that you have asked or simply posted to a mailing list or newsgroup. It is possible, for example, that the comments do not add new content to your research, but do provide a particular personal perspective that you could not possibly find in published journal articles, books, or websites. An apt quote can often add the particular emphasis you want to make to a point, even if the attitude revealed by the quote is shared by others. Of course, as you may already have discovered, some newsgroup comments may be categorized as nonsense or diatribes not worth considering.

 TRY IT NOW

1. Interview at least one expert about your topic either in person or through email. Take notes during a personal interview and capture electronic communications to disk. Then apply the criteria that you have developed to determine whether the source is a valid and worthwhile one to use in your paper. Share what you learn and what you decide about the value of the interview with your classmates. Did the interview result in a particularly good quote to use when you write your research? What was the quote and why was it a good one? How do you intend to use it?

2. Do the same with a posting to a newsgroup or mailing list.

CONCLUSION

Now that you know more about what "evaluating sources" entails, you can pursue your research with an evaluative frame of reference for everything that you read. After you locate a source, take time to evaluate it. Evaluation is a crucial step in the research process. Although there are differences in the way you evaluate library sources and Web sources, the basic criteria are the same.

The techniques you use for evaluating Web sources and print sources have much in common, for the basic question you are asking yourself of each source is this: Will the source be credible for *my* purposes in *my* paper. In other words, will the source help you explain your point or demonstrate that your work makes a contribution to a reader's growing understanding of your topic. As the last Critical Bibliography entry reveals, readers will judge your ability to evaluate your sources well when they examine your total bibliography. They will be less interested in whether you have found many sources (you will automatically when you search the Internet) than they will be in the overall quality of the sources that you select and the manner in which you use them.

At first, you may find it difficult to determine whether sources you locate are valid. Over time, however, most students become expert at "sniffing" out the problems. With experience, researchers develop a second sense for spotting inaccurate or inappropriate sources. It may be that inexperienced researchers simply haven't yet learned how to read the sign system of the Web or may assume that all library sources are good sources. As you gain experience searching and judging your sources, you will notice things like the domain names that help indicate bias, you will be able to spot writers' biases through their word choice, you will begin to ask whether a particular source is the most current or the most balanced, and you will develop your own standards to determine the value of a source. Your research will constantly grow stronger the more you search, the more you question your sources, and the more you ask yourself whether your sources are helping your reader understand your thesis.

SUGGESTED ACTIVITIES

1. Gather as many potential sources as you can to contribute to your research project, including sources found in the library and on the Web. If personal interviews or interviews via email are appropriate for your course, include them. Then create a critical bibliography of your sources and submit it to your professor.

2. In your research log, as you enter sites that you find, make notes on your evaluation of each site, indicating its value or weakness, so that you can determine better which to use as you begin developing your research paper or project.

Organizing Sources and Notes: Preparing to Write

After completing this chapter, you should be able to do the following:

- Organize and annotate your bookmarks.

- Set up an electronic workspace.

- Create research folders for your files.

- Create electronic note cards.

- Organize your computer files as you write.

- Organize your notes before you begin to write the first draft.

L et's review all that you have been doing up until this point and all that you have learned to do.

- You have determined what the format and expectations are for the research paper or report that you will submit.
- You have created a research journal in which you keep your research notes.
- You have learned to browse efficiently and effectively in both the library and the Internet.
- You have narrowed your topic and developed the key research questions that you want to pursue.
- You have identified sources online and created bookmarks that you save in an organized fashion.
- You have identified library sources and, when appropriate, sources outside both the library and the Internet.
- You have been able to evaluate the sources to determine which are the most credible and reliable as valid sources.

Now we come to that phase of research that distinguishes those who master research from those who struggle every time they are assigned a research paper: taking good notes, documenting your sources, and organizing that information so that you can write about your research both systematically and flexibly.

WEB ACTIVITY

Before proceeding with this chapter, go to the companion website for this book and complete the exercise reviewing effective note-taking strategies.

ORGANIZING YOUR BOOKMARKS

In Chapter 4, we introduced bookmarks and how to save bookmarks. You know now that a "bookmark" is an electronic tag that allows you to go quickly to the source that has been tagged without having to search all over again. The browser that you are using allows you to bookmark sources from the Internet and automatically stores those bookmarks at the bottom of your list of bookmarks. That will do when you first begin using bookmarks, but as you use the Internet more and more, your bookmarks will grow to a point where, if you do not organize them, it will be just as quick to search for the site all over again as it will be to find the bookmark. You'll have bookmarks for this research project and for other research projects. You probably won't want to delete bookmarks from previous projects because you may want to return to them for other purposes. You'll have bookmarks for personal purposes, bookmarks for sites that you find as you are searching that are interesting but not related to the research itself. Therefore, you need to organize them so that you can find them easily when you look for them again.

Creating Bookmark Files

The first thing you probably want to do is collect your bookmarks in different folders—your electronic filing system—for different purposes. For example, if you are working on a research paper, you will want to have a bookmark file for your research project. When you have a collection of bookmarks all related to the topic of your research project, you can save the entire list of bookmarks as a bookmark file by simply selecting the **Save as** command in the bookmark file menu and giving your list whatever name you want so that you can identify it and come back to it later. You can save as many bookmark files as you want, saving collections of bookmarks related to other topics such as hobbies or research projects or personal subjects. Figure 6.1 shows you just such a "master collection" of electronic file folders. Notice that it contains personal interest folders, folders with research sources, and a folder related to a research project on NAFTA.

Creating Folders

Within your collection of bookmarks, or bookmark files, you can organize your bookmarks by first creating folders and then filing your bookmarks in these folders. You can create a folder by going to the bookmark section of your browser and clicking on the area that allows you to add a folder. When you do this, you will be asked to give the folder a name. Name your folders with a more general name than the specific title of the bookmarked website or sites within that folder. Before you find all the sites you want to bookmark for your research topic, you might even brainstorm a set of other folders that might relate to your research topic and create those folders before you have bookmarks to fill them. For example, notice in Figure 6.1 that there are folders for "Style guides" and for "Search engines." As you search, you may think of folder topics that you have not thought about at the beginning of your research.

Figure 6.2 is an example from Netscape Navigator of folders and bookmarks ready for editing. After you create bookmarks and file them, you may decide that some are better positioned in a different folder. In this case, all you

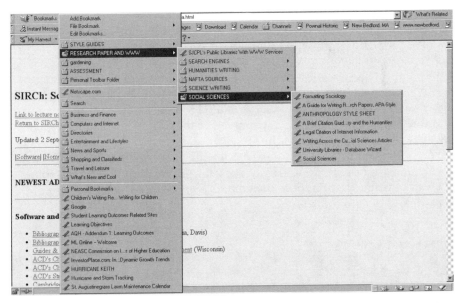

FIGURE 6.1   Bookmarks organized into electronic file folders. Netscape Communicator browser window © 1999 Netscape Communications Corporation. Used with permission. Netscape Communications has not authorized, sponsored, endorsed, or approved this publication and is not responsible for its content.

FIGURE 6.2 Bookmarks organized for editing into folders and subfolders. Netscape Communicator browser window © 1999 Netscape Communications Corporation. Used with permission. Netscape Communications has not authorized, sponsored, endorsed, or approved this publication and is not responsible for its content.

have to do is "click and drag" the bookmark to the folder in which you want it. Notice that in Figure 6.2 the bookmark file is not only organized according to folders, but also according to subfolders. You can create subfolders as you gather more and more bookmarks and decide upon new categories that fit within the categories you have already created. You can click and drag not only bookmarks, but also folders and subfolders. As you begin to develop new folders and subfolders of bookmarks related to your research topic, you will find that you will also be helping yourself to think of ways in which you can organize your research report. In this early stage of your research, be as creative as you want to be, for adding and deleting folders and subfolders is easy once you learn how to do it. (If you are using Favorites in Internet Explorer, you can organize your favorite bookmarks by selecting **Favorites→Organize favorites→Move to folder.**)

TRY IT NOW

Go to the bookmark section of Your web browser and file your bookmarks into folders and subfolders.

1. After you have collected several bookmarks on any topics that you want, save a bookmark file with a general title. Then, collect more bookmarks and save them in new folders. Practice moving from one bookmark folder to another.
2. Create a folder for your research topic. Begin sorting your bookmarks and gathering those that relate to your topic within this folder.
3. After you have collected a variety of bookmarks related to your research topic, begin thinking of ways that the bookmarks provide sources for different subtopics within your research project. Create subfolders for each of those that you organize under the folder for your research project. Move the bookmarks into their appropriate subfolders.
4. Once you have completed that, study the folders and subfolders. Ask yourself whether they suggest ways that you can organize your paper. Add new folders and subfolders as you find new sources and as you think of new or different categories for your written report.

Annotating Bookmarks

In addition to collecting and filing bookmarks in folders and subfolders, annotating them in Netscape Navigator will help when you need to return to them in the future but cannot remember exactly what was contained within a particular site that you had bookmarked. While you might easily remember the purpose of the bookmarks you save when you first start saving them, after a while you may have a great number of bookmarked sites, many with similar or almost identical titles. If you have to go into each bookmark to determine what is in it, you can find yourself spending more time than you may want to. But, by jotting down a brief description and reaction to each site, your bookmark collection becomes a set of electronic note cards. The annotations remind you of the content as well as the merit of each site. (*Note:* Internet Explorer does not allow annotations.)

To annotate a source using Netscape Navigator, click on **Bookmarks,** then **Edit Bookmarks,** then **Edit,** and then **Bookmark Properties.** You should then see a screen where you can write a brief description of your bookmark. Type a summary of what is in the source within the description section of the screen. Figure 6.3 shows you a sample of a bookmark that has been annotated. Note all that is included in the Bookmark Properties box: the title of the original source, the URL, even the time and date when the bookmark was added to the list of bookmarks.

Note the type of comments contained in this annotation: a concise summary of the content, plus an evaluation of its usefulness.

If you are creating bookmarks and organizing them into folders on a computer in a computer lab at your college, a local library, or some other public

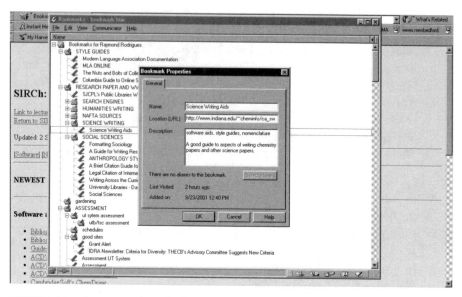

FIGURE 6.3 An annotation of a bookmark. Netscape Communicator browser window © 1999 Netscape Communications Corporation. Used with permission. Netscape Communications has not authorized, sponsored, endorsed, or approved this publication and is not responsible for its content.

computer, you should not leave those bookmarks on that computer, for someone else may erase them before you return to that computer. Remember that the bookmarks are saved on your computer's hard drive. Therefore, save your files on a computer disk so that you can take your disk with its bookmarks home or to another computer in the lab to work on it when you next have time. To save your bookmark file to a disk, click on **Bookmarks,** then click on **Edit Bookmarks,** then **File,** and finally **Save As.** Save the bookmarks to the appropriate disk drive. For example, you might type in "a:research topic name" and the computer will save your bookmark file to the A drive.

Your bookmarks are automatically saved as an HTML file every time you exit your browser. Netscape automatically names the file in a way that recog-

TRY IT NOW

Bookmarks→Edit Bookmarks→Edit→Bookmark Properties

Call up one of the bookmarks that you have saved for your research paper and create an annotation by selecting the above commands. Once you are satisfied that you know how to annotate your bookmarks, continue annotating other bookmarks.

nizes it as a bookmark file. But remember that you are not saving the text or the pictures of the websites that you have bookmarked. You are only saving the Web addresses, so if you want to have separate notes or quotes from those websites, you will have to save them into word-processing files.

SETTING UP YOUR ELECTRONIC WORKSPACE

Whether you will be working on your computer at home or working on a computer in a computer lab and therefore saving everything to a computer disk, you will want to create folders and files for various parts of your research project. A folder is simply a collection of files. Once you have a folder, you can store more than word-processing files: you can also store images, email messages, material copied from online sites—in short, everything related to your project.

- To create a folder using Microsoft Word, go to your **File** command, select **Save As,** and then, in the **Save in** box, select the directory and folder into which you want to place your new folder. Click on the yellow folder icon and give your folder a name.
- To move a file from one folder to another, the simplest way is to open the file and then save it to the new folder, deleting it from the original folder only after you have saved it to the new folder.

Take time to organize an effective workspace either on your home computer's hard drive or on a computer disk that you can move from computer to computer, or both. We recommend that you save files both on your computer and on a computer disk as a backup. Even if you do not have your own computer, try to think through ways of organizing your files into folders on a disk. Use that disk or set of disks exclusively for your research project. Also, write the names of your files on your disks. When you collect a large number of disks, knowing what is on each without having to load each to find out will save you time.

Although you will probably want to refine the techniques we suggest below to suit your own work style, some version of it may be useful to you. Figure 6.4 illustrates what such a workspace might look like on a computer. So, consider establishing these kinds of files and folders for your work:

- A folder for your research project.
- A *research log or notebook* folder or file where you keep notes to yourself about your research and ideas on how to organize your research (see Chapter 2 to review research logs).
- A folder to store bookmarks and to collect information you have gathered in your research.
- A folder or file that serves as a combination *note card* and *bibliography card* file—with template note cards that you use to take notes from your sources.
- A folder for drafts of your research paper, with each draft saved as a separate file (e.g., NAFTA paper 1, NAFTA paper 2, and so on).

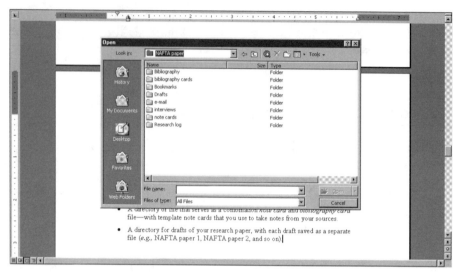

FIGURE 6.4 Example of an electronic workspace. Screen shot reprinted by permission from Microsoft Corporation.

In any folder, you can also have subfolders, that is, folders within folders. So you can have subfolders for each subtopic of your paper, if it is fairly long with major parts. Or you can have subfolders for any of the above, but organized according to the type of material you want to use, such as images, email messages, and Web pages. Don't make your organization so complex that you forget where you put your material, but do organize it to be most useful to you as you retrieve information for your paper.

Notice that all of the folders pictured in Figure 6.4 are subfolders of a folder titled "NAFTA Paper," the topic of a specific research project. The "NAFTA Paper" directory might itself be a subdirectory of another directory titled something like "Research Papers." The possibilities are many.

YOU TRY IT

After you have created your electronic workspace for your research, share that organization with others and discuss pros and cons of different organizations.

Electronic Note Cards

Electronic note cards are just like paper note cards, except that you create them as files in your computer and save them either on the hard drive or on a computer disk. We recommend that you use a particular design for your note cards

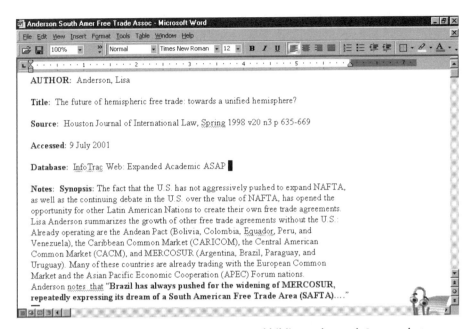

FIGURE 6.5 Example of an electronic note and bibliography card. Screen shot reprinted by permission from Microsoft Corporation.

that is easy for you to follow, copying it repeatedly in the file so that you have many to work with. Figure 6.5 illustrates an electronic note card with bibliographic information included.

Notice that what matters here are the categories of information to be saved:

- The author's name or authors' names.
- The title (since this example is from a database, only the title of the article is included here); if the source is an article or a book, you would include different titles within the "source":
  - article title
  - book title
- The date that you accessed the source.
- The name of the database where you located the source.
- These may be summaries, paraphrases, or direct quotes; be sure that you distinguish between them so that you can eventually cite them correctly.

If you want to keep notes and bibliography cards separate, your note card might consist simply of the author's last name, the page where the information was found, and the summary notes themselves (see Figure 6.6). In such a case, be sure to create a corresponding bibliography card with full bibliographic data (see Figure 6.7).

To design a master template file for your note cards, follow these steps:

1. Open a new file with your word processor.

Burfisher	
p. 130	Reports International Trade Commission (1997) of 120 manufacturing sectors in U.S., 7 negatively impacted by NAFTA 4 positive; all others no discernable difference
p. 130	U.S. Dept. of Ag: rural employment up 0.07% due to NAFTA

FIGURE 6.6   An example of an electronic note card.

2. Type the categories that you want to use. Do not fill them in.
3. Save the file with an identifiable name, such as "notes-TOPIC" for notes on the topic you are researching.

To use the template file:

1. Load the master template file (e.g., "notes-TOPIC").
2. Copy as many copies as you want.
3. Use the **Save as** feature of your word processor to give the file an appropriate name (e.g., "notes-NAFTA").
4. *Note:* Be sure that you rename the master file ("note-TOPIC" or whatever name you've given it) whenever you write notes into it or else, when you save it, you will write over the original master template file.

If you want to save a quote from an electronic source such as a website or a library database, all you have to do is block out the material to be quoted, go to **Edit** and click on **Copy.** Then go to your electronic note card file, open **Edit,** and click on **Paste.** Be sure that you indicate that it is a quote and include the page where the quote was found if the page is specified.

Sometimes you will want to type notes and quotes directly into your template file. At other times, you will want to copy text directly from the website or library database onto your note card template. As always, to avoid plagiarism, be sure to distinguish your direct quotes: use quotation marks, a different font, or boldface.

TRY IT NOW

Create a template for an electronic note card. Go to a source on the Web or in your online library and save a quote to the electronic note card.

Block→Edit→Copy
Open notecard file→Edit→Paste

You can keep all your notes in one file or in several files, but we recommend that you combine all your notes into one file. In that way, you can move back and forth between your notes and your draft of your paper, using the Copy and Paste commands to put the notes right by your writing while you are writing. If you are quoting, paraphrasing, or summarizing, by copying, you have those ready to be inserted as is or revised to fit your text and can make an in-text citation immediately. You can then delete anything from the electronic notes that you do not need. Don't delete the original notes in your note file in case you need to return to them.

As you are putting each of your notes in your file of notes, we recommend that you identify each set of notes by a keyword or words that you can remember. Then, when you are writing your paper and need to find a particular set of notes, you can use the **Find** command of your word processor to go directly to the set that you need.

Electronic Bibliography Cards

Some researchers prefer to keep bibliography cards separate from note cards. By doing so, they save time when writing note cards by not having to have all the bibliographic information on each card. We recommend that you design your bibliography templates so that they match the documentation style that you will be using for your research report (APA, MLA, CBE/CSE, CMS, COS, or whatever style you have been directed to use—see Chapter 8, "Documenting Sources"). Figure 6.7 illustrates an electronic bibliography card template:

Author's name: Last, First Initial	
Book Title	
City of Publication	
Publisher	
Date of Publication	
MLA Format	Last name, First Initial. *Title.* City of Publication: Publisher, Date of Publication.

FIGURE 6.7   Example of an electronic bibliography card template.

Notice that this template is designed to reflect the information that you will need in your bibliography. It even contains the model for the bibliographic entry, in this case in MLA style. Figure 6.8 illustrates what such a card would look like when filled in. In this example, APA style is used:

Author's name: Last, First Initial(s)	Burfisher, M. E., Robinson, S., & Thierfelder, K.
Article title	The impact of NAFTA on the United States
Journal/Periodical	*Journal of Economic Perspectives*
Vol., No.,	*15*(1)
Page nos.	125–144
Date of Publication	2001
Database/source	Hwwilsonweb.com
APA Electronic Article Format	Last name, First Initial (date). Title of article. *Title of Periodical, xx,* xxxxx. Retrieved month day, year, from source. Burfisher, M. E., Robinson, S., & Thierfelder, K. (2001). The impact of NAFTA on the United States. *Journal of Economic Perspectives, 15,* 1. Retrieved September 5, 2001, from WilsonWeb.

FIGURE 6.8　Example of an electronic bibliography card.

Notice how helpful it is to have the format specified on the electronic bibliography card so that you can follow it exactly when you create the bibliography entry on the card. When this information is actually translated into the bibliography, it will appear as follows:

Burfisher, M. E., Robinson, S., & Thierfelder, K. (2001). The impact of NAFTA on the United States. *Journal of Economic Perspectives,* 15, 1. Retrieved September 5, 2001, from WilsonWeb.

Using and Organizing Email for Your Research

Take time to organize your email into folders just as you organize your writing and bookmarks into folders. For purposes of your research, you can organize

WEB ACTIVITY

Go to the companion website for this book. There you will find electronic bibliography cards that you can use in your research or adapt to your bibliographic needs.

YOU TRY IT

1. Since each word-processing program is slightly different, develop a way to organize files, folders, and directories that will work for your program. How, for example, do you insert a new file into an existing folder? How can you capture a portion of an online source and copy it into your word-processing file? Share your strategies with others who may use the same word-processing software.

2. Practice capturing your library searches to a file so that you can incorporate the results into electronic note cards and bibliographic card files.

3. Practice capturing portions of your Web searches onto electronic note and bibliographic cards.

4. Review the way you organized your bookmarks in preparation for your research. Do you need to reorganize them now that you have had more time to think about your research report? If so, do so.

5. Review your directories and subdirectories in your electronic workspace. Consider whether you need to reorganize them in preparation for writing the first draft of your paper.

6. Study your electronic note cards and bibliography cards. Put them in the order that you intend to use them while writing your first draft.

your email folders to correspond with your other research folders or files. Save your email using Microsoft Word or whatever other word-processing program you use. If you are accessing email in a computer lab, be sure to save your email messages to a disk so that you do not lose them once you leave that computer for someone else to use.

Even if you are saving email on your own computer, learn to file the email messages into folders. You may be amazed to see how rapidly email messages can build up if you are keeping them and not deleting them. Indi-

TRY IT NOW

1. Save your email messages into different email folders.

2. After you have created several different email folders and saved email messages into them, open each message and save it as a file in your research folder. Figure 6.9 illustrates a screen just prior to saving an emailed database source.

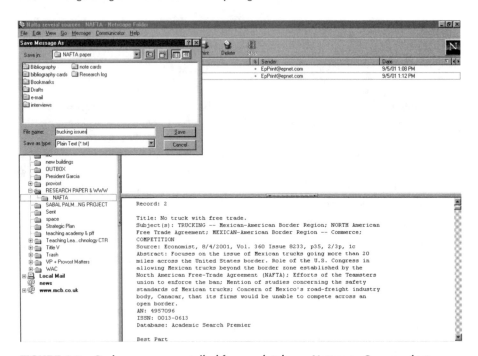

FIGURE 6.9 Saving a source emailed from a database. Netscape Communicator browser window © 1999 Netscape Communications Corporation. Used with permission. Netscape Communications has not authorized, sponsored, endorsed, or approved this publication and is not responsible for its content.

viduals who do not file their email into folders find that they spend much unnecessary time searching through the messages to find exactly the one that they want.

If you are working away from your home computer, searching for sources and finding good ones, many browsers, such as Netscape or Internet Explorer, allow you to send the text of the page that you are viewing to someone. That someone in this case can be you. If you use email from within Netscape or Internet Explorer, you can attach any Web page to an email message, send the page to yourself, and then retrieve the message with the Web page at your own computer. Once you open the email and the attached Web page, be sure to save it in an appropriate folder on your computer.

USING YOUR COMPUTER TO ORGANIZE YOUR WRITING

In the next chapter, we discuss the actual writing of your paper. Before you begin, consider how you might want to save your writing as you begin drafting it.

Draft Files

Open a separate file to draft your paper. If you keep your note cards file (perhaps in a note cards subdirectory) open as you draft, you can move files from one point to another as you work. Many authors create an outline file to guide them as they work. Microsoft Word, for example, allows you to work in "Outline View." This allows you to create the headings and subheadings of your paper and then type the paper into the Outline View.

Each time you prepare a new draft of your paper, you should give it a new name so that you do not eliminate the original draft. The reason for this is that you may decide at a later point that there was something in the original draft that you should have kept. By saving earlier drafts, you can always go back to them to retrieve whatever it is that you want. Another way of doing this is to copy the original draft, revise it however you want to, and save it with a new name, for example, "Topic draft 1," "Topic draft 2," and so on. This uses up more space on your computer disk or hard drive, but it will save you much work in the long run.

Writers can use their word-processing program to keep themselves organized while also allowing themselves the flexibility to change their ideas or organization as they proceed. Two broad methods are available for you to use: one file or many files.

Writing in One File

If you write and save your work in one file, you can move back and forth within that file with ease. If you want to add a part that you think of as you are writing, you simply move back up through the file until you find that part and create it. Or you quickly write it where you are, block it out, and use the **Cut** or **Copy** and **Paste** capability of your word-processing program to move it. If you do that, we recommend that you *copy and paste* it rather than cut and paste it. Then, once you have successfully pasted the material in its new position, you can return to the original place where you wrote it and delete the text from the place where you wrote it originally. Using the copy-and-paste method rather than the cut-and-paste method prevents the possibility of losing the original material before it is successfully pasted in its new position.

If you want to find a particular section of your long file, but don't want to have to scroll through the entire file looking for it, use the **Find** command. In Microsoft Word, click on **Edit** at the top of the screen and then click on **Find** in the drop-down menu that appears. Fill in the box that appears with a word or phrase that is in the section you are looking for, and the program will help you locate the appropriate text quickly. For example, we would look for "copy and paste" if we wanted to find the paragraph above.

You will need to find a way to stay organized if you use one long file. If you are working from an outline, we suggest that you put your outline of your paper either at the beginning of the file or at the end. Some writers prefer putting it at the end because it will be closer to where you are probably writing—at the end of your draft—and you will not have to move very much to go to it and then back to your writing. However, the choice is yours to make, and largely a matter of preference.

Be sure to keep saving your file regularly in case you lose power to your computer or something else happens to cause you to lose your file. Many writers also save the file to both the hard disk in the computer and to a floppy disk. They do so in case something very serious happens to the computer. Saving to a floppy disk allows you to simply go to another computer and keep working.

Writing in Many Files

Earlier in this book we recommended that you create a research log in which you keep separate files as your research proceeds, such as a file with electronic note cards and a file with bibliographic entries. We recommend now that you keep the parts of your draft in separate files as well.

Many writers find that one long file is much too cumbersome to work with, so they save different sections of their writing to separate files. A natural set of files would consist of the introduction, body, summary, and references. But even the body of your research report might be broken into several different files if it is going to be fairly long. We recommend giving the files names that are easily recognizable, such as "research_outline," "research_intro," "research_body_1," "research_body_2," "research_conclusion," and "research_references." Of course, you will probably use names more closely related to your topic, such as "NAFTA_intro" or "Frost_intro."

In case you want to move between files to work on more than one file at once, two techniques will work. The first technique involves loading more than one file at once. After working in the first file, you minimize the first file you are working in and open the second file that you want to work in. In Microsoft Word, for example, there is a box in the upper right-hand corner with an underscore mark in it. Click on it, and the file you are working on is minimized, with the title appearing in a smaller box at the bottom of your screen. If you want to bring it back up, all you have to do is click on that smaller box. Once you have minimized one file, load your second file. You can copy material from the second file, minimize it, and click on the first file. Then you paste the new material in the new file. You can actually use this technique with more than two different files, alternatively minimizing and loading the file you want to work in.

The second technique is to split the screen so that you can see parts of two files at once. If you want to work in two sections of the same file at once, you go to the "split box" at the top of the "vertical scroll bar" on the left side of your screen. Your arrow pointer will change to an icon symbolizing a split screen, and at that point you can drag it down to the point on your screen where you want it to split. Then, by moving your cursor from one screen to the next, you can work in each screen separately. You use your Copy and Paste commands to move sections of your file around, even copying from one screen and pasting in the other screen. If you want to save both your original file and

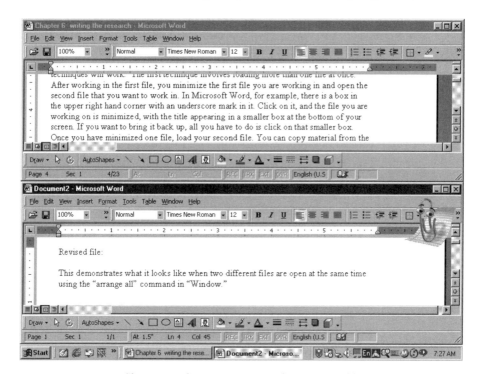

FIGURE 6.10   Two files on a split screen. Screen shot reprinted by permission from Microsoft Corporation.

the revised file, you will have to save the revised file with a new name. (*Note:* Some word-processing programs will have a "split screen" command that you can use instead of using the split box. You should use your "help" suggestions to learn how best to use your word-processing program.)

If you want to split the screen and work in two different files, you use different commands. First, open both files at the same time. Only one at a time will show on your screen. Then, with both files open, move your pointer to the "Window" button at the top of your screen and click on "Arrange all." You will immediately see both files, one on top and one on the bottom. You will be able to work in each file separately, copy and paste from one file to the other, and save each separately. Figure 6.10 shows what the split screens look like.

SUMMARIZING THE ORGANIZATIONAL PROCESS

1. Begin browsing through the Web and through your library online to locate possible sources to include in your research project. Use search engines to narrow the possible sites on various aspects of your topic. Do not restrict your topic too much when you begin.

2. Bookmark your sources as you locate them by using the Bookmark command of your browser. Add as many as you want: they do not take up too much space, and you can always delete them later.

3. Annotate your bookmarks so that you can remember what they were about and how useful they might be. (*Note:* This cannot be done with Internet Explorer.)

4. As your bookmark file begins to grow, and as soon as you have a sense of the categories into which you might sort your sources, organize your research project bookmarks into folders and subfolders. Click and drag your bookmarks into the folder or subfolder where you think each belongs.

5. Organize your electronic workspace into directories and subdirectories, including your research log or notebook, electronic note cards, electronic bibliography cards, bookmarks, drafts of your paper, and other areas that you will find useful as you conduct your research, such as interviews or email messages.

6. Make electronic note cards and electronic bibliography cards on the sources you think you will use so that you can quote and/or cite your sources accurately.

7. Begin drafting your research paper when you have read enough to understand your subject well. Move back and forth between your notes and the draft, copying and pasting from one file to the next as appropriate.

8. For each draft of your paper, create a new file with a new name, thereby keeping the earlier drafts in case you need to refer back to them.

CONCLUSION

Systematic strategies for finding, capturing, and organizing information from your searches in the library and on the Web enable you to make your computer a major research tool. As you develop your research topic, you should think of various ways to organize the information you find so that you can pull it together later into a meaningfully organized research paper. The computer allows you to establish the organizational categories you want and store information in those categories, whether the information be from library searches, Web searches, email messages, field notes, or other sources. The computer also allows you to rearrange your information efficiently once you have determined what organization you want to use and if you have reconceptualized your research after you have started gathering information and had time to think about your topic more.

The same points may be made as you begin writing your research paper. You should consider each version of the paper as a draft that can be revised and reorganized. You will begin to think of the computer as an important research tool, one that will facilitate your gathering, saving, and organizing the information you discover. The flexibility that the computer allows will facilitate your ability to rethink and reconceptualize aspects of your writing.

This, in turn, will enable you to write a more effective research report, and your ability to continuously improve that paper will follow.

SUGGESTED ACTIVITY

Organize your notes and share them with one other person. Talk through the organization of your paper: how you will start, what comes next, next, and so on. Review each other's organization and notes by using the following guidelines:

1. Do there appear to be any gaps in the information that you read? That is, as a reader, what else would you like to know?
2. Does any of the information that you read seem unrelated to the topic or not essential to the research topic? Is there any unnecessary information?

Can the research be organized in a different way? Consider whether you, as the reader, can follow the logic of the research organizational pattern. If not, discuss alternative ways to organize the information.

Turning Your Research into a Written Report

After completing this chapter, you should be able to do the following:

- Pace your writing so that you write what you are able to write and do not suffer "writer's block" by trying to accomplish every stage of writing when you are not ready.

- Focus your thesis statement so that it is clear and manageable.

- Organize your notes and ideas so that the reader can follow your logic, perhaps creating a topic or sentence outline before you begin.

- Quote, paraphrase, and summarize your sources so that you do not accidentally plagiarize those sources.

- Base your conclusions upon the supporting information that you have discovered, while recognizing that there may be other possible conclusions and while being clear about why you have chosen your conclusion rather than the other ones.

- Address your topic in an objective and evenhanded manner, being sure to recognize your own biases as you are compiling your information and writing about what you have learned.

- Recognize and address the questions and different perspectives that others have.

- Present tables and figures clearly.

- Interpret the information that you have gathered so that the reader gains a clear perspective of your thoughts.

- Make your conclusions *yours*, not simply the compiled opinions of the sources you found.

- Write an introduction that prepares your reader for what follows.

R emember one of the themes that we have often repeated in the earlier chapters: The more you know your subject, the better your writing will be. Assuming that you have read broadly and in depth and have taken notes that you can organize in a logical pattern, this chapter will help you prepare the first draft of your report so that your final paper will exhibit the clarity that good scholarship demands.

WRITING OVER TIME

We introduced the need for you to establish a time schedule in Chapter 2. Now, we'd like to revisit the time schedule one more time so that you can think about a writing schedule that is both realistic and efficient. If you can organize your time without commitments beyond your other classes, our best advice on your writing schedule would be for you to set aside a specific time every day and write during that time, no matter what. But we realize that everyone's life is not always that systematic. Some of us have jobs that we have to maintain, a family to take care of, or activities such as sports that we participate in. Given that, it may not be possible to keep a systematic schedule. However, you should still establish a broad time schedule with specific deadlines so that you know how much time you have to complete parts of your work and so that you finish your research and writing on time. As soon as you know your assignment and when it is due, you should have laid out a weekly schedule to

- Begin reading broadly so that you can determine what your topic will be and narrow your thesis statement;
- seek approval for your topic, if that is expected of you;
- conduct your research;
- organize and evaluate your ideas, notes, and sources;
- write your first draft;
- revise what you have written; and
- edit the final draft before turning it in.

Now you are probably at that stage where you need to complete the last four items on the list above. This time you need to lay out a *daily* schedule for your writing, with the due date at the end.

WRITING IN INCREMENTS

Some people can write something from beginning to the end, but most writers don't work that way. You should have a general plan for how your final product will be organized, but you don't have to force yourself to write the parts of the plan in the order that you will finally compile the paper. Begin writing with those parts that you know best and that you are most prepared to write. You will find yourself writing pieces before you put it all together, but doing so will prevent you from being "blocked" by a part that you are not ready to write. If you guide yourself with a general outline for your paper, you can write each part separately and use the plan to keep track of what remains to be written. Like many professional writers, you will probably even write your introduction after you have written the rest of the paper, for, by that time, you will have organized your thoughts, perhaps discovered more about your topic and what you want to say, and had time to revise both your thoughts and your writing as the topic begins to make more sense to you.

Now is the time when your having kept accurate notes, with the essential information about your sources, will matter. If you have to go back to find a complete quote or the date of a source or a specific fact that you need, you'll be using valuable time. When you are writing, think of ways that you can strengthen what you have written. Sometimes you may think of something else you want to include, but not have the information at hand. As you write, include notes to yourself about what you want to do but cannot while your words are flowing easily. For example, you might decide that a good quote would make the point better than the way you just tried to say it. Write a note to yourself to find that quote. Perhaps there is an important argument that you want to make, but you lack the solid facts to back it up; make a note to yourself. Or you may want to remind yourself that you need to refer to a source that contradicts your most important point, as a way of recognizing that there are opposing viewpoints. When your thoughts are coming fast, if you stop writing to find that information, you may have to take more time to remember what it was you wanted to say when you return to your writing. That could cause you to lose the clarity of your original thoughts. And if you don't write the note to yourself, you may forget exactly what it was you needed to accomplish. If you are writing with a word processor, type the notes to yourself in a different font style or a different font size or a different color so that they jump out at you.

There may be times when you suddenly think of something that you want to say that applies to another section of your paper. You probably don't want to go to that section and risk losing your train of thought where you are. In that case, quickly write down what you just thought of—or at least the gist of it—and move it to the top or bottom of your page, marking it with "NOTE:" in uppercase letters, again using a different font to find it easily. Then return right away to the part you were working on. Once you finish your writing, you can return to that idea and move it to the place where you want it. You don't have to read through the entire file looking for it if you use the Find command of your word-processing program. In Microsoft Word, click on **Edit** at the top of the screen and then click on **Find** in the drop-down menu that appears. Fill in the box that appears with a word or phrase that is in the section you are looking for (such as "NOTE:", if that is the word you remember), and the program will help you locate the appropriate text quickly. For example, you might look for "different font" or "remind yourself" if you wanted to find the paragraph above.

As we suggested in the previous chapter, if you are writing a long section using an outline, keep the outline at the end of your file or at the beginning so that you can keep track of your organization. In addition, save your file often, just in case the electricity goes off or something else happens that could cause you to lose the file. Finally, make copies of your files on computer disks in case something happens to the file on your hard drive.

REVISITING AND REVISING YOUR THESIS STATEMENT

Before you begin writing, look at the preliminary thesis sentence that you created during your work with Chapter 3. Does that thesis sentence now capture exactly what you want to say? You have been reading more sources, taking notes, and thinking about your topic for a while now, so your concept of the point you want to make, your thesis, may have evolved as you learned more and thought more about the topic. Look at the latest version of your thesis statement and ask yourself this:

■ Does it capture the exact point you want to make in your writing?
■ Does it give the reader some idea of what the reader can expect to find in your writing?
■ Can the reader understand it clearly?

Consider this example:

Terrorism is an evil that must be overcome.

If you were to ask yourself the three questions above about this particular thesis statement, the answer would probably be "no" to all three questions. Clearly it is much too broad to write about in a brief paper, but it also doesn't help the reader understand what the reader can expect to find in your paper. Here are some more focused thesis statements:

1. Recognizing that terrorism will always exist when groups believe that they have no other way to protect their values, our country must develop foreign policies that address the root causes of those feelings that lead to terrorism.
2. When we say that we will "go to war" to overcome terrorism, the type of war that we conduct will have to be vastly different from the wars we have fought in the past.

Once you have drafted a thesis sentence that meets the criteria addressed above, you can begin your writing because you know what information and arguments you will have to provide the reader. Your writing will flow more easily.

MOVING FROM NOTES TO FIRST DRAFT

Be sure that you have all your notes and at least a preliminary outline of the paper you are about to write before you begin drafting. Your notes should include complete and accurate citation information.

You may have created an outline of your topic before you actually began your research, but it is most likely that any outline written before you have done your research will no longer be appropriate. You will have learned more as you read more, listened to speeches, talked to experts, or even sent email messages to individuals seeking their advice. So begin by reading through your notes, whether they are on separate cards, in a research journal, or in separate files on your computer. As you read, think about what should come first and the sequence of ideas to follow. Write a rough outline. You may change it many times before you are done. Your outline may be as simple as a list of keywords or phrases:

Title: Robert Frost as a "Nature Writer": "The Oven Bird," "Hyla Brook," and "The Exposed Nest."
   I. Introduction
      a. How to know?
      b. My discovery as a reader
  II. A soft romantic or a hard realist?
      a. Arguments for soft romantic
      b. Arguments for hard realist
 III. The evidence from three poems
      a. "The Oven Bird"
         i. Biographical evidence
        ii. Evidence in the text
      b. "Hyla Brook"
         i. Biographical evidence
        ii. Evidence in the text
      c. "The Exposed Nest"
         i. Biographical evidence
        ii. Evidence in the text
  IV. Conclusion
      a. Biography or text?
      b. Believe what you want

Or your outline may be key sentences that capture the themes you want to communicate:

   I. Introduction
      a. Robert Frost has been called both a romantic nature poet and a hard realist.
      b. By the end of this paper, I will demonstrate which he really is. [*NOTE: Tell the reader here?*]

II. The evidence from three poems:
   a. "The Oven Bird"
      i. Note that the oven bird is actually a type of finch and that Frost has captured this bird's behavior accurately.
      ii. Then note that the "The question . . . / Is what to make of a diminished thing" is a very human concern.
   b. "Hyla Brook"
      i. Frost's attention to the details of nature, such as dried leaves and the scientific name of spring peepers, demonstrates the realist in him.
      ii. But his last line reveals the poem to be a love poem.
   c. "The Exposed Nest"
      i. "We turned to other things" reflects the realism of life: Though we romantically want to preserve life, other things happen to us.
      ii. Note the warm, tender way in which Frost speaks to "you"—his wife?
III. Conclusion
   a. In his poetry, we see Frost grounding the poem in objective observations of both nature and people, thus being very realistic.
   b. But the softness of his themes are very romantic.
   c. Therefore, romantic grounded in realism.
   d. [NOTE: Find a good quote to really sum things up—Amy Lowell, 1915?]

Notice that the person drafting this outline drafts it as both ideas that might be written directly into the draft and as notes about what to do. Though they are not parallel, this does not matter, for this is a working outline for the writer, not the reader. As you proceed to write from your outline, you may find yourself changing the organization or even the ideas. As long as the logic of the organization remains clear to the reader, you can always change your plan to make your writing more effective.

To help you develop components of your outline, ask yourself whether any of the following can help you build a stronger paper and, at the same time, help the reader understand it better:

- Key terms should be defined;
- events should be organized chronologically;
- causes and their effects should be explained;
- comparisons or contrasts of the opinions of experts in the field, the data you have gathered, or themes in the literature about this subject should be included; or
- processes should be explained.

Don't write paragraphs that are composed entirely of your source material. Remember that your professor—or any other reader—will be wondering what you think and will want to know why you have included a particular source. Always include your own words in each paragraph, no matter how many sources you are referring to at the moment. Give the reader some idea of

TRY IT NOW

Organize your notes into the order that you think makes the most sense. Check to be sure that you also have the bibliographic information that should accompany each source. Now write a preliminary outline for your paper.

the purpose of including that source, what the context was for it, or how it fits into the overall scheme of your organization.

Writing from an Outline

As you write, remember that you will be revising your draft, either as you are writing or later when you return to it. If you are writing on paper, skip lines so that you can insert new material later. If you prefer reading the hard copy or paper version of your drafts, print them out double- or even triple-spaced to allow you to insert new comments. Writing with a computer simplifies revision greatly, for you can insert and delete easily during the revision and editing stage. You can write from an outline that you have created in two primary ways: (1) copying the outline into the file that you are drafting; and (2) using your word processor's "outline view."

Method one is to begin writing by copying your outline directly into the files where you are writing your drafts. You can put your outline at the top or at the bottom of the file so that you can return to it repeatedly to remind yourself of where you are going and where you have been. By using a keyword at the top of the outline, such as "OUTLINE," you can use the Find command of your word processor to return to it easily as your draft grows longer.

Method two is to use the "outline view" of your word processor. In Microsoft Word, with a new file opened, click on **View**, and then click on **Outline**. You can then create your outline, using the arrow commands at the top of the screen to move sections of it to lower or higher levels on the outline (see Figure 7.1). Once you have created your outline, you can go to **View→Normal** and start drafting your paper right in the outline that you have created. As your file grows longer, you can go to the **View→Outline** again, collapse the section that you have finished drafting, and move to the next section of the outline that you want to write. In fact, you can actually draft your paper in **View→Outline**, allowing yourself to keep the outline in view as you write.

Writing from Your Notes

In your electronic research journal or log you have a file of notes that you were taking while you were conducting your research. Now you can use those notes to write your paper. Some writers find using the outline to be helpful as

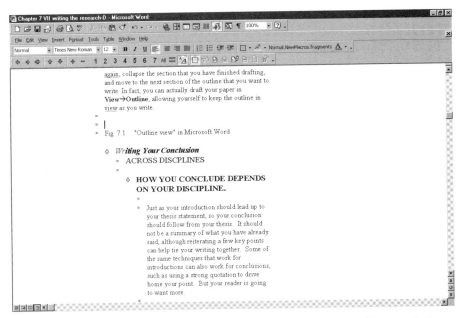

FIGURE 7.1 "Outline view" in Microsoft Word. Screen shot reprinted by permission from Microsoft Corporation.

they write. They simply use the outline as their headings and write between each level of the outline. Whether you are following an outline to write the paper or not, all you have to do is go back and forth between your draft and the notes, copying notes from your note file and paste them into your draft to either use directly or rewrite to fit your writing context at the moment.

There are two ways that you can move between your notes file and your draft file:

1. You can have one file at a time on the screen. Load both files at once. Only one will show on the screen at the same time. To see the other file, you simply diminish one file and use the other file. When you are ready to return to the first file, you diminish the file you are working in and enlarge the second file.

2. You can work in two screens at once by splitting the screen (see pp. 114–115 in Chapter 6). To move between files, you click on the file you want to work in.

The technique of copying and pasting from one file to another works the same way in either of the two methods. You decide which method works best for you.

Writing a Conclusion Appropriate for Your Academic Field

Just as your introduction should lead up to your thesis statement, so your conclusion should follow from your thesis. It should not be a summary of what you have already said, although reiterating a few key points can help tie your writing together. Some of the same techniques that work for introductions can also work for conclusions, such as using a strong quotation to drive home your point. But your reader is going to want more.

Let's assume you have demonstrated that your thesis is true. So what? The answer to that question is what will help make your conclusion a strong one. Several approaches can help at this point:

- Apply what you have demonstrated in your paper to the future;
- Argue for some action to be taken as a result of what you have shown, such as future research needed or some social action.
- Restate your thesis so that your readers recognize how it applies to them.
- Discuss what still needs to happen, regardless of the strength of your thesis.

Regardless of the methods that you employ in your conclusion, some things should be avoided:

- Don't make overt statements such as, "In conclusion, I want to say . . . ," "In this paper, I have demonstrated that . . . ," or "The three points I have made are . . .".
- Don't bring up a totally new thought that you have not discussed in the body.
- Don't indicate that your thesis is the only one that can be correct.
- Don't end the paper just to end it; close it in a way that your reader knows that you are done.

Conclusions in Non-Scientific Research Papers and Reports

In fields such as the humanities and the arts, you are allowed some latitude on how you write your conclusions. The examples below are designed to illustrate options that are available to you. As you read them, think about what would make a clear and interesting conclusion for your research paper or report.

Consider the following conclusion to a paper on illegal immigration from Mexico:

> In summary, I have demonstrated that the continuing and substantial illegal immigration of Mexican citizens has had a negative effect upon our educational system, our social service agencies, our criminal justice system, and our health care system. I have shown that the intentions of NAFTA have been good intentions, despite the flaws in the way that NAFTA has been implemented, but that NAFTA has not gone far enough. So, there can only be one direction for the United States to take: We must treat Mexico just as we treat Canada, with essentially an open border, and we must infuse substantial money into the Mexican economy so that Mexico can grow more jobs with better wages for Mexicans. Then the heavy illegal immigration will be a thing of the past.

Nothing is mechanically wrong with this conclusion, but the style can be stronger. The writer tells the reader that the reader needs to know that this is a summary, that the writer has demonstrated something, and that the solution proposed by the writer is the only possible solution. Readers don't need to be told that they are reading a summary, they don't need to be reminded that the writer has made several points, and they probably won't believe that this solution is the only solution for what is a very complex problem. So, even though the research paper may itself be very strong, this conclusion weakens the final impression that the reader will be left with.

Now, compare the conclusion above with the following two conclusions:

(A) What have our experiences with NAFTA taught us that can help both the United States and Mexico to halt the massive illegal immigration into the United States? They have taught us that, when there is work with decent wages, even by Mexican standards, the citizens of Mexico would rather stay in Mexico than enter the United States. When newer technologies have been infused into Mexican industries, not only does their productivity increase, but also their ability to attract workers with more education increases. When Mexicans earn enough to support their families at home, greater economic stability permeates the villages beyond Mexico City.

Thus, the investment of dollars by business in the United States has had a positive effect upon the economy of Mexico, and when that economy has grown, other benefits have followed. It has not been that NAFTA has failed to help Mexico—it is that the positive aspects of NAFTA are not as strong as they can be. More economic support through new NAFTA initiatives, with joint controls by both Mexico and the United States are, until something better comes along, the most promising solution to the problem of illegal Mexican immigration. Until then, no increase in efforts to seal the border or regulations making it harder for Mexicans to enter the United States will stop the flow of illegal immigrants. Jobs in Mexico may be what it takes.

(B) If Emiliano Zapata were alive today, his rallying cry would not be "¡Tierra o muerte!" ("Land or death!") It would be "Better jobs or more migration problems!" The demographic and economic studies of Mexican immigration reflect the need for a stronger Mexican economy if illegal immigration is to be curtailed. We have noted such estimates as the following: that as many as or more than 300,000 illegal immigrants enter the U.S. each year from Mexico, that the family wages of illegal immigrants are typically in the $30,000 range or slightly above, that they send back to Mexico as much as $3 billion a year, that most of the illegal immigrants return to Mexico after being here a little over a year, and that the U.S. spends $4.3 billion a year to control immigration, with $800,000 of that paying to detain illegal immigrants who are caught. In short, the cost of restricting immigration is enormous.

Therefore, the United States needs to rethink its economic policies toward Mexico so that they strengthen Mexican capacity to offer jobs at decent wages. Among many potential solutions, the proposal that our economic plan be a Mexican "Lend-Lease," similar to our efforts to help Europe rebuild after World War II, appears to be the most promising way we can slow or even hope to stop illegal immigration. *Maquiladoras* demonstrate that Mexicans will flock to jobs if they are available, but *maquiladoras* cannot be the mainstay of the Mexican economy. When the U.S. recognizes that substantial business aid will have long-term benefits to both the U.S. and Mexico, then the perceived "threat" our southern border poses will be no more.

Conclusion A summarizes the major arguments that were made in the paper and ends with the writer urging a reconceptualization of economic policy toward Mexico. The writer summarizes the concepts that the reader should remember before rephrasing the thesis. Conclusion B begins with a famous quotation and then selects a few of the key facts that the research has revealed. It closes with the refined thesis, not just that the United States should work to strengthen the economy of Mexico, but that the effort should be as massive as the "lend-lease" program that followed World War II. Notice that neither conclusion summarizes the paper point by point, but both select what the writers consider to be most important for the reader to remember. And each restates the thesis introduced at the beginning of the papers.

Good conclusions:

- reiterate the thesis sentence;
- don't simply summarize what has already been said;
- don't add ideas that were not discussed in the paper;
- establish a "so what?" position, telling the reader the importance of what has been discovered by the research;
- may suggest future studies or ideas to pursue; and
- leave the reader with words to remember, whether a quote or the writer's own words.

Conclusions in Science and Social Science Research Papers and Reports

How you format your conclusion for a science or social science report depends in part upon the length of your paper. The "conclusion" in these reports often consists of several major parts: the results of the experiment or survey, a discussion of the experiment or survey, and conclusions. In shorter papers, the discussion and conclusion sections are often combined. Consider the following questions when you are writing your conclusion:

- As concisely as possible, what has the experiment or survey demonstrated?
- Why was it important to conduct this experiment or survey? What are the implications of your findings, for a real-world application or as part of a continuing set of studies? Because the research of scientists follows from

previous research and is intended to lead into the next stages of research, you might propose additional research that should follow from your work.

■ What qualifications would you make that your reader should be aware of? If your paper is a report of an experiment, discuss what you have *not* demonstrated as a result of the experiment as well as what you *have* demonstrated.

The following conclusion is from the preliminary draft of the sample science paper in Appendix E:

> Our results are inconclusive at this time. From the data we have already collected, however, we have found that there is no significant difference between the number of pollinators that visit each flower color. There is a difference, though, in the amount of time spent at each flower, depending on their color. The yellow flowers seem to retain the pollinators for longer periods of time. The pink flowers follow, while the peach flowers were the ones where pollinators spent the least amount of time.

Here the researchers clearly summarize what their preliminary conclusions were, but they do not discuss why it was important to conduct this study or qualify their results in any way. In the final draft, you will note that this preliminary conclusion was expanded to include separate results related to separate conclusions and implications for future research.

Conclusions in Case Studies

If your paper is a case study, intended, for example, for a business, social work, or anthropology course, then you will want to remind the reader of what the purpose of doing the case study was and what you learned. But, just as in the conclusion for a science report, you will still be able to argue for some future action, urge the reader to apply what you have learned to the reader's personal situation, or indicate what you think businesspersons or social workers or anthropologists should change as a result of your observations. In addition, suggesting new case studies, perhaps designed to refine what you have done, is always helpful to your readers.

TRY IT NOW

If you have completed writing the main body of your research, write a draft of your conclusion now. Compare it against the characteristics of good conclusions above.

Writing Your Introduction

Once you have written the body of your paper and your conclusion, you are ready to write your introduction. Introductions are not always written first. In fact, it is best for you to write your introduction after you have completed at least the first draft of your paper. You may discover half way through your writing and research that you have changed your mind about your thesis statement. You may have refined it as you learned more about your subject. Even though it may not be exactly what your professor may have originally approved, professors recognize that thesis statements evolve as writers learn more through their research. However, if you completely change your *topic*, then you should consult with your professor.

Before writing the introduction, reread what you have written. Have you argued for and supported a clear thesis? Does your paper flow from the initial statement of the topic through to the conclusion? Or do you change ideas or focus in the middle? If the paper does shift its focus by the end, then you may need to rewrite parts of it so that it consistently concentrates upon a clear topic and set of arguments. Once you are satisfied that the paper accomplishes what you set out to accomplish, then it is time for you to write that introduction.

Introductions in Non-Scientific Research Papers and Reports

You can introduce your paper in a wide variety of ways, but, regardless of the methods that you use, your introduction should introduce your reader to the subject, interest the reader in your subject, and include your thesis statement.

Your introduction can be one paragraph or several paragraphs. Your thesis sentence can appear at the beginning of the introduction or at the end. Most writers tend to write their thesis sentence near the end of their introduction, for they design the rest of the introduction to provide information that will engage the reader and provide the basic information that the reader needs to be interested in the topic and to understand why you are writing about it. A number of methods are available to you to engage the reader. You can:

- summarize the history of the topic;
- explain the nature of the problem you will be discussing;
- summarize the debate that exists about your topic;
- use an anecdote or two to bring life to your subject;
- introduce some key quotations from your sources that capture the essence of what you will write about;
- use facts and data that capture the interest of the reader;
- personalize the topic by explaining your connection to it;
- define key terms and issues related to the topic; or
- combine two or more of the above approaches.

The style of your introduction can establish you as a writer who is in control of your subject and who knows how to make the reader want to read on or, if poorly conceived, as a writer who is mechanically putting together information for a research paper. Some markers of the mechanical approach that you want to keep away from are statements like the following:

■ I am going to write about . . .
■ The purpose of this paper is to . . .
■ There are three points I want to make about . . .

Your reader knows that you are going to write about something, right? Your reader assumes that you have a purpose, and your reader knows that you will be making various points in the body of your paper. So use at least one of those introductory methods listed above. For example, read the following draft introduction to a paper titled "Solving the Dilemma of Illegal Mexican Immigration":

> My purpose in writing this paper is to explain the reasons why Americans seem to feel ambivalent about illegal immigration from Mexico. I will write about the different jobs that illegal Mexican immigrants hold in America and the reasons why we need them to hold those jobs. I will show the drain on the economic resources of our nation that this illegal immigration causes and the gap that it fills in our job market. And I will, after having explored the evidence and conclusions of leading experts in the field, show that there is an economic solution to the dilemma of wanting and not wanting illegal Mexican immigrants, one we all can live with.

Now read the introduction below for the same paper:

> He's the person who mows your lawn. She's the woman who comes once a week to clean your home. They and their children stoop over the vegetable crops that keep us well fed and healthy. They work in the chicken factories, cleaning and cutting up the chicken that we now prefer to beef to keep our cholesterol low. They wash dishes, pots, and pans in the fast-food joints of America. And they do it all for lower wages than the typical American wants to work for.
>
> Their presence drains our resources: our hospitals must take them in and care for them even when they can't afford to pay. If their children are born in the United States, they are automatically citizens entitled to all the benefits of other American citizens. Their children sit alongside American children in school and have to be educated through bilingual education. Our social-service agencies spread their services thin in trying to help them. Their willingness to work for less takes jobs away from American workers.
>
> They are the illegal immigrants who find their ways across our southern border regardless of the risk, and we need their labor even though we don't want to support their health care, education, or housing. We want them here, and we want them gone. Illegal immigration from Mexico has been both a blessing and a curse, a dilemma that bothers us morally and economically, yet a dilemma that does not

have to be. However, there is a solution, and that solution lies in our redefining the ways that we manage the joint economies of Mexico and the United States.

Or consider the following introduction to the same paper:

Writing in *Time* magazine, reporter Nancy Gibbs described the United States/Mexico border as "a barbed-wire paradox, half pried open, half bolted closed" (39). Mexican President Vicente Fox and United States President George Bush have met several times to discuss the relationship between the two countries, realizing that their futures are bound to each other. While no one knows what the best solution may be to address the illegal immigration of thousands of Mexicans every month, most experts agree that the United States needs those workers, even though many people have serious concerns about their impact upon our health care, education, and social services. The evidence is clear: we cannot stop the illegal immigration, Mexicans would remain in Mexico if their economy provided them the jobs and wages that they need, and we need a strong Mexico to help keep our economy strong. The solution is not a legal one. Only an economic solution that will benefit both countries.

Notice how the latter two introductions move immediately into the subject, the first painting a picture of the dilemma by illustrating the conflicting views of illegal Mexican immigrants, and the latter beginning with a quote that captures the dilemma and then summarizes the key issues that must be addressed. All end with the thesis that an economic solution would be the best way to solve the dilemmas of illegal Mexican immigration.

Good introductions:

- are often written last, after the writer knows what the paper really says;
- do not use overt cues for the reader, such as, "This paper's purpose is to . . .";
- give the reader the first impression that the writer truly knows the subject;
- are designed to be interesting, with good quotes, facts, or anecdotes;
- clearly let the reader know what the paper is about; and
- usually end with the thesis statement.

Introductions in Science and Social Science Research Papers and Reports

If you are writing a report of an experiment, such as a science project, then you want to be as objective as possible. Summarize the purpose of the research or the problem addressed by the research, the hypotheses to be tested, and the experimental design that you are going to describe. Your purpose may refer to previous research (which you will summarize more clearly in the body of the paper) and may explain how your research follows from that previous research, but it should be summarized, not explained in detail.

Introductions in Case Studies

If you are writing a case study, such as for a business or social work class, you are allowed more freedom than you would take in a report of an experiment. But your reader will still want to know as clearly as possible what the purpose of the case study is, whether it follows from a pattern of previous case studies, and the problem or issue that it will address. Although you may choose to write more dramatically than you ever would in a science paper, the anecdotes, the quotations, or the selection of facts should help the reader understand the purpose of your case study.

TRY IT NOW

If you have completed writing your paper, write your introduction. Check it against the characteristics of good introductions above.

PREPARING TABLES AND FIGURES

The social sciences and the sciences value tables and figures in research reports, for they help to clarify information in text form within the document. Although it is not common for papers in the humanities to contain tables and figures, they are being used more and more, as knowledge about visual effects and about effective communication becomes more widespread within the fields of the humanities.

We recommend that you consult the style guides of the Modern Language Association (MLA), the American Psychological Association (APA), the Council of Science Editors (CBE or CSE), or the Chicago Manual of Style (CMS) for more detailed guidelines on preparing tables and figures.

Tables

Tables typically are used to present numerical data in some easily understood format. Percentages, total numbers of elements studied, and amounts of money are typical elements found in tables. Most word-processing software now make the preparation of tables fairly easy. Practice drawing tables with your word processor. For example, in Microsoft Word, there is a **Table** button on the screen that takes you step by step through the preparation of a table. By selecting **Table** and then **Insert** and then **Table**, you can design the table to have as many columns and rows as you want. Here are some general formatting guidelines for tables:

- Table numbers and titles go above the tables, flush with the left margin;
- the tables are numbered with Arabic numbers, from the beginning to the end of the report;

- numbers with decimal points and commas should be aligned by the decimal points and commas;
- do not focus on more than one category of information or dependent variable in a table.

Table 7.1 illustrates the categories for columns and rows. An independent variable is a factor that does not change, such as the age categories. For example, if you are reporting on the number of automobile accidents and your study is attempting to determine whether accidents occur among younger people more than older people, your independent variable would be the age categories you have defined. The dependent variables (which will vary depending upon the age groups you have defined) will change. In this example, dependent variables might be factors such as male and female or alcohol involved or not.

As shown in Table 7.1, there are no vertical lines. This has become a standard practice in publishing since the creation of those vertical lines added to the cost of production. If the categories and numerical data are properly aligned, the table should be clear without vertical lines. *Note:* In most word-processing programs, you can create tables using horizontal and vertical lines, but there usually is a command you can learn to eliminate the vertical lines after you have entered your data into the table.

TABLE 7.1   An Example of a Table[a]

	Dependent Variable 1	Dependent Variable 2	Dependent Variable 3	Dependent Variable 4
Independent Variable A	xxx.xx[b]	xx.xx	xxx.xx	xxxx.xx
Independent Variable B	xxxxxx.xx[c]	xxx.xx	xxx.xx	xxx.xx
Independent Variable C	xxxx.xx	xx.xx	x.xx	xx.xx
Independent Variable D	x.xx	x.xx	xx.xx	xxx.xx

[a]This is an example of differences in guidelines: CMS and MLA recommend that the table number be placed above the title, while APA recommends that the two be on the same line. Titles should be capitalized like a title, not all in caps.

[b]Type footnotes below the table, flush left, and double spaced, with an extra space between the footnotes. Note the use of lowercase letters as superscripts.

[c]Footnotes are used in tables to explain such matters as where data was found, anomalies in the data, and other information that helps the reader understand the data.

If you copy a table directly from a source, you should cite that source just as you would cite any source from which you have drawn information. CMS recommends noting the source directly under the table as *"Source:"*. APA recommends including the source in a *"Note."* directly below the table. If the report is going to be published, you should request permission of the original author before publishing the table in your report.

If you draw data from a table or report that someone else has written, you should specify that in the *Source* or *Note* as "From . . ." with appropriate documentation (see Chapter 8 on documentation).

Figures

Generally, everything that is not a table is considered a figure. So, illustrations, screen shots (which we have used throughout this book), photographs, drawings, bar graphs, and pie charts all are considered figures. Figure 7.2 is an example of a figure taken from a report on the assessment of academic programs.

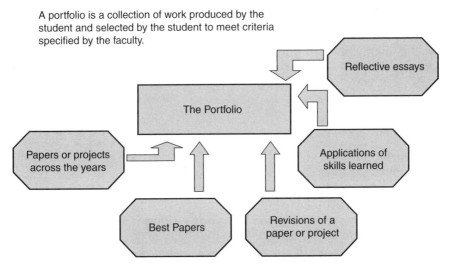

The Portfolio

A portfolio is a collection of work produced by the student and selected by the student to meet criteria specified by the faculty.

Reflective essays

The Portfolio

Papers or projects across the years

Applications of skills learned

Best Papers

Revisions of a paper or project

FIGURE 7.2   The elements of a student portfolio.[1]

[1]You should follow the guidelines for captions and footnotes that the particular style manual recommends. This example follows the guidelines of APA. If you were to follow the guidelines of CMS, however, the caption would be as shown in the example below:

Fig. 7.2. The Elements of a Student Portfolio.

Be sure to cite figures or sources of data in figures that you have created just as you would cite other information taken from your sources, following the documentation style recommended by the particular style manual.

Here are some guidelines for figures:

- Figure numbers and titles go below the figures;
- the figures are numbered with Arabic numbers;
- the figure should be clearly produced.

Tables and Figures: Other Considerations

Check the style guide you are using to determine how you should place your tables and figures in your research report. Many publications ask that tables and figures be placed at the end of the manuscript, with the location of the table or figure indicated within the text.

Your instructor may have a preference on where tables and figures should go, so you should first determine which is preferred.

You should explain or discuss your tables and figures within your text. Don't assume that the table or figure will be so self-explanatory that the reader will not need to know anymore. Think of figures and tables as further evidence of what you are writing. Some readers may understand what you mean when you write it; others may need visuals to help understand what you are saying. Don't discuss all the data in your narrative, but do discuss trends, conclusions to be drawn from the data, or major concepts that the data prove. In the case of figures, no amount of words can capture what the visual image communicates, so your discussion will be reinforced by the figure.

REVISING AND EDITING

While you are writing the first draft of your research, don't worry too much about whether you have chosen the correct words. The important point is that you need to write your paper so that it is clearly organized and incorporates the information that you have gathered from your sources in the most effective manner. When you recognize that your writing is not clear, redraft it immediately. But often you will not have the ability to be objective during the writing of this first draft. It's normal for all writers to become emotionally attached to their words. So how can you be more objective and recognize weaknesses in your writing?

Earlier, we recommended that you block out a calendar of activities to keep your research and writing on track and to make sure that you finish it on time. If you have any time, we recommend that you put your first draft aside for as long as you can afford. By not beginning the revision and editing of your paper immediately after finishing the first draft, you lose some of your emotional attachment to your original words or organization and can more objectively recognize weak writing such as confusing syntax, gaps in your logic, or ambiguous meanings.

However, do be as accurate as you can when you include your source material, whether through summarizing, paraphrasing, or quoting. Keep your note cards, your research notebook, or your computer files with your sources and citation data in case you need to verify the accuracy of how you report your sources and your citations.

Suggestion: As you are writing, make multiple copies of your draft, saving it on your computer hard drive and a floppy disk. Sometimes computers break down, so having an extra copy on a disk will save you if that happens.

WEB ACTIVITY

Go to the companion website for this book and complete the exercises for this chapter.

MAINTAINING ACADEMIC HONESTY

Academic writing places a very high premium on intellectual honesty. Academic research has a long tradition of building upon the work of previous researchers. The reasons for this are clear: seldom is there a discovery that does not depend upon the previous work of researchers, new insights are built upon the ideas of others, and showing where your ideas come from puts you in the company of others who also have struggled with the same issues that you are dealing with. Remember that "research" is not just doing something original or carrying out an experiment. Research involves knowing what others have thought, discovered, and written or said. Your professor will expect you to have found sources of ideas to support your topic, so citing those sources is a critical part of your research.

You should cite your sources

- whenever you quote someone;
- whenever you put someone else's ideas in your own words; and
- whenever you summarize what someone else has written or said.

Don't overuse sources for your writing. That is, a research paper should not be just a collection of other people's thoughts and discoveries. Weak research papers often are a compilation of quote after quote, citation after citation. Your professor will not grade your paper based upon the number of citations that you have, but, rather upon the quality of your argument, judicious use of key sources, and your ability to blend your ideas and sources to back up your ideas so that the research ultimately is yours. You might think of your writing as a quilt. A quilter does not simply sew together people's old clothes to make a quilt. Rather, the quilter carefully selects pieces from the fabrics available, studies how they might best fit together, and may even fit them together in a traditional pattern (like the case study or the report of an experiment), but ultimately produces a quilt that reflects the quilter's concept of the final product, not someone else's.

Copyright Law

Copyright law has been developed to protect the rights of authors. An intent of copyright law is to keep the knowledge produced by authors and inventors public. If an author fears that someone may use his or her words without attributing them to the original source, that author might not want to publish the work in the first place. Therefore, in research we have accepted certain standards that apply to our using the work of others. We must cite or document the work so that others know where we acquired the ideas or words. Copyright law goes further than simply requiring that authors recognize the original sources. It speaks to the number of copies that may be used without seeking permission of the author, the number of times we may use such works, and other matters designed to ensure that the work that authors' produce is appropriately recognized.

WEB ACTIVITY

For more information on copyright law, go to the companion website for this book and follow the links in the bibliography on copyright.

Plagiarism

Plagiarism is passing off someone else's ideas or words as though they are your own. Basically, there are two broad categories of plagiarism: intentional and unintentional. Plagiarism is intentional when the writer purposefully hides the fact that his ideas and choices of words are those of someone else. It is a form of stealing. Unintentional plagiarism typically occurs when the writer does not cite the sources correctly—in other words, just plain carelessness. For example, perhaps the writer uses too many of the original words in trying to put an idea in his or her own words. The writer should be using quotation marks and telling where the words were found. Perhaps the writer does put the original words in his or her own words, but fails to note where the ideas came from. If the ideas are someone else's ideas, then you need to cite the source. Failing to do so may result in your being accused of plagiarism, even though that was not your honest intent.

Note: As a result of the technology now available to us, there are a number of "paper mills" online that may be able to provide you with a copy of a paper that will satisfy the demands of a course. Many students know about these sites and use them. Keep in mind that professors know about them as well. Just as students can go online to find a paper on a topic that meets the requirements of a course, so professors can also go online to determine whether the paper was indeed found at one of these sites (such sites as TurnItIn and Eve2). Passing off another student's paper as your own is an egregious form of plagiarism. Likewise, professors realize that there are so many materials on the Internet that the temptation of some students just to copy what they find and pass it off as their own is substantial. Ultimately, one sign of a scholar is that scholar's citation of sources that he or she used. It makes more sense to cite the online source than to copy it without citing it. Passing off anyone else's work as your own is an egregious form of plagiarism.

SUMMARIZING, PARAPHRASING, AND QUOTING

You need to know how best to incorporate information or ideas into your writing. You have three choices available: to quote, to paraphrase, or to summarize. Regardless of which you choose, you must cite the sources to be academically honest.

In the samples below, we use MLA style to note the source of the summaries. MLA style cites the page number in parentheses when the author is mentioned in the text and cites the author and page number when the author's name is not mentioned in the text. APA style does not use page numbers, but uses the year of the publication instead.

Summarizing

A summary is a short, concise version of the main idea or ideas of your source. Summarize when you want to refer to the general idea of what you have read, but do not want to go into detail or use all the words of the original. It may be, for example, that the writer has so many details that it would only confuse or bore your reader to include them all. Summarize only the essence of those details. It may be that the writer's style is not particularly memorable or different from what others have written on the subject, so quoting would not make sense. Regardless of the reason, to summarize well, be sure that you understand the author's point. After you write your summary in your notes, reread the section you are summarizing to be sure that you have done so accurately.

Sometimes you read several sources that are all making the same point. In this case, it would make sense to summarize all of them together and cite them as a group (e.g., Bradley, 1996; Roser, 1998; Smith, 1999).

When you summarize, use your own words, leave out specific details and facts, and be brief. Do not add your own interpretation to the summary. It is acceptable to add your own interpretation before or after the summary, but not as part of it. Respect the original author's ideas and efforts.

Assume that you want to use the following excerpt from a book on the prehistory and history of American Indians in Vermont:

> According to the U.S. census, there were in 1970 all of 229 Native Americans living in Vermont. A mere five years later, the Boston Indian Council's Manpower census reported 1,700 Native Americans living in Vermont, 80 percent of whom were Abenakis. Yet, there was no great influx of Native Americans from other places into Vermont, nor is there any more reason to doubt the veracity of the Boston Indian Council's figures than there is those of the Census Bureau. What happened simply was that, between 1970 and 1975, there was a resurgence of pride in their ethnic identity on the part of Vermont's Abenakis (247).
>
> —Haviland, William A. and Marjory W. Power. *The Original Vermonters: Native Inhabitants Past and Present*. Hanover, N.H., and London: University of Vermont Press, 1981.

Here is an appropriate summary of the excerpt from Haviland and Power:

> As Haviland and Power point out, in the early 1970s the Abenakis of Vermont developed a sense of self-respect and began to report themselves as Abenakis in the U.S. census (247).

However, the summary below is not appropriate:

> As Haviland and Power point out, between 1970 and 1975 the Abenakis of Vermont experienced a resurgence of pride in their ethnicity (247).

The problem with the summary is that the writer has copied directly too many of the authors' original words. The writer should have put "a resurgence of pride" in quotation marks so that the reader would know that the phrase is that of Haviland and Power. Even "between 1970 and 1975" is a quote, one that could be rewritten in more than one way.

Consider the following summary:

> Although Haviland and Power claim that the increase in the number of persons designating themselves as Abenaki was due to the growth in ethnic pride during the early 1970s, they offer no proof (247).

As a summary, this does not reflect another characteristic of good summaries: good summaries do not interpret or judge the material being summarized. While the writer does cite the source appropriately, the writer mixes judgment with summary, and the reader gets the impression that the entire content is on page 247.

You may find yourself summarizing your sources more than paraphrasing or quoting, so it is critical that you take notes well. Like any other use of a source, a summary should be cited appropriately by referring to the name(s) of the author(s) and page number(s). When you are writing your original notes on information from a source, be sure that you clearly indicate to yourself whether you are quoting or summarizing. Use quotation marks in your notes to designate any words that are taken directly from the original source. If you don't do that, you may be unintentionally plagiarizing when you write your paper.

In short, good summaries

- are written in the researcher's words, not the original words of the source;
- capture the essence of the original accurately;
- do not repeat key phrases from the original without quoting those phrases;
- are cited accurately, even though the words of the summary are different from those of the original; and
- do not add interpretations that are not the interpretations in the original source.

Suggestion when taking notes: When you have summarized a passage in your research journal or on a note card, be sure to note where the entire original passage was found in case you need to return to it later. If you are summarizing on your computer from a source online, you may want to block out the original and use your Copy command to copy it to a disk or to your hard drive, assuming that it is not excessively long. If you are using note cards, write down all the information you will need to make an accurate citation later on either the note card or on a separate note card. Include the correct citation information if you are using a research journal or your computer copy.

Paraphrasing

Unlike the summary, which encapsulates the essential concept of a longer source, a paraphrase attempts to capture all the ideas of the original. When you paraphrase, you put the original ideas in your own words. To use your own words, you should translate technical jargon into language that your reader is more likely to understand and write in your own style. That is, don't try to copy the style of the original writer, but try to keep the style of your own writing the same when you are paraphrasing a source. Generally, the paraphrased item will be roughly the same length as the original.

Paraphrase as a way of avoiding too many quotations in your paper. Paraphrase when the original meaning is what you want to capture, but not necessarily the way that the original is written. Paraphrase when you want to use details from the original, but not necessarily all of them, and not necessarily in the same order as the original. And lead into the paraphrase as you would a quote or summary: Use some "tag phrases" to let the reader know you are starting to use a source, such as: "Snyder says . . ." or "According to Snyder . . .".

There is a danger in paraphrasing: If you are not careful, you may be using the original writer's words or ideas or facts in such a way that you are actually quoting. If you can't find a way to put the original in your own words, you are probably better off quoting. When an author says something in a way that deserves using the very same words, then put those words in quotation marks and continue with the paraphrase.

Here's a suggestion on how to paraphrase. Read the original so that you understand it well. Then, stop reading it and try writing what the author said in your own words. When you finish, go back to the original, check to see whether you have left anything out, and check to see whether you have inadvertently quoted any of the author's key words.

Read this example from an article discussing why teachers do not always adapt new technologies in their teaching immediately and then read the paraphrase that follows:

> For them to use the technology more, teachers have to be convinced that teaching and learning literacy will be more effective after the introduction of computers. Any efforts to modify classroom practice need to be well informed. Teachers' repertoires, which are both resilient and efficient, have been shaped "by the crucible of experience and the culture of teaching" (Cuban, 1986, p. 109). Policy makers need to understand that altering pedagogy requires a change in what teachers believe to work.
>
> —Snyder, I. (1999). Integrating computers into the literacy curriculum: More difficult than we first imagined. In J. Hancock (Ed.), *Teaching literacy using information technology* (pp. 11–30). Victoria, Aus: Australian Literacy Educators' Association.

A paraphrase:

> Snyder argues that those who want to reform teaching should understand that teachers will not change until they are convinced that the change will be better than what they currently do. If what teachers currently do works, they may not see a need to change. So those who want teachers to introduce computers into their pedagogy need to understand the ways that teachers think and what it takes to have them accept something new (28).

Contrast the above paraphrase with the following:

> According to Snyder, teachers won't begin to use computers in their teaching until they believe that it will be better than what they currently do. Teachers are resilient and efficient. So reformers of education need to be patient and take their time in trying to convince teachers to change. They will change eventually (28).

Although the latter paraphrase does capture the essence of what Snyder writes, it has the following problems. First, the person attempting the paraphrase quotes "resilient and efficient." If those words really do say things better than using synonyms, then they should have been put in quotation marks. Second, the writer goes beyond what Snyder says when the writer talks of being patient because teachers will eventually change. In fact, Snyder does write later of teachers gradually changing, but does not say that they *will* change. And third, the paraphrase omits another point that Snyder makes, that "efforts to modify classroom practice need to be well informed." The first paraphrase captures that by noting that reformers "need to understand the ways that teachers think . . . ."

In short, a good paraphrase:

- needs to be introduced just as you would introduce a quote or summary;
- captures what the original author said in the writer's own words;
- does not necessarily follow the same sentence structure as the original;
- uses quotation marks if key words are quoted exactly;
- does not add new ideas to the original; and
- is approximately the same length as the original.

Suggestion when taking notes: You should clearly note that you have paraphrased the original on your note cards or your research journal. Check your paraphrase to make sure that you have not inadvertently quoted anything. If you have quoted, indicate that with quotation marks in your notes. If you are taking notes on a computer, you can block out the original if you are online and copy it, noting that it is the original. Then you can paraphrase it then or make a note to paraphrase it later. As always, include all the information you need for an accurate citation.

Quoting

A quote is an exact use of the original writer's words and is indicated by the use of quotation marks before and after the quoted words. Use quotes when a writer says something so well that you could not possibly capture the idea as well by paraphrasing or summarizing. Quote when your paraphrase would end up being longer or more confusing than the original. Quote when the original words carry with them some importance that helps make a point, such as when the writer is an absolute authority on the subject or when the writer is so well known that your reader will understand the importance of that person's words.

Do not, however, fill your research report with quote after quote. If you do, your reader is likely to conclude that you really have few or no ideas of your own on the subject or that you have not studied and understood the subject well enough to begin to form your own opinions. It will seem as though you are saying, "Here's one person's ideas on the subject and here's another and here's another and . . . ." We think Sarah Kaufman captures this weakness well when she writes in a book review that the author ". . . comes across not as an authority . . . but as the moderator of an extended panel discussion that voices different views but arrives at no conclusions (9)."

In addition to using quotes sparingly, use quotes that are not excessively long. Seldom does all of an original paragraph (unless it is short) need to be quoted. If the entire long paragraph is worth citing, then paraphrase most of it and quote the key parts.

Before you include the quote, you should indicate something about it so that your reader understands why you are quoting and the context of the quote within your paper. Introduce quotations with words such as the following: "In contrast to those who have argued against NAFTA, Woodrow believes . . ." or "Gallegos purposefully intends to shock us when she writes . . .". As an alternative to establishing an attitude or clear context at the beginning of the quote, you might introduce it briefly with a standard introduction such as "Tafolla writes . . ." or "Warhol argues that . . ." and then comment on the importance or reason for the quote afterward. Your intent should be to incorporate the quote easily into your writing so that it maintains the flow of your style.

If you are quoting only a few words, then they should fit effectively into a sentence, for example,

> Since the pedagogical practices of teachers tend to be "both resilient and efficient" (Snyder, 28), they are slow to change.

Finally, be careful to punctuate your quotations correctly. Place the in-text citation after the quotation mark, but before the punctuation mark if one needs to be used immediately.

If you omit parts of the middle of the quote, use *ellipses*, or a string of periods with spaces between each, to indicate that a gap occurs. Follow these guidelines for using ellipses:

- Use three periods to indicate an omission of words within a quoted sentence or at the beginning of the sentence.
- Use three periods plus the terminal punctuation (a period, question mark, or exclamation point) when you omit the end of a sentence that you are quoting.
- Use four periods when you omit entire sentences between the quoted parts.
- *Note:* The *MLA Handbook for Writers of Research Papers,* 5th edition, suggests that you use brackets around ellipses so that the reader can distinguish your ellipses from those that the original writer might have used. The *Publication Manual of the American Psychological Association,* 5th edition, does not. Below we illustrate an example of an ellipsis in MLA style.

> Snyder offers reasonable advice for those who would change teaching practices when she writes, "For them to use the technology more, teachers have to be convinced that teaching and learning literacy will be more effective after the introduction of computers [. . . .] Policy makers need to understand that altering pedagogy requires a change in what teachers believe to work" (28).

In short, good quotes are most worth using when the writer's words are exceptional or especially meaningful; are not used excessively; include some introductory words or explanatory words after the quote; are relatively short in length; are incorporated smoothly into the writing; use ellipses to indicate omitted words; and have the citation after the final quotation mark, but before the end punctuation of the original.

WEB ACTIVITY

Go to the companion website for this book and complete the activity on quoting, paraphrasing, and summarizing.

Quoting Primary Sources

A "primary source" is an original document, rather than someone's interpretation of the document or research based upon the document. The guideline that good quotations should not be very long may be ignored when you are using primary sources such as parts of an important speech, a work of literature, or an official document. When you do quote long parts of such works, be sure to use the same punctuation, spacing, and spelling of the original. If you are quoting more than four lines of prose or three of poetry, indent the entire quote 10 spaces.

> "Hyla Brook"
> By June our brook's run out of song and speed.
> Sought for much after that, it will be found
> Either to have gone groping underground
> (And taken with it all the Hyla breed
> That shouted in the mist a month ago,
> Like ghost of sleigh-bells in a ghost of snow)—
> Or flourished and come up in jewel-weed,
> Weak foliage that is blown upon and bent
> Even against the way its waters went.
> Its bed is left a faded paper sheet
> Of dead leaves stuck together by the heat—
> A brook to none but who remember long.
> This as it will be seen is other far
> Than with brooks taken otherwise in song.
> We love the things we love for what they are.

If you decide when writing your paper that you only need to quote a short excerpt of the original, then you should treat it as you would a normal quote, with ellipses if you leave any portions out and with quotation marks. The standard practice (or convention) when you quote short segments of poetry within your sentence is to use a slash, or diagonal mark, after the ending of each line because not every line will end with punctuation. Put a space before and after the slash:

> In Frost's "Hyla Brook," the poet speaks to us of enduring love when he describes our memory of the brook, ". . . A brook to none but who remember long. / . . . We love the things we love for what they are."

Suggestion when taking notes: Since you may not know exactly how much of a work you will quote directly when you are still gathering your information, it is best to copy as much of the original as possible if you know you are going to quote it. When working online, this is made easier by your ability to block the entire passage you may take your quote from and copying it to your disk or hard drive. Be sure that you include all the information for your citation when you do so.

WEB ACTIVITY

Go to the website for this book. In the exercises section, you will find an exercise on quoting, paraphrasing, and summarizing. Read the selection that is provided and find a good part to quote, find another part to paraphrase, and then summarize the entire selection. Share the results with your classmates, discuss them, and, as a result of your discussion, draw some conclusions about the best ways to quote, paraphrase, and summarize. In your discussion of the paraphrases and summaries, be alert for inadvertent plagiarism. Discuss ways to avoid such inadvertent plagiarism.

YOUR RHETORICAL STANCE

By "rhetorical stance," we refer to the relationship that you establish with your readers by the way that you structure your paper, the arguments that you make within your paper, and your word choice. Generally, a paper in the humanities or the arts may offer you greater latitude than a paper in the sciences. It is very likely that your professor in the humanities, arts, or social sciences will expect you to make an argument, that is, to take a position on one side of an issue or another. In so doing, you will be expected to develop a personal opinion about the issue, but to back up that opinion with objective research to support your position. Many professors want your "voice" to come through and will allow you to speak of yourself and your beliefs in the first person. That is, you can introduce your thoughts with expressions such as, "I believe that . . ." or "I conclude . . .". Before you do use "I" in your writing, however, find out what your professor prefers.

    In the natural sciences, and often in the social sciences, you will be expected to be objective in your choice of words and the ways that you present your research findings. In the natural sciences, you may not have to argue a position or attempt to persuade your reader of your opinions, for you are presenting information as knowledge that has been observed, analyzed, and recorded. In the social sciences, you may also have to present information objectively, such as your observations of a particular social phenomenon, but you may also be expected to argue for a particular action or policy as a result of your objective observations. And while the first person "I" has been discouraged in much science and social science research, many scholarly works now use "I" fairly freely. Thus, the question of whether you may write in the personal first person or must write in the more objective third person is one that you should determine before you complete your writing.

The best advice we can give you to determine the rhetorical stance of your research paper or report is to read published research in the discipline you are studying. Note the ways that the authors organize their writing, note whether they present information in an objective fashion, and note how they may argue for a particular action or not. Pay particularly close attention to the details of your research project assignment: Is there a particular format that you are to follow? What documentation style should you use? What kinds of topics can you select? And are there any intermediate steps expected of you, such as submitting a research proposal, an annotated bibliography, or a preliminary draft? Are you expected to make a strong argument in your paper or not?

WEB ACTIVITY

Please go to the companion website for this book and complete the exercise on developing a rhetorical stance and style appropriate for your discipline.

REVISING YOUR PAPER

When you return to your early draft, read it with as critical an eye as you can. Try to put yourself in the place of a new reader who is reading your paper for the very first time (and perhaps the only time). Is your overall organization and paragraphing as clear as it can be? Here are some suggestions to consider as you reread to revise:

■ Don't be afraid to cut material that you do not need. If you keep separate copies of each draft as you write and revise it, you can always return to it in case you have cut something that you wish you had kept.
■ Review the guidelines for good introductions (p. 132) and conclusions (pp. 128–129) to make sure that you have included all you need to include.
■ Read each paragraph to determine whether one paragraph follows logically from another within your organization.

- If a paragraph is very short, read it to determine whether there are more details or explanations that you can include within it to support the main point of the paragraph.
- If a paragraph is very long, determine whether it is possible to divide it into two or more paragraphs to make the reading easier.
- Look at your use of transitions within and between your paragraphs to determine whether they guide the reader smoothly from one thought to another.
- Determine whether a paragraph includes any of your thoughts or whether the paragraph is composed of material taken entirely from a source. Your thoughts should be included so that the reader understands how *you* think about the subject and does not get the impression that you have only used the thoughts and material of others.
- Confirm that you have cited your source whenever you have used a research source.
- Use your spell-checker program to identify *possible* spelling errors. Be alert for homonyms that you may have misspelled and that your spell checker will not catch because the homonym will be spelled correctly even if it is used incorrectly.
- Use your style-checker program to look for suggestions. (Search the **Help** area of your word processor to learn how to change your style checker.) Be aware that the style-checker program may be set to a style that is inappropriate for your paper, for example, set for *casual* when you may want a *formal* style. Also be aware that the style-checker program has been programmed by someone else and may not give you the best suggestions for the way *you* want to say something. Be in charge of your own writing. Don't let the style checker be in charge.

If you know that you have certain types of sentence structure weaknesses in your writing, you can use your computer to help you look for possible places where those weaknesses might occur. To do so, use your **Find** command to help you look for those weaknesses:

- "There is/are . . ." and "It is . . ." often introduce sentences that are wordy or vague. Use the **Find** command to find those and then revise the sentences by eliminating the "There is" or "It is" structure and rewriting the sentence to be stronger. For example, "There are many ways that this event can be caused" can be rewritten as "Many factors can cause this event," or "Many causes led to this event."
- Forms of *to be* verbs often indicate weak sentences. Search for *is, was, are,* or *been* to locate possible weak sentences, such as, "One of those who argues against this point of view is the author John Smith." Instead, the sentence might be stronger as, "John Smith argues against this point of view when he writes . . .".
- If you often write run-on sentences or use comma splices, use the **Find** command to find commas and then reread the sentence in which the comma appears to determine if you have punctuated it correctly.

A CHECKLIST FOR YOU TO JUDGE YOUR OWN WRITING

- Used the appropriate format for your discipline.
- Focused your thesis statement so that it is clear and manageable?
- Organized your writing so that the reader can follow your logic?
- Summarized, paraphrased, or quoted in an academically honest fashion?
- Based your conclusions upon the supporting information that you have discovered, while recognizing that there may be other possible conclusions and while being clear about why you have chosen your conclusion rather than the other ones?
- Addressed your topic in an objective and evenhanded manner, being sure to recognize your own biases as you are compiling your information and writing about what you have learned?
- Recognized and addressed the questions and different perspectives that others have?
- Interpreted the information that you have gathered so that the reader gains a clear perspective of your thoughts?
- Created tables or figures (when they are appropriate) that are clear to your reader?
- Made your conclusions yours, not simply the compiled opinions of the sources you found?
- Revised your paper by reading it with a critical eye to find weak organization, weak transitions, weak supporting information, or weak sentence structure?

SUGGESTED ACTIVITIES

1. Find three magazine articles or essays in a book of essays and look at their conclusions. Which of the three do you believe is most effective? Why? Discuss effective conclusions with your classmates and develop a list of techniques that you could use in the future.

2. Find three magazine articles or essays in a book of essays and examine their introductions. Which of the three do you believe is most effective? Why? Discuss effective conclusions with your classmates and develop a list of techniques that you could use in the future.

3. After you have drafted a beginning outline for your research report, share your outline with a group of your classmates. Ask each other whether they can understand what the research reports will be about as a result of read-

ing just the outlines. Offer suggestions to one another on how to improve the organization or ask questions of one another to help each writer develop a more effective outline.

4. As you develop your own conclusion and introduction to your research paper, share them with a group of your classmates. Point out parts of your conclusions and introductions that you like, telling each other why you like them. Make suggestions to each other on ways that the conclusions and introductions might be improved.

5. Pair up with a classmate and exchange the first drafts of your writing when you finish them. Note parts that you like in each other's papers and parts that are confusing or that need more information. Help each other prepare the next draft by asking questions like, "Can you tell me more about . . . ?" and "What do you mean when you say here that . . . ?".

CHAPTER 8

Documenting Sources

By the end of this chapter, you should be able to document your paper using one of the following style guides:

- The Modern Language Association (MLA)

- The American Psychological Association (APA)

- The Columbia Guide to Online Style (COS)

- The Council of Science Educators (CBE/CSE)

- The Chicago Manual of Style (CMS)

Ultimately, your ability to document your sources will demonstrate to your readers that you understand that writers must recognize the work of others honestly and accurately. In support of that, "style guides" have been developed by a number of professional organizations. These style guides are designed to present documenting information, or documentation, in a consistent manner so that any reader can learn where the source may be located and find that source if the reader wishes.

The summaries for each style guide begin with recommendations for internal (or parenthetic) citation and then move to recommendations for Works Cited or Reference lists, beginning with electronic documents and then moving to the citation of print documents and other types of sources, such as books and speeches.

Remember, when you write a research paper or report, you are required to let readers know the source of the texts you paraphrase, quote, or refer to. In the body of your research report or paper, you use a different technique for indicating the location of your sources than you use in the bibliography at the end of your paper. This is referred to as "internal citation." Depending upon the style you are using, you indicate where you found your source either at the end of a sentence that uses material from your source or in a footnote. Then, at the end of your text, in what is called either the "Works Cited" or "References," you provide your reader with a full description of each of the sources that you cite internally in your paper.

As a reader reads your report, your internal citations let the reader know where you found the sources that help you make your point. Then, if the reader wants to locate any of those sources, the reader can turn to the References or Works Cited to find the complete information on that source.

GUIDELINES FOR CITING ELECTRONIC DOCUMENTS

Because online and other electronic sources such as CD-ROMs continue to evolve, citation styles also have been evolving. However, those who develop the styles try to adhere to traditional citation styles as much as possible, adding information that applies to the electronic sources of the references. As with print documents, the citations of electronic sources attempt to provide as much information as possible to enable the readers to find the original sources, if they still exist.

The Modern Language Association (MLA) and the American Psychological Association (APA) have provided style guidelines for citing electronic sources. The MLA has long been the key source for citation guidelines in the fields of literature, languages, and humanities. New MLA recommendations regarding online citations are explained in the *MLA Handbook for Writers of Research Papers,* 6th ed. (2003). To access the MLA guidelines online, go to http://www.mla.org and click on the **MLA Style** button, and then click on the button **Frequently Asked Questions about MLA Style.** Then click on **How do I document sources from the World Wide Web in my works cited list?** The APA is the key source for citation styles in the social and behavioral sciences and the sciences. You can access APA's electronic reference formats at http://www.apa.org/journals/webref.html.

As you conduct your research, gather the following information if it is available:

- Author's name.
- Title of the Web source (scholarly project, online book, editorial, etc.) or name of the listserv posting or subject of the email message.
- Title of the website (if your source is part of a larger resource with its own title).
- Date of publication or posting to the Web (if specified).
- Publication information (such as the name of the listserv, CD-ROM, or database).
- Web address (URL).
- Date you accessed the Web source.

WEB ACTIVITY

You may find it useful to copy the charts provided on the companion website to guide you as you record this information for each of your sources. If you are using a loose-leaf binder for your research notebook, you can insert the pages as you need them. If you go to the companion website for this book, you will find these charts, which you can copy.

Regardless of which style you use, you need to indicate the date the source was published or last revised as well as the date that you accessed this source. The version of the Web source that you saw may bear little resemblance to the way the site will look when your reader goes to it. By providing the date you accessed the source, you indicate to your reader that you have tried to be as accurate as possible, but are not responsible for changes after the date in your citation. Because websites are not permanent, you should make copies of the sources you use in your paper.

Should one underline titles or use italics? The Modern Language Association suggests that you use underlining for materials that will be graded or edited, but we recommend that you use italics if you are publishing your work to the Web. The reason is that the use of underlining online is usually intended to designate a hyperlink that you can click on to go to another site. By using italics for titles, you avoid any possible confusion. APA has officially endorsed the use of italics for titles.

DATA ON SOURCE	
Title of article or chapter or other Web source	
Title of book, newspaper, journal, or Web source	
Title of website, such as a database	
URL	
Date of publication	
Publisher and city where published	
Volume and issue number	
Date I accessed this Web source	
Other information	

MODERN LANGUAGE ASSOCIATION (MLA) STYLE

Internal Citation

When using MLA style, use the author–page method of citing sources. Often referred to as parenthetic citation, this method requires the name of the author and the page number of the source where the specific quote appears or where the summary or paraphrase is based. For example:

> Summarizing current university preparation of students to use technology for research or writing, Breivik notes that a common weakness is that there is no campus-wide organized approach (43).

> Most campuses have not organized the ways that they prepare students to use technology for their research or writing (Breivik 43).

> As Breivik notes, "A chief weakness of all the approaches described . . . is their failure to fit into any overall curriculum planning for information literacy" (43).

In the last example, the student includes an ellipsis (. . .) to show that material has been omitted from the quotation. Note that the page numbers are always in parentheses, but the author's last name only appears in parentheses when it is not used in the sentence. Note also the punctuation: no punctuation is used in the parenthetical citation. End punctuation occurs after the parentheses. And, if a quote appears in the sentence, the citation in parentheses occurs immediately after the citation and before the end punctuation. The complete information on the source cited should appear in your Works Cited section at the end of the paper.

Works Cited

MLA Electronic Citation Style

The MLA Handbook for Writers of Research Papers, 6th edition (2003), gives considerable coverage to electronic citation style. The style that MLA recommends includes angle brackets <> to enclose Web addresses (URLs) because they do not want the URL misread. For example, URLs do not end with periods, so a URL at the end of a sentence might appear to end with a period unless the end bracket > appears before the period.

Here are some typical examples of MLA electronic citation style (note that they should be double spaced and that there is a hanging indent, with the second and subsequent lines indented five spaces):

Article in a Journal

Quinlan, Kathleen M. "Generating Productive Learning Issues in PBL Tutorials: An Exercise to Help Tutors Help Students." <u>Medical Education Online</u>. 5 (2000). 26 Apr. 2001 <http://www.med-ed-online.org/issue2.htm#v6>.

Author's last name, First Initial. "Article Title." <u>Journal Title</u>. Vol. # (date of publication) Date you accessed it <URL>. (*Note:* MLA suggests that you check your instructor's preference to determine whether to underline or use italics for journal or book titles. For publication, they suggest underlining. If you cannot find out, use italics.)

Article in a Reference Database

Jones, George, and Mark Luscombe. "Provisions in 1999 Tax Legislation Have Impact." <u>Accounting Today</u>. 3 Jan. 2000. Lexis-Nexis. 27 Apr. 2001. <http://www.lexis-nexis.com/lncc>.

Author's last name, First Initial. "Article Title." <u>Journal Title</u> (if any). Date of publication. Database Name. Date you accessed it. <URL>.

Article in a Subscription Database Search Engine

Herron, Jeffrey. "A Street Guide to Search Warrant Exceptions." <u>Law and Order</u>. Oct. 2000:207–208. ProQuest. ReSearch Engine. 27 Apr. 2001. <http://researchengine.xanedu.com/xreweb>.

Author's last name, First Initial. "Article Title." <u>Magazine Title</u>. Date of publication: Page range (if known). Database name. Commercial search engine name. Library name (if used at library), City name. Date you accessed it. <URL>.

Personal Site

Rodrigues, Dawn. Home page. 1 May 2001 <http://English.utb.edu/drodrigues>.

Professional Site

<u>Modern Language Association</u>. 1 May 2001 <http://www.mla.org/>.

Site with a Sponsoring Organization

<u>Guidelines & Position Statements</u>. 7 Mar. 2001. National Council of Teachers of English. 28 Apr. 2001. <http://www.ncte.org/positions/>.

Scholarly Project

<u>Spice Islands Archaeology Project</u>. Peter Lape. 17 Aug. 1999. Brown U. 26 Apr. 2001 <http://www.brown.edu/Departments/Anthropology/SIAP/home.html>.

Book

Alcott, Louisa M. <u>The Mysterious Key and What It Opened</u>. Boston. 1867. <u>A Celebration of Women Writers</u>. Ed. Mary K. Ackerman. 25 Apr. 2001. The Online Books Page. <http://digital.library.upenn.edu/women/alcott/key/key.html>.

Poem

Silko, Leslie M. "The earth is your mother." <u>Storyteller</u>. 1981. Voices from the Gaps. Richard K. Mott. 6 Nov. 2000. University of New Mexico. 26 Apr. 2001 <http://voices.cla.umn.edu/authors/LeslieMarmonSilko.html>.

Newspaper Article

Associated Press. "Navy Resumes Bombing on Vieques." <u>The New York Times Online</u>. 27 Apr. 2001. <http://www.nytimes.com/aponline/world/AP-Navy-Vieques.html>.

Email

Seiple, Carl. "Kutztown." Email to the author. 20 Feb. 1998.

Posting to a Discussion List (listserv, newsgroup, or forum)

Carbone, Nick. "RE: Question." Online posting. 21 Apr. 1999. Alliance for Computers and Writing Listserv. 6 May 1997 <http://www.arts.ubc.ca/english/iemls/shak/>.

Sychronous Communication

Crump, Eric, and Dawn Rodrigues. MOO conversation. 20 Feb. 1998 <http://mud. Ncte.org:8888/>.

MLA Nonelectronic Citation Style

Article in a Journal, Paginated by Issue

McClasky, Jane. "Who's Afraid of the Big, Bad TAAS? Rethinking Our Response to Standardized Testing." English Journal 91.1 (2001): 88–95.

Article in a Journal, Paginated by Volume

Rand, L. A. "Enacting Faith: Evangelical Discourse and the Discipline of Composition Studies." CCC: Journal of the Conference on College Composition and Communication 52 (2001): 249–267.

Article in a Newspaper

Benevidez, Rachel. "Blood Drive Tries to Help Young Boy." Brownsville Herald, 20 Feb. 2001: A1.

Article in a Popular Magazine

Cohen, Adam. "Who Swiped the Surplus?" Time, September 3, 2001: 30–33.

Article in a Popular Magazine, No Author Specified

"Beyond NAFTA: A Forum—Toward a North American Economic Community (North American Free Trade Agreement)." The Nation, May 28, 2001: 19.

Book Review

Shermis, Mark D. "Book Review." Rev. of Computer-Assisted Assessment in Higher Education, eds. S. Brown, P. Race, and J. Bull. Assessment Update May-June 2001: 16.

Book with One Author

Hume, Ivor Noel. <u>Martin's Hundred</u> 4th ed. Charlottesville: University Press of Virginia, 1995.

Book with Two or More Authors

Cotterell, Howard H., Aldophe Riff, and Robert M. Vetter. <u>National Types of Old Pewter</u>. New York: Weathervane Books, 1972.

Edited Book

Salay, David L., ed. <u>Hard Coal, Hard Times: Ethnicity and Labor in the Anthracite Region</u>. Scranton, PA: Anthracite Museum Press, 1984.

Book with No Author Specified

<u>Sintra and Its Surroundings</u>. Lisbon: Sage Editora, 1994.

Work in an Anthology

Bleich, David. "The Unconscious Troubles of Men." <u>Critical Theory and the Teaching of Literature</u>. Ed. James F. Slevin and Art Young. Urbana, IL: National Council of Teachers of English, 1996. 47–62.

Speech

Fuentes, Carlos. Untitled Speech at Distinguished Lecture Series. Tape Recording. Brownsville, TX: University of Texas at Brownsville and Texas Southmost College, September 11, 2001. [Note: If the speech is titled, the title should appear in quotation marks after the speaker's name.]

Personal Communication

Last, First. Telephone Conversation with Author. Bennington, VT: September 15, 2001.

AMERICAN PSYCHOLOGICAL ASSOCIATION (APA) STYLE

For more detailed information on style, we recommend that you go to the *Publication Manual of the American Psychological Association*, 5th ed. (2001) or to the APA website at http://www.apa.org/journals/webref.html.

Internal Citation

APA style values brief and concise documentation within the text itself. Using the author–date citation style, you will only indicate the year of the source. The detailed information about the source will appear in the Reference section, listed alphabetically. Thus, the style follows a version of these three examples:

Quinlan (2000) argued that . . .

In a report on electronic tutorials (Quinlan, 2000) . . .

As recently as 2000, Quinlan showed how . . .

If there is only one source in the report by the author, the date only needs to appear the first time that you cite it. After that, simply use the author's name. If, however, you have used more than one source by the same author, then you will need to specify the year of the particular source you are referring to in subsequent internal citations.

If the work you cite has 3–5 authors, cite all the authors the first time you cite it. If there are more than 6 authors, use only the first author's name and *et al.* or *and colleagues* (with a period after *al.* since it is an abbreviation for alia).

In their study of Neanderthal DNA, Ovchinnikov, Gotherstrom, Romanova, Kharitonov, and Lidéns (2000) found that . . .

Subsequent citations in the text use only the first author's name and *et al.* The date is included if it is the first citation in a paragraph.

A central finding of Ovchinnikov et al. (2000) demonstrated that . . .

If you cite the same source again in the same paragraph, do not include the date:

However, Ovchinnikov et al. note that they were not able to . . .

If you have two or more citations of works by authors with the same surname, use the authors' initials each time the name appears.

Reference Citation

APA Electronic Citation Style

APA style for citations begins with the same patterns that APA recommends for printed sources, but then adds the information that a reader would need to find the actual source. The date of publication appears after the author(s) name because articles in the sciences or social sciences may become dated, and date of publication is therefore important. Note that quotation marks are not used for works within larger works such as articles or poems. Only the first letter and proper nouns are capitalized in those works as well as in titles of books or main sources.

APA recommends that citations be double spaced and that hanging indents be used for citations, with the lines after the first line indented five spaces. If the URL has to be divided at the end of a line, it should be divided after a diagonal or slash mark. Here are some typical examples of APA electronic citation style:

Article in a Journal

Quinlan, K. M. (2000). Generating productive learning issues in PBL tutorials: An exercise to help tutors help students. *Medical Education Online, 5.* Retrieved April 26, 2001 from the World Wide Web: http://www.med-ed-online.org/issue2.htm#v6

Author's last name, First Initial(s). (Date of publication—year, Month day). Article title. *Journal Title, Volume number: pages (if known).* Retrieved (date) from the World Wide Web: URL

Article in a Reference Database

Jones, G. & Luscombe, M. (2000, January 3). Provisions in 1999 Tax Legislation have impact. *Accounting Today.* Retrieved April 27, 2001, from on-line database Lexis-Nexis on the World Wide Web: http://www.lexis-nexis.com/lncc

Author's last name, First Initial(s). (year, Month day). Article title. *Journal Title. Volume number: pages (if known).* Retrieved (Month day, year) from (source) database (Name of Database, item no. if applicable) on the World Wide Web: URL

Article in a Subscription Database Search Engine

Herron, J. (2000, October). A street guide to search warrant exceptions. *Law and Order. 207-208.* Retrieved April 27, 2001 from ProQuest database ReSearch Engine on the World Wide Web: http://researchengine.xanedu.com/xreweb

Author's last name, First Initial(s). (year, Month day). Article title. *Journal Title. Volume number: pages if known.* Retrieved (Month day, year) from (database name) database (Search Engine Name) on the World Wide Web: URL

Email, Synchronous Communications, and Discussion Lists

Personal communications, synchronous communications, and postings from discussion lists are not cited in the reference list, but are noted in the text as follows: R. Rodrigues (personal communication, May 2, 2001) or J. Honeyman (posting to University of Texas Assessment Forum, June 4, 2001).

Note:

- Although APA style calls for the references cited section to be typed in double space, it allows single spacing when there are browser or word processor limitations.
- Do not put a period at the end of the URL. By not putting a period, no one will think that a period is part of the URL.
- APA allows either *italics* or <u>underlining</u> for titles of major works, but recommends that they be used consistently throughout.
- Regarding indents, APA allows either hanging indents or paragraph indents, but recommends that they be used consistently throughout.

APA Nonelectronic Citation Style

For more detailed information on APA citation style, see the *Publication Manual of the American Psychological Association*, 5th edition. Double space all entries in the reference section. Use a hanging indent for all entries.

Article in a Journal, Paginated by Issue

McClasky, J. (2001). Who's afraid of the big, bad TAAS? Rethinking our response to standardized testing. *English Journal, 91*(1), 88–95.

Article in a Journal, Paginated by Volume

Rand, L. A. (2001). Enacting faith: Evangelical discourse and the discipline of composition studies. *CCC: Journal of the Conference on College Composition and Communication, 52,* 349–267.

Article in a Newspaper

Benevidez, R. (2001, February 20). Blood drive tries to help young boy. *Brownsville Herald,* p. 1.

Article in a Popular Magazine

Cohen, A. (2001, September 3). Who swiped the surplus? *Time, 158,* 30–33.

Book Review

Saba, M. S. (2001). [Review of the book *Goddess of the Americas: La Diosa de las Americas: Writings on the Virgin of Guadalupe*]. *Hispanic Outlook in Higher Education, 11*(22), 48.

Book with One Author

Hume, I. N. (1995). *Martin's Hundred* (4th ed.). Charlottesville: University Press of Virginia.

Book with Two or More Authors

Cotterell, H. H., Riff, A., & Vetter, R. M. (1972). *National types of old pewter*. New York: Weathervane Books.

Edited Book

Salay, D. L. (Ed.). (1984). *Hard coal, hard times: Ethnicity and labor in the Anthracite region*. Scranton, PA: Anthracite Museum Press.

Book with No Author Specified

Sintra and its surroundings. (1994). Lisbon: Sage Editora.

Work in an Anthology

Bleich, D. (1996). The unconscious troubles of men. In J. F. Slevin & A. Young (Eds.), *Critical theory and the teaching of literature* (pp. 47–62). Urbana, IL: National Council of Teachers of English.

Speech

Fuentes, C. (Speaker) (2001). *Untitled Speech at Distinguished Lecture Series* [Tape Recording]. Brownsville: University of Texas at Brownsville and Texas Southmost College, September 11.

[*Note:* APA does not recommend including any source in the Reference section if the original source cannot be recovered. Instead, it recommends the use of internal citations. Thus, if the source above were not taped, the in-text citation would be: "C. Fuentes (speech at the University of Texas at Brownsville and Texas Southmost College, September 11, 2001), said . . ."]

Personal Communication

Doe, J. (2001). Conversation with author [Audio tape]. Brownsville, TX, 15 September.

[*Note:* If you have not taped the conversation, do not cite it in the Reference section. Instead, within the text, write the internal citation similar to these: "In a personal conversation with this writer, Jane Dow (September 11, 2001) said . . ." or "J. Doe (personal communication, September 11, 2001) argued that . . .".]

COLUMBIA GUIDE TO ONLINE STYLE (COS) ELECTRONIC CITATION STYLE

Some professors prefer Janice R. Walker and Todd Taylor's *The Columbia Guide to Online Style* (1998) as a reasonable guide to citing electronic sources. COS contains guidelines for many more types of electronic documents than we have included here, so we recommend that you consult it when our guidelines do not address a type of source that you have.

Here are the COS generic styles for citing electronic sources in the humanities and in the sciences.

General Style for Online Sources

For the humanities style, Walker and Taylor recommend the following format (43) (Note that the citation is double-spaced, uses a hanging indent, and indents the second and subsequent lines five spaces):

Author's Last Name, First Name. "Title of Document." *Title of Complete Work* [if applicable]. Version or File Number [if applicable]. Document date or date of last revision [if different from access date]. Protocol and address, access path or directories (date of access).

For the scientific style, they recommend the following format (44):

Author's Last Name, Initial(s). (Date of document [if different from date accessed]). Title of document. *Title of complete work* [if applicable]. Version or File number [if applicable]. (Edition or revision [if applicable]). Protocol and address, access path, or directories (date of access).

Here is an example of the citation for an article in the humanities:

Conner, Michael. "African Art and the Internet." *African Arts.* Summer 1999. http://www2.h-net.msu.edu/about/internet.html (25 Apr. 2001).

And here is an example of a scientific article:

Ovchinnikov, I., Gotherstrom, A., Romanova, G., Kharitonov, V., Lidéns, K., & Goodwin, W. (2000, 30 Mar). Molecular analysis of Neanderthal DNA from the northern Caucasus. *Nature.* http://www.2think.org/neanderthaldna.shtml (25 Apr. 2001).

Citations of Databases and CD-ROMs

You are very likely to find worthwhile sources on the databases that your library provides, such as Lexis-Nexis for business, the National Teaching and Learning Forum for education, or Biological Abstracts (Biosis) for the life sciences. Walker and Taylor recommend the following general formats (96–97):

Humanities

Author's Last Name, First Name. "Title of Article." *Title of Software Publication.* Publication information, including version or edition number, if applicable, and date of publication. *Name of database,* if applicable. *Name of online service* or Internet protocol and address. File or version number or other identifying information and directory path (date accessed). [*Note:* Access date not required when the source is a CD-ROM.]

Howell, Vicki, & Carlton, Bob. (29 August 1993). "Growing up Tough: New Generation Fights for Its Life: Inner-city Youths Live by Rule of Vengeance." *Birmingham News.* (CD-ROM) 1A (10 pp.) *SIRS/SIRS 1993 Youth.* Volume 4. Article 56A.

Sciences

Author's Last Name, Initial(s). (Date). Title of article (Version or file number). *Title of database. Name of online service* and path, or protocol and address (file number). (Date accessed).

Bhattathiri, V. N. (1 May 2000). Relation of erthrocyte and iron indices to oral cancer growth. *Radiation and Oncology* 59:2. *Science Direct.* http://www.sciencedirect.com (26 Apr. 2001).

GENERAL ELECTRONIC STYLE GUIDELINES FOR MLA, APA, AND COS STYLES

■ In COS and APA styles, use italics for titles. In MLA style, use underlining.

■ Scientific citations use only the initial of the author's first name and abbreviate the name of the scientific journal (do not abbreviate in APA style).

■ In scientific citations, the date appears right after the name or names of the authors because scientific sources often become dated and more current sources may be more accurate (see APA or COS).

■ In the humanities or social sciences, sources are less likely to become dated, so the date is less important and appears at the end before the URL (see MLA or COS).

■ Titles of works in the humanities or social sciences use capital letters except for conjunctions, articles, and prepositions (except in APA style, where you only use capital letters for the first word and proper nouns).

■ Titles of works in the sciences use capital letters for the first word and proper nouns.

■ In COS, the date that you went to the source (or accessed it) appears at the end in both types of citations. MLA puts the access date right after the publication date. APA puts the access date in brackets at the end of the entry. Contrasting them, COS style is the most concise and clear of the three, but you should not mix styles once you know which style guide you will use. Always include the date you accessed the resource in case the online source disappears. The reader then knows that it existed at the time you accessed it.

■ If no author is indicated, but the source is by a group, a corporation, or a government office, follow the style for sources with authors, but substitute the name of the group, corporation, or government office for the author.

■ If no title for the source is indicated, just use whatever title appears on the Web page, if any.

■ Copy URLs carefully so that they are correct. If possible, copy the URL from the online source and paste it into your electronic note cards so that you don't copy it wrong.

■ If the Web source you are quoting is a journal, current guidelines suggest that you include the number of paragraphs if they are numbered for you.

■ Ask the author of an email, listserv, or forum discussion for permission before you cite it. In APA style, this is treated as personal correspondence in the body of the paper, not cited in the References list. In MLA style it is treated as personal correspondence both in the body of the paper and the bibliography.

THE COUNCIL OF SCIENCE EDUCATORS (CBE/CSE) MANUAL STYLE

If you are conducting research in the natural sciences, it is very likely that you will be required to cite your sources using the *CSE Manual*. We have based our examples upon *Scientific Style and Format: The CBE Manual for Authors, Editors, and Publishers*, 6th edition, published by the Council of Biology Educators (now the Council of Science Educators).

Internal Citation

CBE/CSE style is distinct from the previous styles in that you may be expected to use either of two citation systems: (1) the citations–sequence system or (2) the name–year system.

The Citation–Sequence System

Using the citation–sequence system, you will use superscript numbers ([1]) numbers or a number in parentheses (1) following the reference throughout the text of your paper to refer to the sources that you are citing. In your citation, you will indicate the pages that are referred to. If you are referring to more than one source, then use different consecutive superscript numbers to refer to the appropriate sources, with a comma between each number,[1,4] or (1,4), but no space following the comma. If the numbers note references in a sequence, then use a dash between them[1-4] or (1–4).

In the References section, the date of publication follows the publisher's name if the citation is for a book, or the date follows the name of the journal if the citation is for an article:

[1]Awad IT, Shorten GD. Amniotic fluid embolism and isolated coagulopathy: atypical resentation of amniotic fluid embolism. European Journal of Anaesthesiology 2001; 18(6):410–3. Available from: Medline (http://pathfinder.utb.edu:2239/ovidweb/ovidweb.cgi).

The Name–Year System

Using the name–year system, you will list your references alphabetically in the References section. In your text, you will put the name of the author or authors in parentheses immediately following the reference, and you will include the date following the authors' names, but with no comma separating them: (Diaz and Romeo 2000).

To summarize the difference, the citation–sequence system lists references in the order that they appear in the text, while the name–year system lists them alphabetically.

Works Cited or Reference Citation

CBE/CSE Electronic Citation Style

Below are some typical examples of CBE/CSE electronic citation style.

Article in a Journal

Quinlan KM. Generating productive learning issues in PBL Tutorials: An exercise to help tutors help students. Medical Education Online [Internet] 2000 [cited 2001 May 2]: 2(6). Available from: http://www.med-ed-online.org/issue2.htm#v6.

Article in a Subscription Database Search Engine

Awad IT, Shorten GD. Amniotic fluid embolism and isolated coagulopathy: atypical resentation of amniotic fluid embolism. European Journal of Anaesthesiology [Internet] 2001; 18(6): 410–3. In: Medline [database on the Internet]. Bethesda, MD. [cited 2001 May 2]. Available from: http://pathfinder.utb.edu:2239/ovidweb/ovidweb.cgi.

Government Report

National Institutes of Health (US). [Internet]. Stem cells: scientific progress and future research directions. Washington (DC): National Institutes of Health [updated 2001 June; cited 2001 Sept 14] Available from: http://www.nih.gov/news/stemcell/scireport.htm.

Professional Site

Council of Science Editors Web Site [Internet]. Reston, VA: Council of Science Editors: 2001 [cited 2002 Apr 18]. Available from: http://www.councilscienceeditors.org.

Homepage

University of Texas System Assessment Site [Internet]. Austin, TX: University of Texas System [updated 2002 Apr 15; cited 2002 Apr 18]. Available from: http://ntmain.utb.edu/assessment.

Email

Rodrigues D. Stem cell report [Internet]. Message to: Raymond Rodrigues. 2001 Jul 20. 1:30 pm [cited 2001 Aug 3] [about 2 screens].

CBE/CSE Nonelectronic Citation Style

CBE/CSE "References" or "Cited References" are listed alphabetically by the author's last name. The examples below illustrate the name–year system.

Article in a Journal

Croen LA. Todoroff K. Shaw GM. 2001. Maternal exposure to nitrate from drinking water and diet and risk for neural tube defects. American Journal of Epidemiology 153(4):325–31.

Article in a Popular Magazine

Chadwick D. 2001. Phantom of the night. National Geographic. 199(5): 32–51.

Article in an Edited Work

McFarland WN. 1991. The visual world of coral reef fishes. In: Sale PF, editor. The ecology of fishes on coral reefs. New York: Academic Press. p. 16–36.

Dissertation Abstract

Vera MD. 2000. Synthetic and medical chemistry of didemnins. [dissertation]. Philadelphia: University of Pennsylvania. 407 p. Available from: UMI Services, Ann Arbor, MI; DA9976487.

Edited Handbook

Polk C, Postow E., editors. 1996. Handbook of biological effects of electromagnetic fields. Boca Raton, FL: CRC Press. 618 p.

Book with One Author

Bushong, SC. 1993. Radiologic science for technologists: physics, biology, and protection. St. Louis, Mosby. 714 p.

Book with More than One Author

Bertotti, B, Farinella, P. 1990. Physics of the earth and the solar system: dynamics and evolution, space navigation, space-time structure. Boston: Kluwer Academic Publishers. 479 p.

Conference Paper

Hardy SF. 1987. The primate origins of human sexuality. In: Bellig R. and Stevens G. editors. The evolution of sex. Proceedings of the Nobel Conference XXIII; Gustavus Adolphus College. San Francisco: Harper and Row. p. 101–33.

Speech

Fuentes, C. 2001. Untitled speech at Distinguished Lecture Series. Brownsville: University of Texas at Brownsville and Texas Southmost College, September 11. Tape recording.

Personal Communication

Last, First. 2001. Telephone Conversation with Author. Tallahassee, FL: 2 September.

CHICAGO MANUAL OF STYLE (CMS)

Internal Citation

When you document with the style of the *Chicago Manual of Style* (CMS), 14th Edition rev. (University of Chicago Press, 1993), you will use actual footnotes at the bottom of each page or, if your professor allows, endnotes. The footnote is identified by a superscript number immediately after the end punctuation of the sentence with the reference, whether a summary, a paraphrase, or a quote. This sentence demonstrates that guideline.[1] CMS recommends both a scientific style and a humanities style. The scientific style is recommended for both the natural sciences and the social sciences. The humanities style is recommended for the arts and humanities.

Humanities Style

The humanities style employs footnotes or endnotes. If you are using a footnote, then the footnotes at the bottom of the page are separated from the rest of the text by a line typed 1½ inches long. In the footnote or the endnote, do not use superscript numbers, but do put the number of the footnote or endnote, then a period, and then two spaces. Single space the footnotes or endnotes, start them at the left margin, but indent the first line five spaces.

If you are using the humanities style for footnotes or endnotes, you have two choices for the citing of a source for the second time: (1) shortened form or (2) Latin form.

- Shortened form:
  - If you are using only one work by an author, all you have to do is number the footnote as always, indicate the author's last name, followed by a comma and the page number, ending with a period. For example:

    2. Quinlan, 3.

  - If the work being cited is a different work by an author with more than one work previously cited, indicate the author's name and the title of the work, followed by the page number. For example:

    3. Bhattathiri, "Relation of Erthrocyte and Iron Indices to Oral Cancer Growth," 2.
- Latin form:
  - Ibid. Use "Ibid." (same) if the footnote refers to the source cited immediately before it. If the page is the same, no page need be indicated. If the page is different, indicate the different page. For example:

    3. Ibid., 4.

  - Op. cit. Use "Op. cit." (work cited) if the citation refers to an author and work previously cited, but not immediately before this footnote. For example:

    4. Quinlan, Op. cit., 6.

  - Loc. cit. Use "Loc. cit." (place cited) if the footnote refers to an author, work, and page previously cited, but not immediately before this footnote. For example:

    5. Quinlan, Loc. cit.

Note: If the original source no longer can be seen or heard by your reader, you can make a statement in your text such as:

When I spoke to Carlos Fuentes after his speech at the University of Texas at Brownsville and Texas Southmost College on September 11, 2001, he said . . .

Or you can cite your source in a footnote:

[1]I interviewed Carlos Fuentes after his speech at the University of Texas at Brownsville and Texas Southmost College on September 11, 2001.

Scientific Style or Author–Date System

The scientific or author–date style uses "in-text" references. The standard form is to list the author's last name with no punctuation following it, then the date with a comma and space following it, and then the page number without either p. or pp. For example:

> Technology may make plagiarism easier, but technology also makes detecting the plagiarism easier (Scanlan 2000, 1).

Note: If the original source no longer can be seen or heard by your reader, you can make a statement in your text such as:

> When I spoke to Carlos Fuentes after his speech at the University of Texas at Brownsville and Texas Southmost College on September 11, 2001, he said . . .

Normally, when using the scientific or author–date style, sources that cannot be retrieved are not cited in the References section. However, CMS allows you to do so:

Fuentes, Carlos. 2001. Conversation with author. Brownsville, TX, 11 September.

Bibliography

The bibliography in CMS lists sources alphabetically. (*Note:* CMS style calls for double spacing *everything* in the paper.)

CMS Electronic Citation Style

CMS has not developed its own formats for electronic sources, but subscribes to the recommendations of the International Standards Organization (ISO). For ease of understanding ISO citation style, we include examples for a few of the most common types of electronic sources.

Electronic Journal

Quinlan, Kathleen M. "Generating productive learning issues in PBL Tutorials: An exercise to help tutors help students." In *Medical Education Online* [electronic journal]. 2 (6). [cited 20 July 2001]. Available from http://www.med-ed-online.org/issue2.htm#v6.

Scholarly Article Online

Lape, Peter. *Spice Islands Archaeology Project*. Brown University. 17 Aug. 1999. [cited 26 April 2001] Available from http://www.brown.edu/Departments/Anthropology/ SIAP/home.html.

Online Database

Burfisher, Mary E., Sherman Robinson, and Karen Thierfelder. "The Impact of NAFTA on the United States." *Journal of Economic Perspectives.* 15 (1) [cited 10 August 2001]. Available from WilsonWeb: http://vweb.hwwilsonweb. com.

Email

Rodrigues, Dawn. "Stem cell report." Personal email. 20 July 2001. [Accessed 21 July 2001.]

CMS Nonelectronic Citation Style

Article in a Journal, Humanities Style

McClaskey, Jane. "Who's Afraid of the Big, Bad TAAS? Rethinking Our Response to Standardized Testing." *English Journal* 91, no. 1 (2001): 88–95.

Article in a Newspaper, Humanities Style

Benevidez, Rachel. "Blood Drive Tries to Help Young Boy." *Brownsville Herald,* 20 February 2001, Section A.

Article in a Newspaper, Author–Date Style

Benevidez, Rachel. 2001. Blood drive tries to help young boy. *Brownsville Herald,* 20 February, Section A.

Article in a Popular Magazine, Humanities Style

Cohen, Adam. "Who Swiped the Surplus?" *Time.* 158, no. 9 (September 3): 30–33.

Article in a Popular Magazine, Author–Date Style

Badenhausen, Kurt, and Lesley Kump. 2001. The richest football teams. *Forbes,* 17 September, 82–86.

Book Review, Humanities Style

Saba, Mark Saad. Review of *Goddess of the Americas: La Diosa de las Americas: Writings on the Virgin of Guadalupe,* ed. Ana Castillo. *Hispanic Outlook in Higher Education* 11, no. 22. (2001): 48.

Book Review, Author–Date Style

Saba, M. 2001. Review of *Goddess of the Americas: La Diosa de las Americas: Writings on the Virgin of Guadalupe,* ed. Ana Castillo. *Hispanic Outlook in Higher Education* 11 (13 August): 48.

Book with One Author, Humanities Style

Castillo, Ana. *So Far from God.* New York: Penguin Books, 1994.

Book with One Author, Author–Date Style

Richardson, A. 1995. *Plants of the Rio Grande Delta.* Austin: University of Texas Press.

Book with Two or More Authors, Humanities Style

Kearney, Milo, and Anthony Knopp. *Border Cuates: A History of the U.S.–Mexican Twin Cities.* Austin, TX: Eakin Press, 1995.

Book with Two or More Authors, Author–Date Style

Lockwood, M. W., W. B. McKinney, J. N. Paton, and B. R. Zimmer. 1999. *A Birder's Guide to the Rio Grande Valley.* Colorado Springs, CO: American Birding Association.

Book with No Author Specified, Humanities Style

Sintra and Its Surroundings. Lisbon: Sage Editora, 1994.

Book with No Author Specified, Author–Date Style

Sintra and Its Surroundings. 1994. Lisbon: Sage Editora.

Speech, Humanities Style

Fuentes, C. Untitled Speech at Distinguished Lecture Series. Tape Recording. Brownsville: University of Texas at Brownsville and Texas Southmost College, September 11, 2001.

Personal Communication, Humanities Style

Doe, Jane. Telephone Conversation with Author. Brownsville, TX, 5 September 2001.

EXPLORING CITATION PROBLEMS

Citing sources from the Web poses new problems for researchers. As you now know, if you have visited the same website several times, the content can change, sometimes daily. In the past, someone who wanted to check the sources in a research paper could access the very same source that the writer used. With the Web, it is almost impossible to be sure that your reader will have access to information that is identical to the information you used from the same site.

With website addresses changing, it may be that, when your readers type in the URL that you provided in your research report, they will get a message indicating that there is no known URL with that address or that the server may be down or that they may have typed in the wrong address. For that reason, not only should you provide correct URLs, but also you should indicate the date that you "accessed" or referred to the site. Then, if your reader cannot find the site, they know when it was last working. Also, you should save a copy of your sources on disk so you can submit them to your instructor if asked.

An additional problem is that new types of sites may appear for which no style guide has a recommendation on formatting the citation. Websites vary so much that no style manual could ever anticipate all the variants you will find. What should you do? We recommend that you create your own format if the sites you want to document do not fit the examples. Try to imitate the basic structure of the citation as closely as you can. As long as your teacher knows you have followed the general pattern and you are consistent, you need not worry about whether your version is correct or not.

Yet another problem students report is the use of angle brackets (< >) in MLA citation style. If you try to type angle brackets using Microsoft Word, the default setting in the program removes them and turns the URL into a hyperlink. If you want to remove that setting, click on **Tools** in the menu bar and select **AutoCorrect.** Then click on **AutoFormat as You Type.** Under **Replace as You Type,** click on **Internet and network paths with hyperlinks** to remove the check (and thereby stop the automatic conversion from hyperlinks typed in brackets to hyperlinks).

Finally, there is a logistical problem. It is not easy to keep track of URLs. If you are viewing a page from a site that uses "frames," the URL will show the home page for the site rather than the page you are viewing. Most sites do not include the URL on the page itself. Thus, if you save a Web page to disk thinking that you have captured the URL with your information intact, you may discover later that you do not have the URL. You can conduct a Web search to locate the URL, but you have ways to avoid that extra work:

- Save the file with the name of the URL.
- Open files as soon as you save them and copy the URL into them.
- If you print pages immediately rather than save them to disk, check to see if Netscape or Explorer automatically prints the title of the file and the URL in the header of each page.
- Make your electronic note cards or bibliography cards as soon as you save a site.

COPYRIGHT CONSIDERATIONS

In addition to knowing how to document sources, you need to understand copyright laws. The term *copyright* refers to protection provided to authors for their "copy"—whether a printed text, a movie, a graphic image, or a recording. From 1978 on, copyright protection has been automatic, and a simple statement such as "This document cannot be distributed in its entirety without permission of the author" is all that you have to do to guarantee your rights as the author. This statement should be accompanied by the copyright symbol (©) and the date. Such a statement is not absolutely essential, but it can prevent accidental misuse by others.

Before the Web, students rarely had to worry about copyright laws. The few lines of text from books or journals that are included in student papers are within the "fair use" length guidelines. (You can quote up to 300 words from a book or 150 words from a magazine or newspaper, if the total that you quote is not more than 20% of the original.) But if you link a source on the Web to your text, you can be considered to be "distributing" the source. It is always advisable to get permission to link to a given site. Most importantly, if you are writing a hypertext research paper that includes links to copyright-protected essays or poems that you have photocopied and included in an appendix to your research project, do not scan the text into the computer and link it to your writing without receiving permission from the author. If you do, you may be guilty of copyright infringement.

CONCLUSION

Citation conventions for print-based sources have been set in place for years; Internet citation style, however, continues to evolve. When you use the Web for research, you should continue using the same processes for citing sources that you have always used, but it is essential that these processes be adapted to the Internet-specific needs of readers. Clearly, it is not always easy or even possible for a reader of a research paper filled with Internet sources to track the original source. But it is incumbent upon you, the writer and scholar, to do your best to provide clear and accurate guidelines for your readers.

If you have some doubts, include an explanatory footnote in which you let your reader know the context of the source. For example, you may already know that the original source no longer exists. Use an unavailable source if you believe it to be critical to your paper, but be honest to the reader about the situation regarding that source.

Above all, continue to use the Internet for your research. Do not let concerns about validity and citations stop you from including the results of your Internet-based research in your finished paper.

SUGGESTED ACTIVITIES

1. Working from your note and bibliography cards, develop a bibliography (Works Cited for MLA; References for APA) for your paper.

2. Return to the latest draft of your paper and make sure that you have used correct internal citation style. Check for the following: (1) Have you listed page numbers according to the style you are following? (2) Have you mentioned the author that you have cited, either in the sentence or in the parenthetic citation? (3) Have you been consistent in following one particular style guide?

Appendix A:
Writing for the Web

If you are told at the beginning of a course that you will be publishing your research to the Web, you may wonder what your teacher means. There are many possibilities: you may be asked to submit your writing to online forums; you may be expected to develop Web publishing skills and upload your assignments to a website; you may be expected to save your work in Web format so that instructors can upload student files to a class website; or you may be asked to work in teams on your Web writing project. In this appendix, we explain how you can create Web pages to give your research reports the capabilities that the Web environment allows.

To get started, take time to learn about copyright law, in particular acceptable use of information on the Web. In general, you should request permission before using a copyright-protected article or graphic on your website. If the website you create is password-protected, you can include copies of articles you collect for projects on a one-time-only basis. If you plan to keep them on the site permanently, you must immediately attempt to secure permission to use them. Learn more about copyright and intellectual property on the Web at the Copyright and Fair Use website at http://fairuse.stanford.edu.

WRITING: IN PRINT AND ON THE WEB

What changes when you write for the online world? Much depends on whether you intend your writing to be read online or whether you are merely making your writing available online. If you intend your research to be read online, you should consider designing it exclusively for the Web environment. Usually, Web writing is *hypertextual*; that is, writers design texts that contain links to supplementary information (pictures, sounds, or text); or, they design texts with multiple points of entry. To facilitate that, they divide their topics into many chunks and then allow their readers to enter at selected points.

How does reading online differ from reading print information? People expect to be able to skim through Web text, to read headings and subheadings and click from section to section. Readers of Web texts do not necessarily start at the top and move in a sequential order through the text. Instead, readers skip around, reading what appeals to them. If they know that they will be expected to remember what they read, they will probably choose to print portions of the file or the entire file.

DIFFERENT KINDS OF WEB WRITING PROJECTS

Below, you can explore different kinds of Web writing projects, ranging from those that require minimal technical skills to those that encourage students to develop their own Web pages.

Posting to Online Forums or Submitting to Online Journals

You can find a list of sites where you can "publish" drafts of your essays to a public area at the companion website. When you submit your work to a Web log or an online magazine, you need to take time to analyze the audience for your writing. No longer are you writing solely for your classmates. In many cases, your forum responses are available to everyone with access to the Web. Be sure to proofread your writing. You don't want readers to think you are careless.

Using a Word-processing Program to Transform a Traditional Essay or Research Paper into a Web Text with Links

With a standard word processor, you can create documents that tap the information resources of the Web. Even if you have no plans to post your writing to the Web, you can create hyperlinks in your essay that lead the reader to key information, such as the sources you are referring to or the websites you mention in the text. For instance, if you are writing on the Web, you can include a reference to a site called "Learn the Net" by clicking on Insert/Hyperlink, as shown in the screen in Figure A.1, and then entering the address of the site that you want to link to in the blank text box with the heading "Type the file or Web page name."

In your word processor file, when you create a Hyperlink, it is displayed with underlining, as shown in the example of a hypertext link in the sentence below:

> If you want to learn about the Web on your own, you can explore many online areas, such as <u>Learn the Net</u>, an excellent tutorial for beginners.

When you are reading that sentence online, all you have to do is click on the underlined link and it will take you to the website that it is linked to.

You can insert images into your text, too, and create a visually appealing Word document that is ready to publish to the Web after you save your file as a Web page.

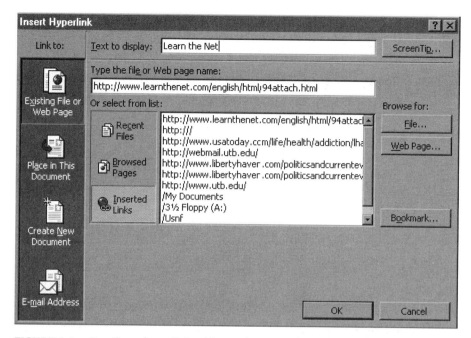

FIGURE A.1 Creating a hyperlink with Word. Screen shot reprinted by permission from Microsoft Corporation.

To transform a standard Word document into a Web page, follow these directions:

1. Click on **File/Save As.**
2. Highlight **Web Page,** as shown in Figure A.2.
3. Save the page.

You can also link to files that you create yourself. For example, if you are writing about teen drinking, you might want to link to a page that contains

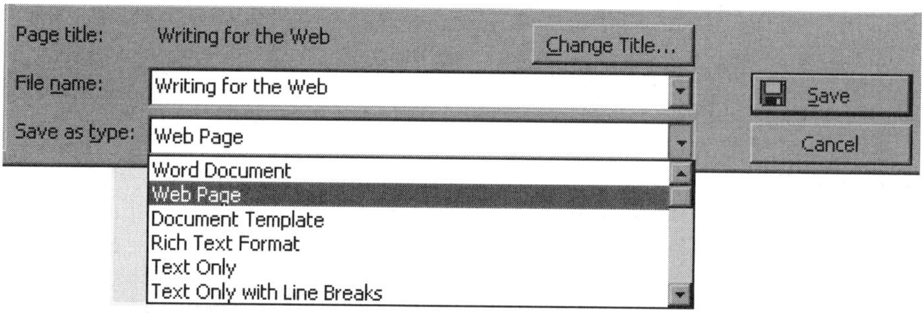

FIGURE A.2 Saving a document as a Web page. Screen shot reprinted by permission from Microsoft Corporation.

interviews you have conducted with parents of teenagers. Or, you might want to link to a page that includes an interview you have had with an Alcoholics Anonymous counselor. You can simply type the interview in a separate file and save it in the same directory as the first file. Then, when readers click on the hyperlink in your essay, they will retrieve the second file.

When research is published to the Web, some uses of hyperlinks have now become conventions. For example, whenever you cite a source, you should create a link from the in-text citation of the source to its target, the bibliographic entry at the end of your paper. Then, if that source can be found online, you can create a link from the bibliographic entry to its target, the online source itself. (See the companion website for examples.)

In addition, you may choose to provide links within your paper to online sites that give the reader more background information, even if that background information is not specifically used in your paper. For example, if you are writing a paper on illegal immigration from Mexico, you might link to a site that provides a map of the Mexican border from Brownsville, Texas, to Tijuana, Mexico. Or you might link to a site with economic data about Mexico. Those may simply be background material for your reader, but it helps provide a fuller picture of your subject for those readers who want to explore more. Footnotes, as you know, usually provide information that may be background information for your topic, so now those footnotes can contain hyperlinks to additional information.

Hypertext Essay

There are major differences between an essay with a few links and a project that has been specifically designed as a hypertext document. If you are planning to include links freely, wherever they add content to your main page, then you are probably designing in a free-association hypertext style. You may not even think ahead of time about what you want to include in your essay or whether you should redesign it for the screen. On the other hand, you may want to write a structured hypertext essay, one that is designed to allow readers to enter at a variety of points in the essay. In that case, you will probably provide a menu of choices to your reader, such as the menu shown in Figure A.3.

- Free association hypertexts allow readers to link to supporting information as necessary.
- A structured hypertext essay project with multiple entry points must be written in a multilinear manner. That is, authors cannot assume that readers will start at the beginning and proceed to the end. Instead, readers might start in the middle and move to whatever parts of the project interest the reader. Thus, an author must write each section so that it can stand alone. Authors should not assume that readers have read any parts of the text before they enter a given section.

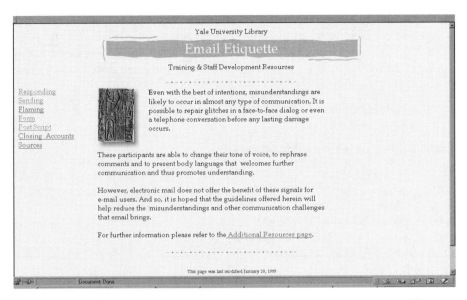

FIGURE A.3   Links in the left column are examples of a menu in a structured hypertext document. © 2000 Yale University Library. Reprinted with permission.

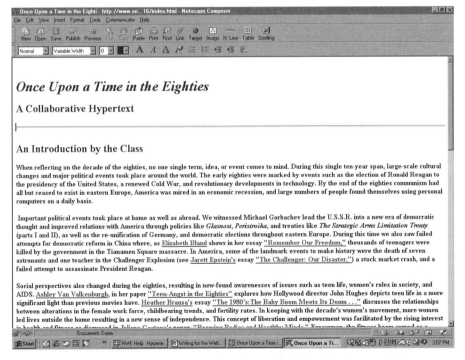

FIGURE A.4   Sample hypertext project in a free-association hypertext style. Reprinted with permission.

■ The links in hypertext essays may be to other parts of the document itself, to sites on the Web, or to multimedia components created either by the writer or available on the Web. Hypertext projects frequently integrate images, audio, and video at key points—to illustrate or comment on a concept in the text.

For examples of hypertext essays, see Figures A.3 and A.4.

Class E-Zine or a Class Anthology

Your class can create an electronic magazine (e-zine) or an anthology of class writing projects. How you proceed depends on the nature of the assignment. If students work individually on different projects with different audiences and purposes, a class anthology would be a good choice. Students in future classes would be the audience for your writing, and you can think of their needs and interests as you write and as you design the look and feel of your Web anthology.

If you decide to collaborate as a class (or with students in a group) to produce a specific kind of Web magazine, you have a fascinating challenge. You will need to decide not only on the topic of your publication, but also on the nature of your readers. A good way to proceed is to examine a range of e-zines available on the Web, noting the ways each attempts to target specific groups of readers. Here are some sites to explore as you begin to consider your own publication:

Gettingit
http://www.gettingit.com

Bohemian Link
http://www.levity.com/corduroy/index.htm

Katharsis
http://www.katharsis.org/

Zines, Zines, Everywhere
http://www.zinebook.com/

Zine Resource Starting Page
http://www.zinebook.com/main.html

After you target a specific audience and choose a specific topic, you should design the visual look of your publication. What colors, images, or pictures will you use on the cover? What kinds of interactivity will you include in the pages? For example, many e-zines now include a discussion forum within each issue. If your class has access to an online bulletin or forum, perhaps you want to create an area for discussion of your finished writing.

Here is a simple procedure that a group of students can follow to produce their own magazine:

1. Ask students to upload their own pages to a website.
2. Ask students to provide instructors or group leaders with the URL for their sites.
3. Ask each classmate to write a brief autobiographical sketch so that you can create a contributor's page.
4. Create a template file that includes places for each student's name and the title of the student's project. Insert the correct URL into the hyperlink box for each title, as shown below:

Class Anthology	
Jane Doe	Bush Daughters Drinking Creates a Stir
Jose Garza	Should Humans Be Cloned?

Collaborative Course Projects

If you have the freedom to experiment, consider a collaborative course project, one in which each student conducts research on a different component of the background or contexts of an article or a topic. For samples of a collaborative project, see Figure A.5.

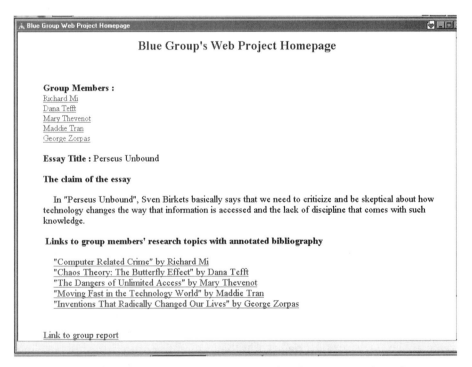

FIGURE A.5 Collaborative project page. Reprinted with permission from the authors, Lee Sung Yoon, Lindsey Fifer, and Kim Bell under the instruction of Lisa Justine Hernandez, University of Texas at Austin.

CREATING WEB PAGES

If you haven't created your own Web pages, here are some ways you can proceed.

1. **Use a page-builder site.** Some sites provide tutorials and simple forms to create Web pages and require very little computer expertise. The drawback of most of these sites is that since they are free, they rely on advertising for support. Each page thus usually has a "banner ad" on it—either in a pop-up window or at the bottom of the screen.

The list of sites below gives you the option of creating pages from scratch or using either templates or page-builder "wizards." A template is a completely formatted file that can be edited with your information. Wizards are automated sets of directions that you follow to build a page based on one of a set of templates offered in the program. Templates are often fine for personal home pages, but of limited use for course projects, for they often allow too little customization. (Alternately, try using a wizard in PowerPoint to create a basic page there and then upload that page to your website.)

Geocities
http://www.geocities.com

Homestead
http://www.homestead.com

Tripod
http://www.tripod.com

CNET's Builder.com
http://www.cnet.com

2. **Create your Web page with a word processor and then upload it to a server.** Remember, you need to have permission to publish on a server. At your college or university, this usually involves filling out an application and following directions for posting. If you do not have access to a Web server at your institution, you can publish to one of many free websites that offer free server space, as long as you don't mind pop-up ads and banners on your pages.

You can create your Web page on your own computer or disk and then upload it to the Web server whenever you are online. If you do create a website, take time to learn how to maintain your pages. Many people learn how to create a Web page or set of pages, but they forget the procedures for revising their pages and do not keep their sites up-to-date. If your instructor has created a website for the papers created by students, then it is your instructor's responsibility to keep up the site.

3. **Use page editing software.** Web page editing programs, such as Netscape Composer, Front Page, and DreamWeaver, make Web page creation easy, even for novices. Even so, you will probably need some help if you are new to Web page creation. See if you can attend a seminar at your college or university, or ask a classmate or friend to help you get started.

DESIGN BASICS

Most students have little or no experience in what is called "document design"—the effective placement of text and images on a page or screen. If you are designing an entire website, you should design the interface before you do any actual writing to the site. What does this mean? It means that you need to sketch out what the screen will look like and what screens you want to link to. It also means that you need some kind of navigational guide, either on the side or on the top of the page, to lead people through your site. And you need consistent page design so that people will know that all the pages you design go together.

Designing a Website

Designing a website is different from designing a Web page. If you will be designing an entire site, you should think through the overall design before developing individual pages. Here are some guidelines for you to follow:

■ Establish a common identity to all of the pages by having them all look somewhat alike—the same logo, the same kind of text placement, the same color combination, and so on.
■ Determine a structure for the site in advance, using paper to "story board" the organization of your site.
■ Limit the typeface to one or two sizes from no more than two font families.
■ Sequence the elements on a website in a way that is intuitively clear to users. That is, you can show readers the hierarchy of your site (as shown in Figure A.6).
■ Make it possible for readers to navigate easily through your site:
  1. Create menu structures that allow users to move from one page to any other page on the site.
  2. Let readers know their location within the site (by using different shading on the menu bar, for example).
  3. Indicate when the site links to a page outside the site.
  4. Include site maps so that readers can learn how the site is structured.

Designing a Page

Here are some basic guidelines for designing a single page:

■ Make the topic clear to a reader.

- Create a simple-to-follow structure or organization for your page; for example, use bullets or numbered lists so that your reader can scan the page for main ideas and key points.
- Chunk the text into topical areas that will interest readers. Use headings and subheadings to help a reader locate subsections of text.
- Leave enough white space around the edges and between paragraphs to make your page more readable. (*Hint:* Place your text inside a table and limit the size of the table to 700 pixels or to 75% of the page, then the text will not spread out across the entire screen—a problem on large monitors.)
- Use graphics to aid navigation (e.g., color headings and subheadings).
- Remember to indicate the author of the website and any contact information.
- Include the last date the page was updated.

The samples below illustrate some basic design principles. See if you can determine which is better screen design.

(A)

Computers in the Home
More than 50% of American homes have computers, according to a recent statistic. This data, however, does not explain the reasons 50% of Americans do not have computers. Some of those reasons follow:

- Low literacy skills
- Poverty
- No motivation or reason to use computers

(B)
More than 50% of American homes have computers, but an equal number of people do not have computers in their homes. Certainly computers are not to blame for the lack of high literacy in the inner cities of this country. Instead, low literacy skills, poverty, and lack of motivation are the primary culprits.

REVIEW QUESTIONS: WEBSITE DESIGN

The sample Web pages in Figures A.6 and A.7 are part of a website on email etiquette at Yale University Library. Evaluate the design of these Web pages, using the following criteria:

- Do readers always know where they are in the site?
- Can readers find their way back to the start?
- Can readers exit easily?
- Is there sufficient white space on the page?
- Are individual pages no longer than several screens?
- Does each page indicate that it is part of a larger site? That is, can readers who access only one page recognize that it is part of the larger site?

A. Opening Page of Website

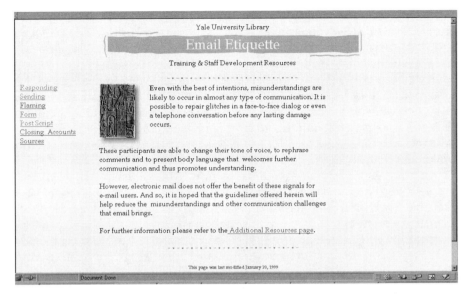

FIGURE A.6 Site to review for design features. © 2000 Yale University Library. Reprinted with permission.

B. Internal Page of Website

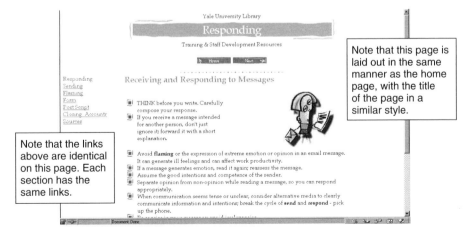

FIGURE A.7 Internal page to review for design features. © 2000 Yale University Library. Reprinted with permission.

THE BASICS OF HTML

The language used to develop Web pages is called Hypertext Markup Language (HTML). Even though you will rarely need to know much HTML, a basic understanding of a few commands will help you create simple pages and will enable you to read the source code of Web pages well enough to make your way through them and revise or add to them. *Note:* To read the source code on a page in Netscape Composer, click on **View/Page Source.** In many cases, you can edit the page directly in Netscape Composer, and avoid using HTML. For expert fine-tuning, you can edit the HTML code. (You need to save the Netscape page; then, after clicking on **File/Edit Page,** select **Edit/ Document Source.**)

Learning just a few basic commands in HTML will enable you to create simple pages without any Web editing software or will allow you to revise a page that has been created with an editing program. Also, since many bulletin board programs allow users to insert basic HTML commands, you can improve the screen design of bulletin board posts by inserting commands such as those in the box text below. Note that HTML tags are often used in pairs—one tag before the page element and one after it. Table A.1 summarizes key commands.

Now try creating a sample page with a text editor such as Word Pad.

1. Type the code shown above.
2. Save the file as a text file with a Web extension: e.g., sample.htm. (Do not save as a Word document.)
3. Open the file with a browser (Netscape or Internet Explorer).
4. Edit the file as needed and post it to a website. (Directions vary at different sites. You will need to have explicit instructions for uploading your page to the server.)

Step One

```
<html>
  <title>Course Essays</title>

<body>

<center>
<h1>
My Portfolio of Essays</h1>
</center>

<blockquote> Below are links to the essays I have written in this course:

To read my essays, click on one of the links below:
<ul>
<li>
```

TABLE A.1 HTML Tags

Page Element	Tags
Begin and end page	\<html> \</html>
Title	\<title> \</title>
Body	\<body> \</body>
Paragraph	\<p>
Line break	\
Web link	\<a href="http://www.something.edu"> nameoflink\</a>
Bold font	\word\
Italicized font	\<I>word \</I>
Unordered list	\<ul> \</ul>
Ordered list (numerical list)	\<ol> \</ol>
Line in list	\<li>
Horizontal line	\<hr>
Heading levels	\<h1>\</h1> \<h2>\</h2> \<h3>\</h3> \<h4>\</h4>
Blockquote	\<blockquote> \</blockquote>

\<a href="http://english.utb.edu/drodrigues/essays/essayone.htm">Essay One\</a>\</li>

\<li>
\<a href="http://english.utb.edu/drodrigues/essays/essaytwo.htm">Essay Two\</a>\</li>

\<li>
\<a href="http://english.utb.edu/drodrigues/essays/essaythree.htm">Essay Three\</a>\</li>

\</ul>
\<p>

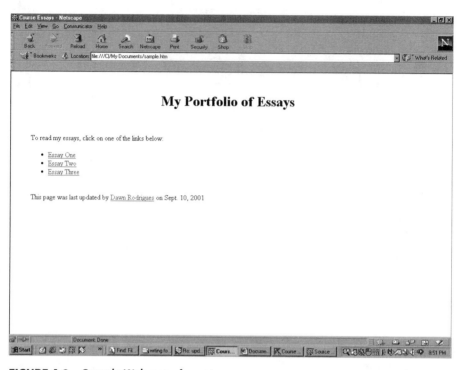

FIGURE A.8   Sample Web page format.

This page was last updated by <ahref="mailto:drodrigues@utb1.utb.edu">
Dawn Rodrigues</a> on Sept. 10, 2001

</blockquote>

</body>
</html>

Step Two

View your page in a Web browser. Open the page using the File/Open
commands of the browser. Your page should look something like the one in
Figure A.8.

ADDING PICTURES OR GRAPHICS

Pictures add much to Web pages, but they also affect the speed with which
your page is loaded on the screen. A recommended maximum space that a
page should take up is 30KB. You can limit your page size in several ways: by
limiting the number of pictures, by not using a background, by using fewer

colors, or by reducing the size of the image (with the help of an image editor). There are two kinds of image files you should learn about: JPEGs and GIFs. JPEG stands for Joint Photographic Experts Group. GIF stands for Graphic Image Format. GIFs only allow 256 colors, and are fine for line graphics or logos. JPEGs are best for photographs.

Keep in mind that in order to use a picture that you did not create yourself or that you did not locate on a copyright-free clip art site, you need to have copyright permission. Some clip art sites allow you to use their work as long as you include a notice on the page indicating who owns the artwork.

Here are some tips and suggestions:

- Avoid distracting graphics. Use graphics and images only if they have a purpose on your page.
- Create graphics using a painting or drawing program.
- Locate clip art on freeware sites on the Web.
- Save any image (JPEG, GIF, or other format) by right-clicking on the image and choosing **Save Image As** from the pop-up menu and saving the file to a space on your disk.
- Use a scanner to transform a picture or a drawing into digital format so that it can be saved to a file.
- Use a digital camera to take pictures that can be included on Web pages.
- Consider giving readers the option of using "text-only" Web pages.
- Use thumbnails as links to larger images. (A thumbnail is a small version of the larger image, which takes up relatively little space.)
- Learn how to use some kind of image-editing software. A trial program called Paint-Shop Pro can be downloaded free and used for 30 days (http://www.paintshoppro.com).

WRITING ON THE WEB: SITES TO EXPLORE

A Guide from the Writing Environment at the University of Florida
http://web.nwe.ufl.edu/writing/help/web/authoring/

Writing for the Web
http://www.iss.stthomas.edu/studyguides

Design Exercises
http://www.cwrl.utexas.edu/~tonya/kairos/integ/wwwsite.html

Untanging the Web
http://www.closeup.org/untangle.htm

TechWeb's HTML Editors
http://htmleditors.com

UC Berkeley HTML Editors
http://www.lib.berkeley.edu/TeachingLib/HTML/editors.html

Web Graphics
http://oswego.org/staff/cchamber/webdesign/web_graphics.htm

Cool Text
http://www.cooltext.com

Yale Guide
http://www.info.med.yale.edu/caim/manual

Copyright Guidelines
http://www.cit.cornell.edu/computer/www/guidelines/copyright.html

Daniel Anderson, From Browsers to Builders: Student Composition on the World Wide Web
http://www.cwrl.utexas.edu/~daniel/browserstobuilders/

Killer Web Sites
http://killer.com

Appendix B: Creating a PowerPoint Presentation

It is very common now for instructors to ask students to present the results of their research using PowerPoint or another type of presentation software. The intent of such a presentation is to inform the rest of your class about the results of your research. It is not to include the entire research paper. A good PowerPoint presentation is fairly concise, making use of graphics and illustrations to clarify the points being made. Therefore, it is critical that a good presentation make full use of good design principles, similar in many ways to the design principles for websites discussed in Appendix A, but designed to be controlled by the person presenting the material rather than the reader. Here are some basic guidelines:

- To learn PowerPoint, attend a seminar at your university or read the materials provided by PowerPoint. Then, practice as much as you can using the features that make PowerPoint a strong presentation tool. Experiment: Try different shapes, try different colors, try the animations that PowerPoint allows, and don't be afraid to do something wrong. You don't have to save anything that you don't like.
- Put yourself in the place of other people viewing your presentation. Design your PowerPoint pages so that they are clearly visible from the back of the room and easy to understand. Use large font sizes and don't write many long, complex sentences.
- Put no more than one or two sentences on each page. Use those to talk from, but don't try to put all your ideas on that page. Those sentences should capture your main ideas, not everything you have learned in your research. You can fill in the details orally. If all you do is read your sentences, you might as well just give your audience a handout and let them read it.

■ Use the graphics capabilities of PowerPoint to draw designs that help explain your points. For example, if you are discussing the causes of an event, show it visually:

■ Use the animation feature to show aspects of your topic one point at a time or to show relationships between those aspects. For example, in the illustration above, you could have the Event on the screen by itself. Then you could have Cause 1 appear and the arrow grow toward the Event, then Cause 2 and its arrow, and finally Cause 3 and its arrow. That forces your audience to focus only on the point you are discussing rather than looking at everything while you are talking and thereby losing your point.
■ If you want to include an illustration, you can copy the illustration from your computer's hard drive to the PowerPoint presentation.
■ If you want to include a screenshot of a Web page, you go to the website itself, find the screen you want to show, press **PrintScrn** (print screen) on

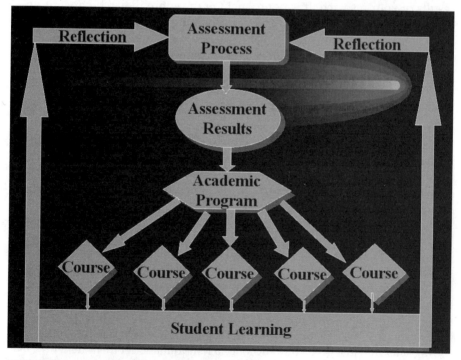

FIGURE B.1 Example of graphics in PowerPoint.

your keyboard, and then go to the blank PowerPoint slide where you want the screen shot, go to **Edit,** and press **Paste.** The screen shot will appear on the PowerPoint presentation.

■ Practice the presentation a number of different times so that you become comfortable with it, speaking from the screen that the audience sees, but not reading everything on the screen. Remember, the screen that the audience sees is to help them understand what you are saying, not to provide a script for you to follow word for word.

■ As you practice, you may realize that you should revise your presentation a bit, perhaps changing the order of the screens. Go ahead and make those changes.

■ If you are asked to provide a handout for your audience, go to **File → Print → Handouts.** There you can select the type of handout that you want. It will print the handout, and you can make as many copies as you want. If you want other students to take notes while you are talking, you should choose a design that provides space for notes. If your instructor wants you to provide a bibliography of sources, make a handout for the class of just those pages from your paper.

Figure B.1 illustrates a PowerPoint screen that is designed to illustrate a process. In this case, it is the process of assessing an academic program. Each of the components appear one at a time as the presenter presses the Enter key.

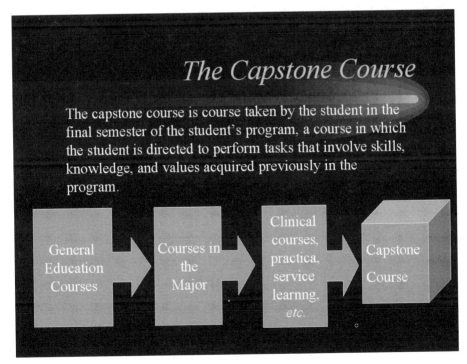

FIGURE B.2 Example of graphics and words in PowerPoint.

The arrows appear to grow because the presenter created them and then used the animation technique "stretch" for each arrow. Notice that there are no sentences included on the slide to describe this process; the presenter does that orally.

Figure B.2 illustrates a PowerPoint slide that combines words with graphics. Notice that there is only one sentence. This length for the number of words that the viewer needs to read is about as long as your text should be if you include text on your screen. The graphics were animated so that one box with an arrow appears at a time and so that the speaker could describe what is happening at each step.

A PowerPoint presentation can interest viewers a great deal or it can bore them and cause them to stop paying attention. Obviously, you want them to be interested. So, as you design your PowerPoint presentation, make as much use as you can of the capabilities of PowerPoint or whatever other presentation software you may have available to you.

Appendix C: Sample Research Paper—American Psychological Association Style

MODEL PAPER, APA STYLE

The Role of NAFTA in Stopping Illegal

Mexican Immigration

First-Name Last-Name

Course number, Section number

Course name

Professor's Name

University name

Month Day, Year

Abstract

For generations, many Mexicans have been crossing the

border of the United States illegally to find work.

Since 1993, when the United States signed the North

American Free Trade Agreement (NAFTA), people have dis-

agreed about whether NAFTA is beneficial to the U.S. The

balance of trade between Mexico and the U.S. has been

cited as proof that NAFTA is working and that it has

failed. The number of jobs in the United States has

either decreased or increased as a result of NAFTA,

depending upon how one calculates loss or gain. And

throughout the history of NAFTA, illegal Mexican immi-

gration has not stopped. Some argue that Mexicans are

filling an "essential worker" category. The efforts to

improve the economic infrastructure of Mexico may pro-

vide a solution, within the terms of NAFTA, to ongoing

illegal immigration into the United States.

Note: The abstract page is optional. Check with your professor to learn whether you should include an abstract.

The abstract is placed on page 2 by itself.

The abstract should not exceed 120 words.

The Role of NAFTA in Stopping Illegal

Mexican Immigration

Use the past tense when indicating what a source has written or said.

Writing in *Time* magazine, reporter Nancy Gibbs described the United States/Mexico border as "a barbed-wire paradox, half pried open, half bolted closed" (2001). Mexican President Vicente Fox and United States President George Bush have met several times to discuss the relationship between the two countries, realizing that their futures are bound to each other. While no one knows what the best solution may be to address the illegal immigration of thousands of Mexicans every month, most experts agree that the United States needs those workers, even though many people have serious concerns about their impact upon our health care, education, and social services. The evidence is clear: we cannot stop illegal immigration, Mexicans would remain in Mexico if their economy provided them the jobs and wages that they need, and we need a strong Mexico to help keep our economy strong. The solution is not a legal one. Only an economic solution that will benefit both countries. Is NAFTA that solution?

From the very first time that the North American Free

Trade Agreement (NAFTA) began to be discussed as an

official agreement between the United States, Mexico,

and Canada, opponents raised serious arguments against

it. Foremost among those arguments was the claim that

the agreement would have a serious negative impact upon

U.S. industries, leading to many American workers losing

their jobs. Ross Perot, running for President of the

United States, expressed the fear through the image of a

"huge sucking sound," as jobs left the U.S. and were

pulled across the border. Labor unions understandably

were concerned because labor was cheap in Mexico, job

safety was a concern, and workers' rights were seldom

protected. Environmentalists also joined the argument,

expressing concerns about uncontrolled pollution result-

ing from unregulated industries in Mexico. Now, approxi-

mately seven years after NAFTA was first implemented in

1974, can we determine whether NAFTA has had a positive

or a negative effect upon the U.S. economy, including

the question of whether jobs and businesses have been

lost as a result of NAFTA? Correlated with that question

is the issue of illegal immigration to the U.S., which

NAFTA 4

many see as taking more jobs away from American workers

and which continues to be a serious issue not only along

our border with Mexico, but deep into the major cities

of the U.S. Because the U.S. has not been able to stem

the flow of illegal immigrants, many point to NAFTA as

having failed. Thus, the loss of U.S. jobs and illegal

immigration are linked in the minds of many Americans.

Although the focus of these questions is economic

in nature, novelist Carlos Fuentes, speaking in

Brownsville, Texas, argued that "Cultures perish in iso-

lation; cultures thrive in the presence of others"

(2001). He was, in fact, arguing the benefits of NAFTA

and the need to maintain close relations with Mexico. He

believes that both nations have and will continue to

derive many benefits from being close to one another,

whether it be in the arts, in business, or in the per-

sonal relationships of humans to humans. Even President

George W. Bush, welcoming Mexican President Vicente Fox

to Washington, said, "El que tiene un buen vecino, tiene

un buen amigo," or "He who has a good neighbor has a

good friend" (Thompson, 2001). It appears that both

When the name of the source is in the sentence, it is not in the in-text citation.

President Bush and Carlos Fuentes recognize benefits

beyond those of trade agreements.

The Issue of the Balance of Trade

Those who have studied the balance of trade between the

United States and Mexico draw very different conclusions

about whether NAFTA has helped the United States because

they base their analyses upon two very different

approaches. On the one hand, some maintain that NAFTA

has failed to help the balance of trade of the U.S. with

Mexico because the U.S. continues to import more goods

from Mexico than it exports. Others argue that we should

not measure the value of NAFTA that way. Rather, we

should measure it based upon whether both imports and

exports have increased (Gould, 2001; Burfisher et al.,

2001). Burfisher argued that concentrating upon trade

balances is actually "irrelevant," for what matters is

trade in the aggregate. She and her colleagues noted

that trade is affected by "other macroeconomic forces,"

not just NAFTA. For example, shortly after NAFTA was

begun, there was the peso crisis and the devaluing of

the peso. But efforts to counteract that opened trade to

Mexico even more. During the eight years since NAFTA was

Internal headings and sub-headings help guide the reader through the sections of the paper.

When the name of the source is not in the sentence, place it in the in-text citation.

begun, the U.S. experienced a booming economy, fueled in part by the growth of technology, not NAFTA per se.

The causes of the peso devaluation were many, not the least of which were restrictions on foreign capital in Mexico, including the ability to invest in Mexican stocks and banking institutions. To work against the peso devaluation, Mexico reduced restrictions on foreign capital in Mexican banks and the stock exchange. Lustig (2001) noted that, as a result of this relaxation of restrictive policies, from 1985 to 1999 Mexican exports rose over six times what they had been earlier. From an increase of $21.7 billion per year in 1985, exports rose to $136.4 billion a year. Furthermore, they were more diversified: no longer was Mexico relying upon exports of oil and minerals primarily, but now other exports began to grow. Another consequence of that, according to Lustig, was that foreign direct investments in Mexico grew almost five times what they had been, to $10 bil-lion during 1998. The Gross Domestic Product (GDP) of Mexico rose 5.4% a year since the peso was devalued.

NAFTA actually protected U.S. exports to Mexico when the peso was devalued, for, as Burfisher noted, NAFTA prevented Mexico from raising tariffs against U.S. goods

(2001). And when the U.S. provided a massive loan to

Mexico to see it through its difficult economic times,

the relaxed restrictions on foreign investment in Mexico

and the continued opportunities to trade with the U.S.

led to a recovery. In a relatively short time, Mexico

repaid its debt to the U.S., something few other coun-

tries have ever done.

Recent summary studies by two economists, Lustig

(2001) and Burfisher (2001), summarized the growth

that has occurred in both the U.S. and Mexico since

NAFTA was implemented. Lustig reports that Mexican

exports to the U.S. rose from $43 billion in 1993, the

year before NAFTA began, to $109 billion in 1999. Its

share of total U.S. imports rose from 6.9% to 10.7%.

On the U.S. side, exports to Mexico more than doubled

during this same period, rising to $105 billion in

1999. Fourteen percent of U.S. exports go to Mexico,

making it second only to Canada in the nations that

receive our exports. Agriculture in the United States

has benefited greatly from NAFTA, according to Bur-

fisher, with other exports to NAFTA partners rising

9.5% and imports rising 13.8%. The U.S. Department of Agriculture (2001) reported that from 1992 to 2000 agricultural exports rose 19%, with exports to Canada and Mexico rising 62%. The total for that period was $7.2 billion a year more than the total for the four years prior to NAFTA. From 1999 to 2000, according to the USDA, exports to Mexico rose $916 milion, while, prior to NAFTA, U.S. agricultural exports to Mexico had actually lost market share.

So, the general conclusion of recent economic studies is that NAFTA has benefited the U.S. balance of trade, not because we export more to Mexico than we import from Mexico, but, rather, both imports and exports have risen substantially during that period. On the surface, a major difference is that the goods that each imports and exports have changed in distribution. Mexico now has a greater variety of exports to the U.S., including agricultural products and apparel, not just oil and minerals, which had been the primary exports to the U.S. in pre-NAFTA days.

There is no question, though, that Mexico's export growth rate has been greater than the export growth rate of the U.S. However, when one examines more closely what

constitutes imports and exports between the U.S. and Mex-

ico, however, the distinctions tend to blur even more,

for what has developed might be described more as a sym-

biotic relationship. For example, the U.S. delivers raw

plastic to maquiladoras in Mexico, which form the plastic

into radio and dashboard parts which are installed in

radios, tape decks, and geo-positioning devises using

American-made electronics. Those are shipped back to the

U.S., where they are installed in American cars, which

are then exported to other countries, including Mexico.

Burfisher reported that, from 1993 to 1998, U.S. imports

of automobiles increased approximately 200%, but exports

of U.S. automobiles increased approximately 1,400%, with

exports of automobile parts increasing 30%.

In general, then, the balance of trade of the U.S.

with Mexico indicates that Mexico exports more to the

U.S. than the U.S. exports to Mexico, but the overall

trade for both countries, both imports and exports, has

risen since NAFTA was implemented. Balance of trade data,

however, do not indicate whether the number of jobs in

the United States has diminished as a result of NAFTA.

> **Use the passive voice when you want the object of the action to be emphasized. Otherwise, avoid it.**

The Issue of Jobs[1]

Jobs in the United States

Just as those who study the balance of trade issues

arrive at different conclusions based upon how they con-

ceptualize economic impact, so the issue of job loss

also depends upon how one conceptualizes it. For exam-

ple, Ensign (1997) reported that, by 1997, 394,835

jobs had been lost in the United States due to NAFTA

and wages in NAFTA-related industries had fallen by

4%. More recently, Struck (2001) summarized a report

of the Economic Policy Institute that jobs in the

states bordering Mexico declined by 135,000 from 1994

to 2001 as a result of NAFTA. The EPI study reports

[1]This discussion concentrates upon the number of jobs that have

been created and lost as a result of NAFTA. It does not consider

a variety of other issues regarding jobs within the NAFTA agree-

ments. For example, Human Rights Watch notes that it is a side

agreement of NAFTA, the North American Agreement on Labor Coop-

eration (NAALC), that is supposed to address many aspects of

worker rights, such as safety issues, child labor, and the right

to strike, but that very few cases have led to any actual

changes (2001). Wallach notes that 90% of the companies that had

promised to increase U.S. jobs have failed to deliver on those

promises (1998).

Footnotes should be used to provide background information that is not directly related to the discussion.

that California lost 82,354 jobs, Texas 41,000 jobs,

and New Mexico 2,970 jobs. During this same period,

over 766,030 jobs were lost across the nation, not

counting jobs in the wholesale, retail, and advertising

fields, which are difficult to tally. Those data appear

to confirm the fears of those who warned about jobs

disappearing in the United States and reappearing in

Mexico where wages and worker protections are substan-

tially lower.

Using data from the NAFTA Trade Adjustment Assis-

tance Program (TAA), Burfisher (2001) confirmed that

jobs have been lost in the United States following the

implementation of NAFTA. The TAA was designed to

retrain workers whose jobs had been lost as a result of

NAFTA. Hinojosa et al. (2000) reported that, by July

1999, 238,051 workers were certified as qualifying for

TAA training, or about 3,662 per month. Counterbalanc-

ing the fact that over 37,000 per year had lost their

jobs as a result of the work moving to Mexico, the U.S.

was creating approximately 200,000 new jobs per month

since NAFTA began, although most of those jobs were

skilled positions that the unskilled or semi-skilled

workers who lost their jobs could not fill. Gould

(1998) argues that it is not trade per se that leads to

these job losses, but, rather, the influences of busi-

ness cycles, and he notes that, from 1994-1996, immedi-

ately after NAFTA began, U.S. employment increased by

3.6 million.

Burfisher (2001) reported on a study by the Interna-

tional Trade Commission in 1997 that indicated that, of

120 manufacturing sectors in the United States, 7 had

been negatively impacted by NAFTA, 4 were positively

impacted, and the rest showed little influence from

NAFTA. Whalen (2001) reported that, since 1995, the U.S.

Labor Department had certified 316,000 jobs as either

threatened or lost due to NAFTA. And while about 20,000

new jobs were being added each month to the U.S. economy

during this period, only about 100,000 of these were new

jobs related to NAFTA trade. Citing data from the U.S.

Department of Agriculture, Burfisher observed that rural

employment, rising only 0.07% since NAFTA was imple-

mented, had essentially no improvement at all.

The Bureau of Labor Statistics reports that unemploy-

ment in the United States was 7.5% before NAFTA, while

it is 4.5% now.[2] Following the start of NAFTA, the U.S.

textile and apparel industry was particularly hard-hit.

Nevertheless, according to Burfisher (2001), from 1980

to 1990, prior to NAFTA, those industries had gone from

1.3 million jobs to 824,000 jobs. In other words, jobs

were being lost prior to NAFTA. Since NAFTA, interest-

ingly, textile production in the United States has actu-

ally risen, even though jobs have decreased. And textile

imports are up. What is happening? The answer is that

importation and exportation within this industry are

closely interwoven, as was illustrated earlier with the

automobile industry. Two-thirds of the content of tex-

tiles imported from Mexico had originally been exported

to Mexico from the U.S. So, in the U.S., agricultural

and industrial producers of fibers had benefited from

NAFTA. Textile producers in Mexico had benefited. Work-

ers who made apparel in the U.S. had lost.

[2]This research report was prepared with sources that were compiled before the terrorist attack on the World Trade Towers and
the Pentagon on September 11, 2001. Unemployment and other economic data may have changed since then, but if it has, it is not
the result of NAFTA.

While the Economic Policy Institute recognized that, overall, employment in the United States has increased since NAFTA was implemented, it also pointed out that the rise has not been directly related to NAFTA and has, in their words, "obscured" the real impact of NAFTA. Furthermore, they caution:

> Unemployment, however, began to rise early in 2001, and, if job growth dries up in the near future, the underlying problems caused by U.S. trade patterns will become much more apparent, especially in the manufacturing sector. The U.S. manufacturing sector has already lost 759,000 jobs since April 1998.
>
> . . . If, as expected, U.S. trade deficits continue to rise with Mexico and Canada while job creation slows, then the job losses suffered by U.S. workers will be much larger and more apparent than if U.S. NAFTA trade were balanced or in surplus (Scott, 2001).

Jobs in Mexico

The evidence is that Mexican exports to the U.S. have increased since NAFTA began. Does the evidence indicate that jobs also increased in Mexico as a result of NAFTA?

Double-space throughout the paper, including block quotes.

Indent block quotations 5 spaces from the left margin.

Whalen (2001) reported that *maquiladoras*, the industries owned by U.S. firms inside Mexico and mostly along the border with the U.S., had created 800,000 jobs. Furthermore, he indicates that there have been 3.5 million new jobs in Mexico since August 1995, of which one-half can be attributed to the influence of NAFTA. Lustig (2001) explained how that job growth has occurred by noting that over 11,000 businesses from the U.S. have invested approximately $35.1 billion in Mexico. Job growth in Mexico has been double that of the growth of the overall Mexican economy, with one-fourth of those jobs in those areas that U.S. businesses have invested in. When U.S. businesses invest in companies in Mexico, those companies, in turn, have more access to credit and therefore more ability to grow.

Nevertheless, Lustig also pointed out that about 20 million Mexicans live below the Mexican poverty level, which is $2.00 per day. Those industries that have been most hard-hit have been agriculture and mining, in part because the trade tariffs that once protected them were eliminated or are being phased out under NAFTA. Poverty in southeastern Mexico is five times more than poverty in northern Mexico, near the border, and forty times

that of Mexico City. Lustig reported that, between 1994

and 1996, poverty rose 19% in Mexico. *Nation* magazine

recently cited Richard Mead, a fellow at the Council on

Foreign Relations, as saying that real wages in Mexico

are now 26% below what they were in 1981.

So, while the overall economy of Mexico has grown as

a result of the benefits of NAFTA, that growth has been

limited mainly to those industries with large invest-

ments by U.S. firms and those sectors that have been

able to increase their imports to the U.S. Most of Mex-

ico remains poor and most Mexicans unemployed. As a

result, illegal immigration to the U.S. continues,

despite attempts by the U.S. government to close the

border. One estimate (Thompson, 2001) placed the number

of illegal immigrants into the U.S. at 3.5 million.

The Issue of Illegal Immigration

Everyone agrees that the continuing illegal immigration

of Mexicans into the United States is because there is

not enough work, especially work that allows the people

to live at a barely comfortable level, for the vast

majority of Mexicans. Politicians are divided over the solution, ranging from those who would close the border and send every illegal immigrant back to Mexico to those who would find a way to allow every Mexican who wants to work in the United States to stay here.

The arguments against illegal immigration consider a wide variety of negative consequences: the schools must find a way to educate the children of illegal immigrants, putting a strain upon their resources. Health services and social services must deal with the human problems that arise among the poor, with those numbers increasing as a result of illegal immigration. Fear that illegal immigrants take jobs away from U.S. citizens continues, but the counterargument is that these are jobs that most Americans do not want to take. Some refer to them as "essential workers."

The American Immigration Lawyers Association (2001) defines "essential workers" as those whom the U.S. needs to keep the economy growing. They work in the hospitality industry, cleaning rooms in hotels and providing janitorial services to businesses and other institutions. They work in fast-food restaurants. And, of course, they are among the migrant workers who weed and pick crops, allowing produce prices to remain low.

AILA argued that we should spend less effort and money trying to police our borders and create a visa program that would allow Mexicans to work in the U.S. legally. This is essentially what President Vicente Fox has asked the U.S. to do. AILA claimed that the H2B visa program cannot address our needs (2001). The H2B visa is designed for temporary workers, but it allows no more than 5,000 temporary workers a year and applying for the visa requires maneuvering a bureaucratic tangle. Instead, AILA called for a new visa program, a "guest worker visa," similar to the H1B visa, which is designed for workers with highly needed skills.

In short, the proposals that guest worker visas be created in large numbers recognizes that no amount of effort or money has been able to stem ongoing illegal immigration. When the Immigration and Naturalization Service strengthened the numbers of immigration officers along the Mexican-U.S. border, illegal immigrants crossed far away from the more heavily populated areas where the agents were stationed. They crossed into the deserts and the mountains, and many have died trying to make that crossing. But providing guest worker visas does not address the underlying cause of illegal immigration: unemployment in Mexico.

Proposals to reduce unemployment in Mexico range from better education to more supportive social and economic services to increased investments in Mexican businesses. The Progresa project is a program to supplement the income of workers in high poverty, low education populations so that the general level of education (literacy) will increase (Lustig, 2001). In exchange for a government supplement, parents must regularly take their children to health centers for check-ups. In addition, the families receive an educational supplement to help them send their children to school up until the third grade. Since Progresa was begun, the percentage of Mexican children going on to their secondary schools has increased 17%.

The Padrino project is a program designed to encourage Mexicans living in the United States to invest their money in business at home (Smith, 2001). For every one dollar or peso invested at home, the local community, the state, and the federal government of Mexico each

match it with another dollar or peso. Smith also

reported a $2 million project of the InterAmerican

Development Bank that is sponsoring 40 small businesses

in several cities of Mexico. Professor Garcia Zamora of

the Autonomous University of Zacatecas believes that if

some of the money[3] that is spent on trying to prevent

illegal immigration into Mexico were to be spent on proj-

ects such as the Padrino project, the result would be to

diminish illegal immigration more.

The case of Andres Bermudez has been reported as an

example of what can happen when Mexicans in the U.S.

invest in businesses back home (Smith, 2001). Bermudez

came to the U.S. illegally in the trunk of a car and

later took advantage of an amnesty program that the U.S.

offered illegal Mexicans. He grew his wealth in the

United States and then returned home to Zacatecas where

he began a tomato packing industry to ship tomatoes back

to the U.S. His business has employed many workers in

Zacatecas. Recently he was elected mayor in his home

[3]President Bush recently asked for $5.5 billion for the fiscal
year 2002 budget of the Immigration and Naturalization Service
(Immigration and Naturalization Service, 2001).

town and is promoting more Mexican investment in
businesses.

The Hinojosa study (2000) of Home Town Associations
(HTAs) in California reported on how they help build the
economies of the communities back home. By raising money
through parties, food sales, and other events, they have
paid for roads back home, schools, and social services.
For example, Smith (2001) reported that there are an
estimated 600,000 to 1 million Zacatecans living in the
United States. They send back to Mexico approximately
$1 million a day to help their families. Unfortunately,
95% of these "remittances" go to pay for basic needs,
such as food and clothing, so little is left to build
businesses. But the concept of Mexicans living in the
United States and investing in entrepreneurial efforts
in their home towns is a good one. Lustig (2001) argues
that Mexican banks are still not flexible enough in
their lending policies and need to take more risks to
support small businesses.

These proposals for more investment in Mexico by U.S.
businesses and Mexicans living in the United States are
similar to the "lend-lease" program that the U.S. cre-

ated to help rebuild Europe after World War II. Building businesses and work opportunities in Mexico may be the only sure solution to the illegal immigration problem in the United States. In fact, Mead (*The Nation*, 2001) argued that by investing in the basic infrastructure in Mexico, as well as reforming currency policies, legal policies, and Medicare availability for Mexican workers, we "would create millions of Mexican jobs, raise wages and living standards and create new jobs in the U.S. and Canada." If Mexicans could remain at home to work for decent wages, they would not want to take the risks they now take to enter the U.S. illegally.

Conclusions

On the issue of the balance of trade, it appears that whether one believes NAFTA has been beneficial to the U.S. depends upon how one calculates the import and export balances. Those economists who believe that you answer that question by totaling the exports of the U.S. to Mexico and then subtracting the imports from Mexico to the U.S. conclude that NAFTA has not benefited our balance of trade. But those economists who believe that one should look at the aggregate of both imports and

exports and determine whether those have increased as a
result of NAFTA conclude differently. They conclude that
our exports have increased substantially, even though
Mexican imports to the U.S have increased more.

On the issue of whether jobs have been lost to Mexico, the answer is again defined differently depending
upon what jobs one looks at and whether total jobs are
considered as well. There is no question that some
industrial sectors, such as the clothing or apparel
industry, have lost jobs. But those losses have been
offset by an overall increase in jobs in the United
States since NAFTA began. Some who have studied this
phenomenon note that jobs in the apparel industry were
declining before NAFTA, and NAFTA only sped up the
decline. They also note that the apparel industry in the
United States has actually grown since NAFTA, while jobs
have declined. The reasons include such matters as the
growth of technology in the industry, and an overall
growth in the U.S. economy across the board during this
time. Some have cautioned against single causes for what
are in fact complex phenomena, noting that world economic trends, or "macroeconomic trends," also influenced

what happened to the U.S. economy since NAFTA. NAFTA alone cannot be credited with job losses in certain sectors, and NAFTA alone cannot be credited with overall job growth and declining unemployment in the United States since NAFTA was implemented.

And finally the issue of illegal immigration enters into any evaluation of the effectiveness of NAFTA. If NAFTA has benefited the Mexican economy, why do so many Mexicans enter the U.S. illegally? And do they take jobs away from U.S. workers? The answer appears to be that the entire Mexican economy has not benefited from NAFTA. The poorest people and the poorest sections of Mexico still do not have adequate work, even while the upper classes of Mexico and some areas have increased their earnings. Furthermore, the evidence seems to indicate that those illegal immigrants take jobs that most Americans do not want to take and thus do not cause more Americans to be unemployed. Nevertheless, if we are concerned about the impact of illegal immigration upon our social service, health, and educational institutions, it appears that NAFTA has so far not solved the problem of illegal immigration.

If Emiliano Zapata were alive today, his rallying cry would not be "¡Tierra o muerte!" ("Land or death!"). It would be "Better jobs or more migration problems!" The demographic and economic studies of Mexican immigration reflect the need for a stronger Mexican economy if illegal immigration is to be curtailed. Reports have included the following estimates: that as many as or more than 300,000 illegal immigrants enter the U.S. each year from Mexico, that the family wages of the illegal immigrants are typically in the $30,000 range or slightly above, that they send back to Mexico as much as $3 billion a year, that most of the illegal immigrants return to Mexico after being here a little over a year, and that the U.S. plans to spend $5.5 billion a year to control immigration. In short, the cost of restricting immigration is enormous.

Therefore, the United States needs to rethink its economic policies toward Mexico so that they strengthen Mexican capacity to offer jobs at decent wages. One proposal that appears to be a reasonable compromise is to provide more long-term visas for "essential workers," workers in the low wage industries. That can be an immediate step, but it does not address the underlying cause for the current rate of illegal immigration. Among many potential solutions, the proposal that our economic plan be a Mexican "lend-lease," similar to our efforts to help Europe rebuild after World War II, appears to be a promising way for us to slow or even hope to stop illegal immigration. If Mexico and the United States also provide incentives for Mexicans living in the United States and for companies in the United States to invest in Mexico, that, too, can help keep Mexican workers in Mexico. *Maquiladoras* demonstrate that Mexicans will flock to jobs if they are available, but *maquiladoras* cannot be the mainstay of the Mexican economy. When the U.S. provides substantial business aid to Mexico and when Mexico continues to reduce its regulation of foreign businesses, then there will be long-term benefits to both the U.S. and Mexico, resulting in a reduction in the perceived "threat" to our southern border and to jobs for American workers.

NAFTA 27

References

American Immigration Lawyers Association. (2001). Es-

sential workers keep the economy growing. *AILA*

Infonet, Doc. No. 39IP1005. Retrieved 10 September

2001 from the World Wide Web: http://www.aila.org/

newsroom/391IP1005.html

Beyond NAFTA: A forum--toward a North American economic

community (North American Free Trade Agreement. *The*

Nation, 272 (21), 19.

Burfisher, M. E., Robinson, S., & Thierfelder, K.

(2001). The impact of NAFTA on the United States.

Journal of Economic Perspectives, 15(1), 125-144.

DeLong, J. B. (2001). A symposium on the North American

economy. *Journal of Economic Perspectives, 15*(1),

81-83.

Ensign, D. (1997). NAFTA: Two sides of the coin. *Spec-*

trum: The Journal of State Government, 70(4), 1-4.

Fitzgerald, S. J. (2001, August 1). The effects of NAFTA

on exports, jobs, and the environment. *The Heritage*

Foundation Backgrounder, No. 1462. Retrieved 10

September 2001 from the World Wide Web: http://www.

heritage.org/library/backgrounder/bg1462.html

Double space, hanging indent

Article titles: no caps except first word and proper nouns.

Divide URLs so that they continue to the end of lines.

Fuentes, C. (2001, September 11). Untitled Speech at

    Distinguished Lecture Series. [Tape Recording].

    Brownsville: University of Texas at Brownsville and

    Texas Southmost College.

Gibbs, N. (2001). The new frontier/la nueva frontera.

    Time.com. June 11. Retrieved 1 September 2001 from

    the World Wide Web: http://www.time.com/time/covers/

    1101010611/opener2.html

Gould, D. M. (1998). Has NAFTA changed North American

    trade? *Economic Review, First Quarter,* 12-13.

Hinojosa-Ojeda, R., Runsten, D., DePaolis, F. & Kamel,

    N. (2000). The U.S. employment impacts of North

    American integration after NAFTA: A partial equi-

    librium approach. North American Integration and

    Development Center, School of Public Policy and

    Social Research, UCLA. Retrieved 1 September 2001

    from World Wide Web: http://naid.sppsr.ucla.edu/

    pubs&news/nafta2000.html

Lustig, N. (2001). Life is not easy: Mexico's quest for

    stability and growth. *Journal of Economic Perspec-*

    tives, 15(1), 85-106.

NAFTA 29

Scott, R. E. (2001). NAFTA's hidden costs. *EPI Briefing Paper, April.* Retrieved 7 September 2001 from the World Wide Web: http://www.epinet.org/ briefingpapers/nafta01/us.html

Smith, J. F. (2001, August 20). Job programs aim to curb migrant flow. *Los Angeles Times Online.* Retrieved 6 September 2001 from the World Wide Web: http://www. latimes.com/news/nationworld/world/la-082001jobs. story

Struck, M. (2001, April 11). Study says U.S.-Mexican border states lost nearly 135,000 jobs to NAFTA. *States News Service.* Retrieved 6 Sept 2001 from InfoTrac Web: Expanded Academic ASAP Electronic Collection: A73238642: http://web2.infotrac. galegroup.com/tw/infomark/558/782/5487848w2/purl= rc1_EAIM_0_A73238642

Thompson, G. (2001, September 6). Mexico president urges U.S. to act soon on migrants. *The New York Times on the Web.* Retrieved 7 September 2001 from the World Wide Web: http://search.nytimes.com/2001/09/06/ international/americas/06PREX.html

Trading away rights: The unfulfilled promise of NAFTA's

labor side agreement. (2001). *Human Rights Watch,*

13(2B). Retrieved 5 September 2001 from the World

Wide Web: http://www.hrw.org/reports/2001/nafta

U.S. Department of Agriculture. (2001, July). Fact

sheet: North American Free Trade Agreement.

FASonline. Retrieved 8 September 2001 from the

World Wide Web: http://ffas.usda.gov/info/

factsheets/nafta.html

U.S. Immigration and Naturalization Service. (2001, May

17). Testimony of acting Commissioner Kevin D.

Rooney Immigration and Naturalization Service (INS)

before the Committee on Appropriations Subcommittee

on Commerce, Justice, State, and the Judiciary

United States Senate concerning the President's

FY2002 budget request. Retrieved 10 September 2001

from the World Wide Web: http://www.ins.usdoj.gov/

graphics/aboutins/congress/testimonies/2001/5_17_

01.pdf

Wallach, L. (1998). NAFTA's broken promises: Failure to

    create U.S. jobs. *Public Citizen.* Retrieved 10 Sep-

    tember 2001 from the World Wide Web: http://www.

    Citizen.org/pctrade/nafta/brokenpr.html

Whalen, C. J., Magnussen, P., & Smith, G. (2001, July

    9). NAFTA's score card: So far, so good. *Business*

    Week, 54.

Appendix D:
Partial Sample Research Paper—Modern Language Association Style

MODEL TITLE PAGE

The Role of NAFTA in Stopping Illegal

Mexican Immigration

First and Last Name

MLA-style papers do not require a title page. Should your instructor request a title page, here is an example of a title page showing the necessary information.

Course Number, Section Number

Professor's Name

Day Month Year

Double space personal and course information at the top left of your paper.

Include the title on the first page.

Double space, including long quotes, which are block indented without quotation marks.

The header includes the writer's last name and page number beginning with the first page of text.

Note: This quote is from the Internet and does not have a page number.

Since this was a speech without a printed version, the speaker's name is all that is needed within the text.

Last Name 1

Your Name

Your Professor's Name

Your Course

Day Month Year

The Role of NAFTA in Stopping

Illegal Mexican Immigration

The Mexican-United States border has become so important that *Time* magazine made it the cover story, describing the border as "a barbed-wire paradox, half pried open, half bolted closed" (Gibbs). Every day, family members visit their relatives on both sides of the border, students cross over to go to the local university, and some Mexicans are prevented from crossing because they do not have the proper identification or visas. Passions always seem to flare whenever people debate whether our economic relations with Mexico should be stronger or not. Inevitably, people cite the massive number of illegal immigrants who cross the border every day, and some ask, "If NAFTA (North American Free Trade Agreement) is so good, why are there so many illegal Mexicans in this country?" The answer to this question is revealed through the interrelationships of jobs, economies, and cultures.

Speaking in Brownsville, Texas, novelist Carlos Fuentes argued that "Cultures perish in isolation; cultures thrive in the presence of others" (Fuentes). He was, in fact, arguing the benefits of NAFTA and the need to maintain close ties between the United States and Mexico. He believes that both nations have and will continue to derive many benefits from being close to one

The format shown in this paper is reflective of MLA documentation style, but has been modified to accommodate space limitations. All MLA student papers are double-spaced throughout, including the works cited list on p. 235.

Last Name 2

another, whether it be in the arts, in business, or in
the personal relations of humans to humans.

Whenever the topic of illegal immigration arises,
passions tend to be strong on all sides of the issue.
Some, such as the Economic Policy Institute, point out
that many jobs have been lost in the United States as
a direct result of NAFTA, as many as 135,000 in the
border states alone since NAFTA was implemented
(Struck). Others argue that unemployment in the United
States actually dropped during that period to the lowest
point in 30 years because the economy was growing, in
part from the stimulus of NAFTA (American Immigration
Lawyers Association). Some who have studied the issue of
job loss related to NAFTA note that, while about 3,662
jobs per month have been certified as lost due to the
effects of NAFTA, about 200,000 new jobs per month have
been created (Burfisher 129). Burfisher goes on to note
that a study by the International Trade Commission found
that, of 120 manufacturing sectors in the United States,
only 7 lost substantial jobs because of NAFTA's
attracting those jobs to Mexico (130).

We need to look at the impact of NAFTA upon jobs in
Mexico as well if we are going to understand why there
is so much illegal immigration of Mexican workers to
the United States. Whalen reports that *maquiladoras*, the
industries owned by U.S. firms inside Mexico and mostly
along the border with the U.S., had created 800,000
jobs for Mexican workers. Furthermore, he indicates that
there have been 3.5 million new jobs in Mexico since
August 1995, of which one-half can be attributed to

> **Use the present tense when citing sources.**

> **In-text citations include the author's name and the page number.**

Last Name 3

the influence of NAFTA (54). Lustig explains how that
job growth has occurred by noting that over 11,000
businesses from the United States have invested
approximately $35.1 billion in Mexico and notes that
job growth in Mexico doubled that of overall economic
growth in Mexico (98).

> When the author's name appears in the sentence, only the page citation appears.

Last Name 4

Works Cited

American Immigration Lawyers Association. "Essential

    workers keep the economy growing." <u>AILA Infonet</u>.

    19 June 2001. 12 Sept. 2001 <http://www.aila.org/

    newsroom/391IP1005.html>.

"Beyond NAFTA: A Forum—Toward a North American Economic

    Community (North American Free Trade Agreement."

    <u>The Nation</u>, May 28, 2001: 19.

Burfisher, Mary E., Sherman Robinson, and Karen

    Thierfelder. "The Impact of NAFTA on the United

    States." <u>Journal of Economic Perspectives</u> 15.1

    (2001): 125-144.

DeLong, J. Bradford. "A Symposium on the North American

    Economy." <u>Journal of Economic Perspectives</u> 15.1

    (2001): 81-83.

Ensign, David. "NAFTA: Two Sides of the Coin. *Spectrum:*

    <u>The Journal of State Government</u> 70.4 (1997): 1-4.

Fuentes, Carlos. Untitled Speech at Distinguished

    Lecture Series. Tape Recording. Brownsville:

    University of Texas at Brownsville and Texas

    Southmost College, September 11, 2001.

Gibbs, Nancy. "The New Frontier/La Nueva Frontera."

    <u>Time.Com</u> 11 June 2001. 1 Sept. 2001 <http://

    www.time.com/time/covers/11010106/opener2.html>.

Struck, Myron. "Study Says U.S.-Mexican Border States

    Lost Nearly 135,000 Jobs to NAFTA." <u>States News

    Service</u>. 11 Apr. 2001. Infotrac Web: Expanded

    Academic ASAP. 6 Sept. 2001. <http://

    web2.infotrac.galegroup.com/tw/infomark/

    558/782/15487848w2/purl=rcl_EAIM_0_A73238642>.

Double space lines, indent 5 spaces after hanging indent.

Work Cited lists should set double space throughout.

Article titles capitalized normally.

Insert space in URL to fill out the line.

Thompson, Ginger. "Mexico President Urges U.S. to Act
Soon on Migrants." <u>The New York Times on the Web</u>.
6 Sept. 2001. 7 Sept. 2001 <http://
search.nytimes.com/2001/09/06/international/
Americas/06PREX.html>

"Trading Away Rights: The Unfulfilled Promise of NAFTA's
Labor Side Agreement." <u>Human Rights Watch</u>. 13.2B. 5
Sept. 2001. <http://www.hrw.org/reports/2001/nafta>

Appendix E:
Sample Research
Paper—Council
of Science
Educator's Style

The following sample is a field study report done in partial fulfillment of the class requirements.

Study on the Polymorphism of Flower

Color of the *Opuntia engelmannii*

in South Texas

Genetics lab 3403.91

Presented to Dr. Alison Abell

By

Eliza Carrasco

Jennifer Carrillo

Marcus Ruiz

Christian Torres

5/7/01

The University of Texas at Brownsville

Carrasco 1

Abstract

We studied the preference of pollinators for flower colors in the prickly pear cactus, *Opuntia engelmannii.* In South Texas, three different colors are present: peach, pink, and yellow. The study was divided into two parts. First, we did a random inspection of fifty flowers from each of the three colors. The numbers of pollinators present in each flower was recorded. Second, we randomly selected three flowers, one of each color, and observed for fifteen minutes. During this time, we recorded the number of pollination visits and the duration of each visit. For the census of multiple flowers, we found that the flying insects preferred the yellow flowers over the peach and pink flowers. However, the crawling insects showed no preference according to flower color. For the observations of individual flowers, we found no significant effect on flower color on the number or duration of pollinator visits.

Note: The abstract should summarize the study briefly and concisely.

Abstracto:

Estuvimos estudiando la preferencia de insectos por el color de las flores del nopal, *Opuntia engelmannii*. En el sur de Tejas, hay tres colores presentes: durazno, rosádo, y amarillo. El estudio fue dividido en dos partes. La primera parte fué inspeccionar cincuenta flores al azar de cada uno de los tres colores. Luego seleccionamos tres flores, una de cada color y las observamos por quince minutos. Durante este tiempo, apuntamos el numero de insectos que visitaron cada flor y el tiempo que duraron en cada visita. Descubrimos que en al parte que tomamos el censo de flores, los insectos voladores prefirieron las flores amarillas sobre las flores rosadas y color durazno. Los insectos ambulantes no tuvieron preferencia por ninguno de los tres colores de flores. Nuestras observaciones individuales no indicaron una diferencia significativa entre el color de la flor y el número y duración de las visitas.

Note: These students provided a translation of the abstract in Spanish because their audience is on the border of Mexico. This is not a standard practice.

Carrasco 3

Introduction

Opuntia engelmannii are among the most common cactus.
They are characterized by modified axillary buds,
spines, flowers, a thick waxy cuticle, fruits, and shallow, wide spreading roots. *Opuntia engelmannii* are pho-
tosynthetic year round, but their growth diminishes when
there is lack of water. Their pads are able to absorb
large quantities of water and store it for when in need.
Opuntia engelmannii provide food, water, and even shel-
ter for certain animal species. About thirteen to twenty
species of *Opuntia engelmannii* can be found in Texas.

A single species of *Opuntia engelmannii* predominates
in south Texas. They usually bloom in April, but their
blooming season can vary from March to June. Its fruit
is a reddish-purple color and juicy. Their flowers vary
in color and shades. The most common are yellow to
yellow-orange flowers, but other shades and colors exist
(Royo 1997). ◄─────────────────

In-text citation includes author and date if the author is not mentioned in the text. No comma between the name and date.

We were interested in the polymorphism of flower
color in *Opuntia engelmannii*. We had seen yellow, pink,
and peach flowers and decided to investigate whether
they differ in their ability to attract pollinators.

Polymorphism is common in all species. Research has suggested that color polymorphisms exist to increase an individual's survival rate and variability (Ekendahl 1998). How the different morphs are preserved in nature is not clear. However, the different environment, predators, and pollinators for a particular species influence the survival rate of the different types of morphs (Sellers and Wolfe 1997).

Experiments have suggested that genes that condition resistance phenotypes might have an impact on plant reproductive success because they might influence traits that attract pollinators (Butcher and Simms 1996). For example, in a study of bumblebee responses to different colored and scented snapdragons (*Antirrhinum: Scrophulariaceal*), the researchers found no significant difference in the preference of the bees toward different scents, but did find that bees prefer yellow flowers over white ones. Both of these flowers are in the bees' visual range. However, bees perceive yellow as green. They tend to be attracted to bright colors, in which the background plays a big role (Odell, Raguso, and Jones 1999). Green matches with most natural backgrounds and

is therefore more appealing. Flowers adapt their colors
to pollinator vision, including bees (Speisbach 1996).
Pollinators and plants follow a circular path: flowers
feed pollinators, which in turn are responsible for the
enormous variability of flowers (Jones 1995).

Bees are common pollinators of *Opuntia engelmannii*.
They are attracted to flowers with exotic shapes, patterns, and bright colorations. When we visited the field
where our study was to be held, we observed many bees
and a vast number of yellow flowers. Since yellow is
brighter than pink and peach, and yellow flowers seemed
to slightly dominate the area, we hypothesized that pollinators would prefer the yellow flowers of *Opuntia
engelmannii*.

Methods

A field about 25 minutes from Brownsville was chosen for
our study due to its abundance and diversity of *Opuntia
engelmannii*. All members of the group took turns visiting
and making observations of the *Opuntia's* flowers. All of
us visited the same place to avoid as much environmental
difference as possible. We caution that there could have
been a difference in pollinators if one flower color pre-

dominated over the other flower colors. We were unable to observe cacti located in different places.

The observations occurred between April 15, 2001, and April 21, 2001, with observations in both the AM and PM. Observers spent an average of two hours in each visit. We made our observations by trying to eliminate as much sampling errors as possible. The project was divided into two parts. The first was to observe fifty flowers chosen from each color. This gave us a total of 150 flowers per visit. The flowers observed in this section could have been any of the ones found in the field, as long as there were fifty of each color. This part did not take very long. We simply checked the flowers to see if there were pollinators inside and recorded the number and type of pollinators.

After this quick "check-up" of the flowers, each observer randomly selected three flowers, a pink, a peach, and a yellow one, to observe for 15 minutes. The observer recorded the number of insects and duration of time that the insects visited each flower. After a week of observation, we reviewed our data and performed a statistical analysis using the statistical program Systat.

Results

The correlation between flower colors in the *Opuntia*

engelmannii and its pollinators' preference seemed to be

significant among the flying insects: bees, flies, mos-

quitos, and others that were not as common. Figure 1

shows that the flyers stopped more often in the yellow

flowers (x^2=12.49, df=2, p=0.0019).

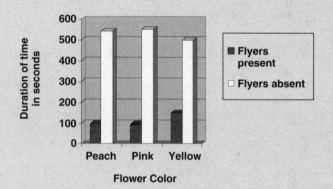

Figure 1. Amount of Time Flying Insects Spent on Each Color

Note: Figures should be both introduced and discussed in the text. The figures also should be clear to the reader.

Figure 2 shows that the number of crawling insects

visiting the pink, peach, and yellow flowers was about

the same (x^2=1.60, df=2, p=0.4488). That is, crawling

insects appeared not to prefer one flower color over

another. The crawling insects also showed no difference

in frequency and duration time of visits to any of the

different colored flowers.

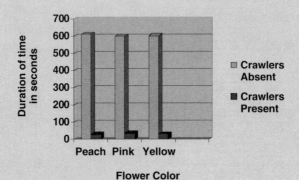

Figure 2. Amount of Time Crawling
Insects Spent on Each Color

Even though the three different colors of flowers had

a similar average number of visitors, as shown in Fig-

ure 3, the yellow flowers had a larger standard devia-

tion and range. The mean for visitors to the yellow

flowers was bigger than those for visits to the pink and

peach flowers ($F_{2,18}=0.94$, p=0.4099).

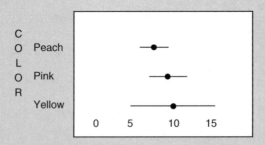

Figure 3. Range and Mean of Number
of Visitors per Color per Minute

Carrasco 9

Discussion and Conclusions

Our research was designed to determine whether different

flower colors of *Opuntia Englemannia* attracted different

insects for different periods of time and for the three

different-colored flowers. Our analyses showed a normal

distribution of insects among the three different-

colored flowers. This could have been because there was

an abundance of the three colors and of insects in the

field where we conducted our study. Enough insects were

attracted to the flowers to enable our comparisons. The

only significant difference found is the preference

shown by the flying insects, especially the bees, toward

the yellow flowers, supporting our original hypothesis

that this would be true for bees, but not the other

insects. The bees have a tendency to feel attracted to

bright colors. Peach and pink are dull in comparison to

yellow. Perhaps this was the cause of the bees and other

flying insects' obvious preference toward the yellow

flowers. The crawling insects showed no particular pref-

erence for any of the three colored flowers. Of course,

it must be taken into consideration that there are other

aspects besides flower color that affect pollination.

Result

In a longer paper, the discussion and conclusions may be separate sections.

Discussion

Result

Discussion

Result

Discussion

Carrasco 10

Conclusion Since not all of our results were significantly different, several other aspects of our study deserve attention, not because the results show no significant
difference, but because this study confined itself to a
limited number of variables.

Result Analysis of our raw data reveals no clear preference
for the time of day when insects visit the flowers.

Discussion Sometimes the insects appeared mostly in the morning,
while other times they appeared mostly in the afternoon.
In comparing the duration of time the insects spent on
the flowers to the time of day at which the data was

Conclusion collected, we found no pattern. Therefore it can be concluded that factors other than time of day must account
for our observations. Maybe the weather affects the
insects' visitation rates and times. Some might like
windy conditions, while others enjoy the hot sun. The
effect that different weather has on pollinators' behavior could be a study of its own.

Implication for future research. Our study has added to previous studies of color
polymorphism in flowers. Given the other possible vari-
ables, there are many other studies that can be done on
the *Opuntia engelmannii.* Further research is warranted.

Our study of polymorphism in flower color of *Opuntia*

engelmannii can be extended to other factors influencing

how pollinators are attracted to flowers. The age of the

flowers could be important. Young flowers might be more

appealing to insects than old flowers. The pH of the

soil or its content, the multiple nutrients that compose

it, can be a factor influencing the amount and type of

flower color present in the area.

References

Butcher M. Simms E. 1996. Pleiotropic effects of flower-color intensity on herbivore performance on *Ipomoe pupurea*. Evolution 50 (2): 957–963.

Ekendahl A. Colour polymorphic prey (*Littorina saxatlils Oliva*) and predatory effects of crab population (*Carcinus Maenas L.*). Journal of Experimental Marine Biology and Ecology 1998; 222 (1–2):239–246. In Science Direct [database on the Internet]. City? [cited 2000 Apr 1]. Available from: http://pathfinder.utb.edu:2141/Science?_ob.

Jones K. 1995. Fertility selection on a discrete floral polymorphism in *Clarkia (Onagraceae)*. Evolution 50 (1): 71–79.

Jones K. Odell E. Raguso R. 1999. Bumblebee foraging responses to variation in floral scent and color in Snapdragons (*antirrhinum: Scrophulariacea*). The American Midland Naturalist 142 (2): 257–265.

Royo A. 1997. Prickley pear cactus. Desert USA. Oct. http://www.desertusa.com/magoct97/oct_pa/du_prkpear.html. Accessed 2000 Apr. 5.

Sellers S. Wolfe L. 1997. Polymorphic floral traits in *Linaria candensis*. The American Midland Naturalist 138 (1): 134–139.

Spiessbach K. 1996. The eyes of bees. Discover 17 (9): 32.

Note: CBE/CSE Style, Name-Year System

Note: Journal, database, and date accessed all included.

Works Cited

Cox, Belinda J., Ellen R. Cowie, & James B. Petersen. "The Cloverleaf Site: Late Archaic Settlement on the Walloomsac River in Southwestern Vermont." *The Journal of Vermont Archaeology*, v. 3, 2000, pp. 17–32.

Kaufman, Sarah. Fancy Footwork. *Washington Post Online*. 1–7 July 2001. 3 July 2001 <http://www.washingtonpost.com/wp-dyn/print/sunday/bookworld/A61398-2001Jun28.html>

Wagner, Daniel A. "Literacy Futures Revisited: Five Common Problems from Industrialized and Developing Countries." In Daniel A. Wagner, ed. *The Future of Literacy in a Changing World*. Cresskill, NJ: Hampton Press, 1999, pp. 3–19.

Index

Academic honesty, 137–139
  copyright law, 138
  plagiarism, 138–139
Academic Search, 54
Alta Vista, 65–66
American Psychological Asso-
    ciation. *See* APA
Annotated bibliography, 94–96
APA style, 5, 133
  citing electronic documents,
      152–153
  internal citation, 159
  quoting, 144
  reference citation, 159–163
    electronic citation style,
        159–161
    nonelectronic citation style,
        161–163
  sample research paper, 197–229
Archives, 22
Archnet, 70
Arts and Letters Daily, 88
Authentic research, 4

Bibliographies, 49–53
Bibliography cards, 24
Bohemian Link, 182
Bookmarks, 59–61
  annotating, 103–105

creating files, 100–101
creating folders, 101–103
saving to a disk, 60–61
Boolean terms/operators, 64–65
  AND, 64
  NOT, 64
  OR, 64
  stem searches, 65

Case study, 9–13
  common components of, 10
  nonparticipant observation, 12–13
  participant observation, 11–12
Category-question technique, 33–34
CBE/CSE style, 133, 166–169
  internal citation, 166
    citation–sequence system, 166
    name–year system, 166
  sample research paper, 237–250
  works cited or reference citation,
      167–169
    electronic citation style, 167
    nonelectronic citation style,
        168–169
Chicago Manual of Style, 6. *See also*
    CMS
Chronicon, 88
Cinahl, 54
Citation problems, 174–175

CMS style, 5, 93, 133, 169–173
  bibliography, 171–173
    electronic citation style,
      171–172
    nonelectronic citation style,
      172–173
  internal citation, 169–171
    humanities style, 169–170
    scientific style or author–date
      system, 171
CNET's Builder.com, 184
Collaborative course projects,
  creating, 183
Columbia Guide to Online Style.
  See COS
Content criteria, 83–84
Copy-and-paste method, 113
Copyright law, 138, 175
  as applies to Web sources, 175
  Copyright and Fair Use website,
    177
  fair use guidelines, 175
COS electronic citation style,
  163–164
    databases and CD-ROMs,
      164
    general style, 163–164
Coverage, 85
Currency, 84

Dewey Decimal System, 21, 49
Dogpile, 66, 68
Draft files
  computer organization for,
    112–115
  many files, writing in,
    114–115
  one file, writing in, 113–114

Earth Resource System, 70
EBSCO, 88
Education Resources Information
  Clearinghouse (ERIC), 22
Electronic bibliography cards,
  109–110
  template for, 109–110

Electronic note cards, 106–109
  master template file for, 107–108
Electronic style guidelines for MLA,
  APA, COS, general, 165
Electronic workspace, setting up,
  105–112
  electronic bibliography cards,
    109–110
  electronic note cards, 106–109
  email, using and organizing,
    110–112
  folders, 105–106
Email, 75–76
  attaching documents to messages,
    76
Excite, 66
Experimental research, 6–8
  standard organization of, 6–8
Expert sources, interviewing, 74–80
  email, 75–76
  mailing lists, 76–78
  newspaper reports and magazine
    articles, identifying
    sources through, 79–80
  online communities, exploring, 79
E-zine or anthology, creating,
  182–183

Fast, 66
Field research, 41–47
  interviews, 42–43
  observation, 45–47
  surveys, 43–45
Field studies or observational
  research, 8–9
Figures, preparing, 135–136
  other considerations, 136
File transfer protocol (ftp), 58
First draft, creating, 122–133
  conclusion appropriate for aca-
    demic field, writing,
    125–129
  case study, 129
  nonscientific, 126–128
  science and social science,
    128–129

introduction, writing, 130–133
  case studies, 133
  nonscientific, 130–132
  science and social science, 132
  notes, writing from, 124–125
  outline, using, 124
Flaming, 78
Focus group, 42
Forums, 75

Geocities, 184
Gettingit, 182
Google, 67
Gopher, 58
Government and legal documents,
  sources for, 53
Graphic Image Format (GIF), 191
Graphics/pictures, adding to web-
  site, 190–191

Hawthorne effect, 13
Homestead, 184
HotBot, 67
HTML, basics of, 188–190
  tags, table of, 189
Hypertext essay, creating, 180–182
Hypertext transfer protocol
  (http), 58

Infomine, 67
Infotrac, 54
Interlibrary loan, 22
Interviews, 42–43
Issue, developing from topic, 32

Joint Photographic Experts Group
  (JPEG), 191

Kairos, 88
Katharsis, 182
Keyword searching, 54

Lawcrawler, 69
Lexis Nexis Academic Universe, 54
Library, using, 21–22
  archives, 22

interlibrary loan, 22
microforms section, 22
reference desk, 21
reference section, 21–22
stacks, 21
Library of Alexandria (Bibliotheca
  Alexandrina), 2
Library of Congress cataloging
  system, 21, 49
Library of Congress Subject Headings,
  55–56
Library research paper, 5–6
  MLA style, elements of, 5–6
Library resources, 49–53
  finding books, 49
  general reference materials, 49–50
  key reference materials, 50–53
LibWeb, 49
LISTPROC, 76
LISTSERV, 76
Literary database, 26
Lycos, 67

Magazines and journals, 87–88
Mailing lists (email lists), 76–78
  flaming, 78
  LISTPROC, 76
  LISTSERV, 76
  netiquette for, 78
  subscribing to, 77–78
*Manual for Writers of Term Papers,
  Theses, and Dissertations,
  A*, 6
Metacrawlers, 68–69
  Dogpile, 68
  Metacrawler, 68
  qbSearch, 69
  Search.com, 69
  TeRespondo, 69
  Vivisimo, 69
Microforms section, 22
MLA style, 5–6, 93, 133
  citing electronic documents,
    152–153
  internal citation, 154
  paraphrasing, example of, 142

MLA style (*cont.*)
　partial sample research paper, 230–236
　quoting, 144
　summarizing, example of, 140
　works cited, 154–158
　　electronic citation style, 154–157
　　nonelectronic citation style, 157–158
Modern Language Association. *See* MLA
Monthly Catalog of United States Government Publications, 26
Multimedia research paper variation, 13–14
　examples on websites, 14

Netiquette, 78
Newsgroups, 74–75
Newspaper reports/magazine articles, using to find sources, 79–80
Northern Light, 68
NOT, 64
Note taking, 106–109
　paraphrasing, quoting noted on cards, 143

Observation, 45–47
OCLC WorldCat, 49
Online Community Report, 79
Online databases
　Academic Search, 54
　Cinahl, 54
　Infotrac, 54
　Lexis Nexis Academic Universe, 54
　locating journals and magazines, steps for, 53
　Proquest, 54
　PsychINFO, 54
　searching, 53–54
Online forums and journals, submitting to, 178
Online journals, 88

Open-ended questions, 44
OR, 64

Paraphrasing, 141–143
Periodical indexes, 22
Plagiarism, 138–139
PowerPoint presentation, creating, 193–196
Précis, 93–94
Preparing to write, organizational process, 99–117
　bookmarks, organizing, 100–105
　electronic workspace, setting, 105–112
　summary of, 115–116
　using computer to organize, 112–115
Primary sources, quoting, 145–146
Print indexes, 49–53
ProfNet, 79
Project Muse, 88
Proquest, 54
Psychcrawler, 70
PsychINFO, 54
Public Access Catalogues, 3, 25

qbSearch, 69
Quoting, 143–146
　APA style and, 144
　MLA style and, 144
　primary sources, 145–146

Reference desk, 21
Reference section, 21–22
Relevance, 85–86
Research journal/research log, 22–25
Research methods, developing, 36–38
Research paper and information age, 1–16
　changes in process, 2–3
　expectations of professors, 3–4
　types of research reports, 4–16
　　case study, 9–13
　　experimental research, 6–8

field studies/observational research, 8–9
  library research paper, 5–6
  multimedia research paper variation, 13–14
Research plans, 31–47
  field research, 41–47
    interviews, 42–43
    observation, 45–47
    surveys, 43–45
  implementing, 40–41
  issue, developing from topic, 32
  preliminary thesis statement, developing, 38–40
  research methods, developing, 36–38
  research questions
    developing, 33–34
    narrowing, 35
  template for, 38
Research questions, developing, 33, 35
  category-question technique, 33–34
Revising paper, 147–149
Rhetorical stance, 146–147
RSNA Electronic Journal, 88

Scientific Style and Format: The CBE Manual for Authors, Editors, and Publishers, 7. *See also* CBE/CSE
Search.com, 69
Search engines, 29, 61–63, 65–68
  Alta Vista, 65–66
  Dogpile, 66
  Excite, 66
  Fast, 66
  Google, 67
  HotBot, 67
  Infomine, 67
  Lycos, 67
  Northern Light, 68
  WebCrawler, 68
Searchlight, 48
Search strategies, 73–74

Source of publication, 84–85
Sources, documenting, 151–176
  APA style, 159–163
    internal citation, 159
    reference citation, 159–163
  CBE/CSE style, 166–169
    internal citation, 166
    works cited or reference citation, 167–169
  citation problems, 174–175
  CMS style, 169–174
    bibliography, 171–173
    internal citation, 169–171
  Columbia Guide to Online Style, 163–165
    databases and CD-ROMs, citations of, 164
    general style, 163–164
  copyright considerations, 175
  electronic documents, guidelines for citing, 152–153
  general electronic style guidelines, 165
  MLA style, 154–158
    internal citation, 154
    works cited, 154–158
Sources, evaluating, 82–98
  annotated bibliography, 94
  critical or evaluative bibliography, 94–96
  drafting phase, evaluation at, 89–90
  information evaluation in early stages of project, 83–86
    content criteria, 83–84
    coverage, 85
    currency, 84
    relevance, 85–86
    source of publication, 84–85
  interviews, email communications, mailing list postings, newsgroup postings, 96–97
  journal or magazine, appropriateness of, 87–88

Sources, evaluating (*cont.*)
    kinds of sources to explore,
        determining, 90–93
    précis, 93–94
    varied sources, importance of,
        88–89
Sources, finding, 48–81
    field research and interviewing
        expert sources, 74–80
    keyword searching, 54
    library resources, 49–53
    online databases, 53–54
    search strategies, 73–74
    subject searching, 55
    Web, exploring, 56–72
Split screen command, 115
Stacks, 21
Subject directories, 28, 71–72
    World Wide Web Virtual Library,
        71–72
    Yahoo!, 71
Subject searching, 55–56
Summarizing, 139–141
Surveys, 43–45

Tables, preparing, 133–135
    other considerations, 136
Telnet, 58
TeRespondo, 69
Thesaurus, 26
Thesis statement
    preliminary, 38–40
    revisiting and revising, 121
Tilde (~), 86
Topic, developing, 17–30
    browsing in library, 25–28
    browsing World Wide Web,
        28–29
    creating research journal or log,
        22–25
    expectations of discipline,
        recognizing, 19–20
    exploring in different ways, 20–21
    exploring possible topics first,
        18–19

skimming sources, 29
using your library, 21–22
Tripod, 184
Turabian, Kate L., 6

Universal Resource Locator (URL),
    57. *See also* URL
URL, 86
Usenet, 79

Validating sources, example of,
    90–93
Vivisimo, 69

Web browsers, 56–59
    location bar, 57
    Microsoft Internet Explorer, 56, 58
    navigation panel, 56
    Netscape Navigator, 56, 58
    protocol, 58
    URL, 57
WebCrawler, 68
Website, designing, 185, 186
Web writing projects, kinds of,
    178–183
Who's Who Online, 76
World Wide Web
    browsing, 28–29
    creating pages, 184–186
    exploring, 56
        bookmarks, 59–61
        Boolean terms or operators,
            64–65
        metacrawlers, 68–69
        search engines, 61–63, 65–68
        specialized searchable
            databases, 69–70
        subject directories, 71–72
        Web browsers, 56–59
    field research and interviewing
        expert sources, 74–80
    search engines, 29
    search strategies, 73–74
    subject directories, 28

writing for, 177–192
  design basics, 185–187
    review questions, 186
    single pages, 185–186
    websites, 185
  HTML, basics of, 187–190
  kinds of projects, 178–183
    class e-zine or anthology,
      182–183
    collaborative course
      projects, 183
    hypertext essay, 180–182
    posting to online forums
      or submitting to online
      journals, 178
    transforming paper to Web
      text with links, 178–180
  pictures or graphics, adding,
    190–191
  sites about, 191–192
  web pages, creating, 184–185

Writing process, 118–150
  academic honesty, maintaining,
    137–139
  checklist, 149
  first draft, notes to, 122–133
  incremental writing, 119–121
  revising, 147–149
  revising and editing, 136–137
  rhetorical stance, 146–147
  summarizing, paraphrasing,
    quoting, 139–146
  tables and figures, preparing,
    133–136
  thesis statement, revisiting, 121
  time schedule for, 119

Yahoo Groups, 79

Zine Resource Starting Page, 182
Zines, Zines, Everywhere, 182

Summary of Changes to the *MLA Handbook for Writers of Research Papers*, Sixth Edition (2003)

The *MLA Handbook for Writers of Research Papers* was recently published in a new sixth edition. Some forms of documentation and citation have been changed. This insert is intended to detail these changes and provide you with the most up-to-date information about MLA style. Be sure to speak with your instructor if you need additional clarification.

PREPARING THE LIST OF WORKS CITED

Full-Text Databases

Most college and university libraries subscribe to full-text periodical and book databases such as the *New York Times Online* and *American National Biography* and to general databases such as JSTOR, InfoTrac, and Lexis-Nexis that provide a wide range of bibliographic and full-text sources. When you cite works from databases, observe the following changes in MLA style.

1. *URL-Specific Document:* When you cite an online source that can be accessed by a short and logical URL, include the full URL in your citation of the source. An article from the *New York Times*, for example, can be easily accessed by the reader using the URL specified in your Works Cited list.

   > Petersen, Melody. "A Respected Face, but Is It News
   >   or an Ad?" New York Times on the Web 7 May
   >   2003. 8 May 2003 <http://www.nytimes.com/2003/
   >   05/07/business/media/07DRUG.html>.

2. *URL of Search Page:* If the URL of your document is long and convoluted, it will be quite difficult for your reader to access the source. Consider this example of a URL from a journal accessed through JSTOR.

   > http://links.jstor.org/sici?sici=00290564%28197512%
   > 2930%3A3%3C305%3AATSOPJA%3E2.0CO%3B2-5

When this problem arises, MLA suggests that it is more convenient to supply the URL of the database's search page, as shown here.

```
Hart, Francis R. "The Spaces of Privacy: Jane Austen."
     Nineteenth-Century Fiction 30.3 (1975): 305-33.
     JSTOR. 5 Feb. 2003 <http://www.jstor.org/search>.
```

3. *No URL:* If your source does not have an accessible URL or the URL is unique to the library, cite the URL for the home page of the subscription service that you used to find your source.

```
Youakim, Sami. "Work-Related Asthma." American
     Family Physician 64 (2001): 1839-53. Health
     Reference Center. InfoTrac. Bergen County
     Cooperative Lib. System, NJ. 14 Mar. 2003
     <http://www.galegroup.com/>.
```

Internet Sources

The new edition of the *MLA Handbook* does not change the style for Internet citations, but it does expand the information to be included. The following citation exhibits the necessary components of an Internet citation.

```
           ❶                            ❷
Hart, Francis R. "The Spaces of Privacy: Jane Austen."
     Nineteenth-Century Fiction 30.3 (1975): 305-33.
                                                      ❸
     JSTOR. 5 Feb. 2003 <http://www.jstor.org/search>.
       ❹        ❺                    ❻
```

❶ Name of author, editor, translator, or compiler of the source.

❷ Title of the article or other short work, enclosed in quotation marks. For a posting to a discussion list or forum, use the subject line as the title.

❸ Publication information for the print version of the source.

❹ Title of the Internet site (scholarly project, database, online periodical, or Web site, underlined).

❺ Date of access.

❻ URL of the source or URL of the site's search page if the URL is exceptionally long.

Remember to include the following details in your citation if such information is given or available for your source.

- Include the name of the editor, translator, or compiler of the source in addition to the author's name.
- Note the name of the editor of the Web site.
- Include the date of electronic publication, latest update, or posting.
- Give the name and location of the library if your site was accessed through a library subscription service.
- Name the list or forum, if your source is a posting to a discussion list or forum.
- Include the name of the site's sponsoring institution or organization.

Other Important Points Concerning the List of Works Cited

1. *Work from a Library Subscription Service:* When you cite material from a library service, be sure to cite the name of the database used, the name of the service, the name and location of the library, the date of access, and the URL of the subscription service home page if it is available.

   Dutton, Gail. "Greener Pigs." <u>Popular Science</u>
       255.5 (1999): 38-39. ProQuest Direct.
       Public Lib., Teaneck, NJ. 7 Dec. 2002
       <http://proquest.umi.com>.

2. *Work from a Personal Subscription Service:* To cite a source that you found via a personal subscription service that allows you to retrieve information through a keyword search, end the citation with *Keyword,* followed by a colon and the date of access. If you used a series of topic labels rather than a keyword end the citation with *Path,* followed by a colon, and the sequence of topics that you used to locate your source. Use semicolons to separate the topics.

   Futurelle, David. "A Smashing Success." <u>Money.com</u>
       23 Dec. 1999. America Online. 4 Oct. 2002.
       Path: Personal Finance; Business News;
       Business Publications; Money.com.

THE MECHANICS OF WRITING: ELLIPSES

The most significant difference between the fifth and sixth editions of the *MLA Handbook* is in the style of ellipses. The fifth edition required that ellipses (three spaced periods used to indicate an omission from quoted material) be enclosed in square brackets. Now the style is to omit the brackets. You should, however, check which ellipsis style your instructor prefers.

*Preferred Ellipsis Style of the **6th** Edition:*

In her article "Living in Two Cultures," Jeanne
Wakatsuki Houston notes: "My husband and I often joke
that the reason we have stayed married for so long is
that we . . . mystify each other with responses and
attitudes that are plainly due to our different
backgrounds" (191).

*Preferred Ellipsis Style of the **5th** Edition:*

In her article "Living in Two Cultures," Jeanne
Wakatsuki Houston notes: "My husband and I often joke
that the reason we have stayed married for so long is
that we [. . .] mystify each other with responses and
attitudes that are plainly due to our different
backgrounds" (191).

Exception: Do enclose ellipses in square brackets if the original passage you are quoting contains its own ellipsis points. The brackets will distinguish your ellipses from those in the source.

Original Source:

In "Living in Two Cultures," Jeanne Wakatsuki
Houston discusses her early questions about marital
roles. She notes:

>   When we first married I wondered if I should lay
>   out his socks and underwear every morning like
>   my mother used to do for my father. But my
>   brothers' warning would float up from the past:
>   don't be subservient to Caucasian men or they

```
will take advantage. So I compromised and laid
them out sporadically, whenever I thought to do
it . . . which grew less and less often as the
years passed. (224)
```

Quoted Source:

```
In "Living in Two Cultures," Jeanne Wakatsuki
Houston discusses her early questions about marital
roles. She notes:
        When we first married I wondered if I should
        lay out his socks [. . .]. But my brothers'
        warning would float up from the past: don't be
        subservient to Caucasian men or they will take
        advantage. So I compromised and laid them
        out sporadically, whenever I thought to do
        it . . . which grew less and less often as the
        years passed. (224)
```

The following paper by first-year student Chassey Wilkins-Hicks demonstrates the changes to MLA guidelines. The format shown in this paper is reflective of MLA style but has been slightly modified to accommodate the space limitations of the trim in this book. Note that MLA-style student papers should be double-spaced throughout. As always, see your instructor if you have any questions regarding the arrangement of this paper.

1"

½"

Hicks 1 ← 1" →

Chassey Wilkins-Hicks

Professor Ezzell

English 112

17 April 2003

Peace by Prescription

←5→ "Sit down at the dinner table!" "Stop
spaces
fidgeting and finish your homework!" "Didn't
you hear a single word I said?" Do these
demands sound familiar? Perhaps you remember
hearing those same words as a child, or
maybe you have even spoken them to your own
son or daughter. They are not uncommon
phrases in the home of a lively, vivacious
child doing nothing more than enjoying life
and burning the energy many adults wish they
could bottle. Yet many adults are beginning
to view any type of bubbly, rambunctious
behavior as unacceptable. More parents are
being swayed toward the idea that if you
have to speak to your children in such a
manner, there must be something wrong with
them. Enter attention deficit hyperactivity
disorder (ADHD). In the past two decades the
diagnosis of ADHD has been on a steady rise.
Independent academic studies as well as
numerous years of research by organizations
such as the National Institute on Drug Abuse
(NIDA) place the proportion of the general
public affected at approximately 3 to 5
percent (United States). The American

1"

Academy of Pediatrics reports that 4 to 12
percent of the nation's school-age children
are affected (1).

A considerable number of the diagnosed
children are prescribed some form of
psychostimulant, such as methylphenidate, to
treat their symptoms. One brand is so
commonly used, it has practically become a
household name--Ritalin. These drugs,
however, do not pave the path to recovery.
Instead, they chemically alter some of the
behavior symptoms associated with ADHD. As I
intend to prove, behavior therapy is a much
safer alternative than psychostimulants in
treating children diagnosed with ADHD. The
process can also prove to be a learning and
rewarding experience for children, as well
as their parents.

A comprehension of exactly how the
diagnosis of ADHD is determined is needed to
understand the treatments offered. Even with
the countless hours of research dedicated to
the study of ADHD, the cause remains a
mystery. Zwi, Ramchandani, and Joughin
attribute the symptoms to a collection of
neurobiological problems in the function and
makeup of the brain rather than just one
disorder (975). Unfortunately, none of my
research reveals a conclusive opinion that
the brains of those classified with ADHD

function differently than the brains of
those who are considered normal. And,
because there is no proven medical
examination or test that can confirm ADHD,
the chance of misdiagnosis remains high.

Jaydene Morrison, a nationally certified
school psychologist and teacher, does a
fantastic job of outlining the standard
practice of diagnosing ADHD in her book
<u>Coping with ADD/ADHD</u>. It requires several
steps and a wide range of IQ and aptitude
tests. A doctor may first want to rule out any
medical disorder or learning disability (9).
The frustration experienced or what
may appear as lack of attention due to a
hearing impairment can be a misconception
of an unruly student. Teachers are often
requested to assist by completing lengthy
questionnaires on the child's behavior as
well as study habits and moods. The next step
is determining whether the child falls within
the academic level of his or her peers.
Reading, writing, spelling, and mathematic
capabilities are analyzed for correctness as
well as speed. IQ testing such as problem and
puzzle solving is utilized in a verbal and
hands-on setting. These different aspects of
testing demonstrate the process by which the
mind computes the problem and transfers the
information to paper (11).

Hicks 4

Symptoms of ADHD include a wide variety of behavior and learning traits. Some of these include being inattentive, easily distracted, unable to organize, forgetful, overtalkative, fidgety, and impatient. Many argue that this list also describes most typical, healthy children at some point in time. In an October 2000 issue of US News and World Report, Nancy Shute quotes Dickie Scruggs as saying, "[T]he diagnosis of ADHD would fit every child in America."

Ritalin, a central nervous system stimulant, is used to treat ADHD based on the speculation that it increases the release of dopamine in the brain. This assumption is founded on laboratory research performed on healthy adults. The InfoFacts sheet on methylphenidate (Ritalin) explains that by use of a type of brain scan called positron emission tomography (PET), researchers confirmed an increase in dopamine levels in what were considered normal, healthy subjects administered with

◄—10—► therapeutic doses of
spaces

methylphenidate. . . . The researchers speculate that methylphenidate amplifies the release of dopamine, a neurotransmitter, thereby improving attention and focus in

Hicks 5

individuals who have dopamine
signals that are weak, such as
individuals with ADHD. (United
States)

Like many others who disagree with the
use of psychostimulants as a primary
treatment for ADHD, I am not out to disprove
the effects of these drugs. In fact, as
described in the research above, Ritalin and
similar drugs can improve attentiveness and
concentration in almost anyone. In a
personal interview, Thomas Mates, PhD, a
respected child psychologist here in
Wilmington, North Carolina, told me that
many college students have admitted taking
these types of pharmaceuticals to improve
their study habits. Improving only the
ability to focus, however, does not teach a
child good learning habits. The chemicals
merely subdue the individual and the
undesirable behavior. David Stein, PhD,
author of Ritalin Is Not the Answer and an
advocate for behavior therapy, asserts, "The
drugs do control the behaviors, but then
they serve to mask the problem behaviors and
thus block the way for effective change"
(35). What parent would envision spending
quality time with an eight-year-old child
that was under the influence of cocaine?
Amazingly enough, though, parents of

millions of children have been convinced
that giving Ritalin to their child is
acceptable. The comparison with cocaine is
not so outrageous when you consider that the
NIDA has placed a Schedule II narcotics
control label on methylphenidate.

As with any drug, the risks of
adverse reactions are always present. A
long list of side effects accompanies these
stimulant medications, including "decreased
appetite/weight loss, . . . transient tics,
stuttering, increased blood pressure or heart
rate, and growth delay" (American Academy of
Pediatrics 12). I can speak only for myself,
but I hope I represent all cautious parents
when I say that I would take dealing with my
child's behavior problem over inducing these
side effects in her.

I question, is the tranquility these
drugs create for the children or for the
parents? The choices between two minutes
of the parents' day to administer the dose of
a tiny pill versus the countless hours of
one-on-one attention needed to find the root
of the problem could appear too easy. The
answer is obvious for those who are willing
to take the time. I don't deny that there
may be children with extreme cases of
inattentiveness and/or hyperactivity that may
require a medical approach. This, however,

should be the last option and used after all other means, methods, and programs have been exhausted. Mind-altering drugs are not a safe alternative in treating children for what is more often than not a behavior problem.

Behavior therapy does work. Stein notes that the treatment of Helen Keller by Annie Sullivan is the "first documented behavior modification case" (13). Helen Keller's motivation and drive were eliminated by a family who pampered her and overcompensated for what they thought were her inabilities to function for herself. Ms. Sullivan removed Helen from these detrimental surroundings and required her to perform activities necessary to everyday existence. In doing so, Helen was able to gain and retain the knowledge to lead a self-fulfilling life.

I recently took my nine-year-old daughter to a psychologist. I was relieved to hear that she does not exhibit the characteristics or enough of the symptoms to be diagnosed with ADHD. Why then was I prompted to have her tested? More than likely it was for the same reasons most parents are succumbing to this decision. She was almost unmanageable at times and seemed easily distracted or frustrated when it came to schoolwork or long projects. Thinking

Hicks 8

back, I was looking for the easy way out. The term "spoiled" now looms in my mind. After reviewing the results of her tests and discussing the doctor's analysis, we concluded she needs more direction in controlling her behavior, study habits, and thinking patterns. The doctor also explained that I may be too lenient with her at times, allowing her to feel entitled to get what she wants. In looking for a way out, I, probably like many other parents, was searching for a cause rather than looking at my parenting skills. We are looking, however, in the wrong direction if looking for a medical answer. Stein writes, "I deeply believe that nothing medical causes children to not pay attention and to misbehave. They simply do not pay attention and they do misbehave" (22). Behavior therapy, therefore, can be a learning and growing experience for the child and for the parent, as well.

There are many behavior therapy treatment programs geared toward and created specifically for children suffering from ADHD. The programs may differ in structure, but are based on modifying the child's current behavior by applying the techniques frequently and consistently. Some programs set goals and rewards for

good behavior and have consequences for
inappropriate behavior. These rewards and
consequences vary depending on the present
and long-term goals set by the parent
and child. The program is individualized
to the child by allowing him or her to
participate. Recognizing behavior, both
good and bad, is an important step in
allowing the child to assist in setting
goals and choosing punishments.

Another program, the Caregivers'
Skill Program, works "by first getting
[children's] behavior under control, so we
can get their full attention, so we can
inspire their motivation" (Stein 41). Lack
of interest, and thus motivation, can
cause anyone to be inattentive, fidgety,
forgetful, and easily distracted. No, it is
not a coincidence that you have heard these
descriptions before. This only reinforces
the fact that these are not symptoms of
ADHD alone. As stated above, the first goal
is to get a handle on the current behavior.
This is achieved in a manner similar to
other programs by identifying the problem
behavior and using reinforcements such as
spending more time with the child and
praising the child. Material reinforcements
such as special privileges and objects are
also an option, but their effects are

Hicks 10

short-lived and can cause another form of entitlement expectancy. Immediate reinforcement of positive behavior leads to a much more pleasant atmosphere than discipline for bad behavior. Ponder this: If your employer only pointed out the shortcomings of your work performance without praising your accomplishments, would you not have a bad attitude?

Stop and smell the roses. The roses in this story are the children. We would not unnecessarily poison our roses just as we should not poison our children. Drugs such as methylphenidate and amphetamines used needlessly are poison to a child's mind and body. Encouragement, interaction, and positive reinforcement are the keys to a healthy, motivated child. Who knows? Many parents may find their children need them more than anything a prescription could ever offer.

Works Cited

American Academy of Pediatrics.

    <u>Understanding ADHD</u>. Elk Grove

    Village: American Academy of

    Pediatrics, 2001.

Mates, Thomas. Personal interview. 27 Mar.

    2003.

Morrison, Jaydene. <u>Coping with ADD/ADHD</u>.

    New York: Rosen, 1996.

Shute, Nancy. "Pushing Pills on Kids?" <u>US</u>

    <u>News and World Report</u> 2 Oct. 2000:

    60. <u>Academic Search Elite</u>. EBSCO.

    Cape Fear Community Coll. Lib.,

    Wilmington, NC. 24 Mar. 2003

    <http://www.epnet.com>.

Stein, David B. <u>Ritalin Is Not the Answer</u>.

    San Francisco: Jossey-Bass, 1999.

United States. National Institute on

    Drug Abuse. <u>NIDA InfoFacts:</u>

    <u>Methylphenidate (Ritalin)</u>. 17 Mar.

    2003 <http://www.nida.nih.gov/

    infofax/ritalin.html>.

Zwi, Morris, Paul Ramchandani, and Carol

    Joughin. "Evidence and Belief in

    ADHD." <u>British Medical Journal</u>

    321.7267 (2000): 975-76. <u>Academic</u>

    <u>Search Elite</u>. EBSCO. Cape Fear

    Community Coll. Lib., Wilmington, NC.

    20 Mar. 2003 <http://www.epnet.com>.